ISLAM, WOMEN AND GENDER JUSTICE

ISLAM, WOMEN AND GENDER JUSTICE

Asghar Ali Engineer

GYAN

GYAN PUBLISHING HOUSE

NEW DELHI-110 002

ISLAM, WOMEN AND GENDER JUSTICE
(Religion, Gender, Women)

ISBN: 81-212-0755-X

Published in 2001 in India by
Gyan Publishing House
5, Ansari Road,
New Delhi-110 002
Phones : 3282060, 3261060, Fax : 3285914
E-mail: gyanbook@del2.vsnl.del.in
Visit Our Web Site At http:\\www.gyanbooks.com

Laser Typesetting at: Sharma Graphics, New Delhi
Printed at: Mehra Offset Printers, New Delhi

Contents

Preface

This book on Muslim women and their problems is a collection of papers presented in a couple of seminars on Muslim women, their rights and empowerment held in different places in India. One of the seminars was of all India level and we are grateful for collaboration of Minority Rights Group, London.

The problems of women in genera and those of Muslim women in particular are of great importance today. These problems are of various natures -legal, religious, economic and educational. They are doubly persecuted -by their own community and also greatly suffer because of majority communalism, particularly because of communal violence.

These seminars were held both to discuss these problems and to bring awareness among the Muslim women. The Muslim women in India are suffering because cf lack of reform and codification of Muslim personal law. Triple divorce in one sitting has become the main form of divorce and polygamy also remains unregulated. Many women suffer a great deal because of triple divorce and polygamy.

Also, a large number of Muslim women belong to poor and illiterate families. Majority of Muslims are poor in India and level of literacy is quite low, particularly among women. Many Muslim women toil throughout the day for a pittance. Divorcees and those, whose near and dear ones have died or beer killed in communal riots find their living an ordeal indeed. These papers collected in this volume discuss all these problems facing Muslim women. This volume will

Women but also among other activists and scholars.

I am extremely grateful to all those scholars who agreed to participate in the seminar and contributed papers based on their scholarly studies or filed work, I am also grateful to those who helped me organise these seminars, particularly Seema Qazi who worked hard for organising the All India Seminar in Mumbai in July 1999. I am also thankful to Irfan Engineer and Asad bin Saif for their active help without which it would not have been possible to organise the seminar. I also owe my thanks to the staff of Centre for Study of Society and Secularism for all the help they readily provided for making the seminar a reality.

15th November 2000 **Asghar Ali Engineer**

Introduction

The women's question is acquiring ever greater importance throughout the world. The women suffer discrimination whichever community or country they belong to. Women in western countries also suffer discrimination in the male dominated society though there may be difference of degree. Women in Islamic countries are perceived to be suffering more compared to other countries. What is happening in Afghanistan at the hands of Taliban has reinforced this perception. The Taliban are treating women in most primitive way. It is hardly Islamic. Yet they do it in the name of Islam.

The orthodox *'ulama* treat the question of women in Islam with hypersensitivity. They are opposed to any kind of change in general and on women's question, in particular. They imitate quite mechanically all the provisions in this respect formulated by the *'ulama* more than fourteen hundred years ago. Any re-thinking on the issue is no less than a sin. Also, the question of women has become an important question of Islamic identity *vis-a-vis* the west as far as the Islamic countries are concerned and also of Muslim minorities vis-a-vis the majority communities in countries like India. Thus, any change in Muslim personal law is opposed vigorously as a threat to Muslim identity and an unwarranted interference in Islam. The agenda of Islamic revolution in Iran included re-assertion of Islamic identity *vis-a-vis* the west and it found expression in enforcing *chadar* (a head-gear) for women.

The Islamic revival throughout Islamic world is compelling women to take to veil. In many cases Muslim women are doing so voluntarily. In Iran too many women who had taken to miniskirts during the Shah's period, discarded them and began to wear *chadar* of their volition to escape the charge that they were opposing the Shah at the instigation of the Soviet Union. Similarly in countries like Egypt the women, particularly the university students have taken to veil to assert their Islamic identity. In fact in an era, of MTV when the western pop culture is being disseminated with all vengeance such a reaction appears to be quite normal. In the west the woman bares as much as she can whereas in the east she hides as much as she can. It is thus more of reaction rather than coercion. Women in Islamic countries assert 'modesty' to fight the western 'vulgarity'. These are two different cultures poles apart. Thus veil should not be seen as mere subjugation of women. The Iranian women are quite assertive of their rights despite wearing *chadar*. They are recruited in all government offices, they are members of parliament, they hold political offices like Masumeh who is vice president of Iran. Not only that the Iranian women are fighting for equal status today and women's movement in Iran is quite strong, as strong as in any other non-Muslim country. Thus veil is a cultural expression of modesty rather than any oppressive measure.

In the modern era, education is spreading fast in all countries including Muslim countries. Muslim women in almost all countries are going to universities in ever larger numbers. These educated women become far more aware of their rights than illiterate women. Thus, there is hardly any country with a sizeable Muslim population, where women are not seen asserting themselves. Even in a conservative Sheikhdom like Kuwait, woman are demanding the right to vote and the right to hold political offices. There is a large number of women in the universities in Kuwait. The woman spearheading the movement for women's rights in Kuwait is the dean of the faculty of arts in the Kuwait University. In Pakistan women have held the highest offices, i.e. offices of Prime Minister and hold offices in various governmental as well as non-governmental organisations. The same is the case in Bangladesh, where the present head of government is a woman.

However, it does not mean there are no serious problems. It is a struggle all the way for women: struggle against orthodoxy, struggle against certain oppressive cultural norms, which do not permit women to enter certain fields, struggle against dowry and bride burning and struggle against dishonour. As women assert their rights and struggle to find a place of honour in the society, the society which is under domination of men, reacts quite sharply and tries to put more restrictions over them. This struggle will go on for a long time to come. What is shocking is that women are being denied even their well-defined Islamic rights.

It is important to note that Islam is the first religion in the world which recognised woman as legal entity and gave her all the rights that man enjoyed. Thus Islam has given women the right to enter into a marital contract on her own conditions. Her father or any male member of the family cannot give her away in marriage to any person of his choice, without her consent. Her consent to marriage in presence of two witnesses is a condition for the finalisation of marriage. She can stipulate certain conditions which must be fulfilled for the validity of marriage. Any violation of the stipulated conditions could lead to the dissolution of marriage. What is most revolutionary is that she can insist on what is known as *talaq-i-tafwid,* i.e., a delegated right to divorce. According to this provision in the marriage contract, she can insist on the delegated right to divorce her husband on his behalf if he violates any of the conditions of the marriage contract. It would be seen that even the most modern laws have no such provisions for the benefit of women.

Divorce is a recognised institution in Islam though it is not encouraged. Both man and woman has right to divorce. The Holy Qur'an has made a very fair provision for divorce. It stipulates arbitration. The Qur'an says:

> "And if you fear breach between the two, i.e., husband and wife, appoint an arbiter from his people and an arbiter from her people. If they both desire agreement, Allah will effect harmony beween them." (4:35)

The very concept of arbitration is quite modern and this was stipulated 1400 years ago by the holy Book of Islam. However, it is highly regrettable that such a fair provision of the Qur'an is ignored by Muslims and they resort to triple divorce in one sitting which was part of pre-Islamic customary law.

Unfortunately at least in India triple divorce has become the most prevalent form of divorce among the Sunni Hanafi and Shafi Muslims. In fact triple divorce is un- Qur'anic and is rejected even by Hanbalis and Ahl-e-Hadith among the Sunni Muslims and all Shi'ah sects as well. Triple divorce being unjust to women was not practised during the Prophet's (PBUH) time and also during the time of the first Caliph Hazrat Abu Bakr (RA) and for two and half years during the reign of second Caliph Hazrat Umar (RA). It was during the later part of his reign that triple divorce in one sitting was enforced again on account of its misuse by some Arabs. Triple divorce has never been a part of Islamic teachings. It was, in fact, part of the Arab customary law. Even according to Shah Waliyullah, a great Islamic thinker with a social vision of eighteenth century India, it is unfair to apply the Arab customary law to non-Arab people. Many Shari'ah provisions include some aspects of the Arab customary law prevailing in the pre-Islamic times. Abolition of triple divorce on which there is no unanimity among Muslims will give great relief to Muslim women. Many men misuse it either to harass their wives or to divorce them most arbitrarily, leaving them in lurch. Hundreds of women are suffering today because of its validity. Fortunately it has been abolished in Pakistan and Bangladesh.

Islam has also given a right to Muslim women to divorce which, is known as Khula. Though this word has not been used in the holy Qur'an, a woman, according to it, can buy her freedom from her husband by giving *fidyah,* i.e., compensation. And this right is absolute. Thus, the Qur'an says:

> "Then if you fear that they cannot keep within the limits of Allah, there is no blame on them for what she gives up to become free thereby." (2:229).

Commenting on this verse Maulana Muhammad Ali says, "These words give the wife the right to claim a divorce. It is one of the distinguishing characteristics of Islam that it gives the wife the right to claim a divorce, if she is willing to forgo the whole or part of her dowry." (*Holy Qur'an,* Lahore, 1973,p.98). The Holy Prophet (PBUH) enforced this right in the case of Jamilah who wanted to free herself from her husband though she found no fault in his behaviour towards her except that she did not like him. According to *Sahih Bukhari* the Prophet (PBUH) allowed her *khula'* by returning the orchards which her husband had given her by way of *mehr*. But unfortunately the orthodox, *'ulama* deprive the woman of this right also by insisting on the consent of her husband. This approach is not in keeping with the *sunnah* of the Prophet (PBUH). Her right to *khula'* should be absolute particularly, when they fear they cannot keep within the limits of Allah, i.e., they cannot fulfil the marital obligations.

There is also a form of divorce what is called *mubarat*. It is in this form of divorce that mutual consent of both husband and wife is required. Unfortunately the, *'ulama* have equated *khula'* with *mubarat* which is not correct. The Muslim personal law as it operates in India also does not grant the women right to *khula'* without her husband's consent and naturally husband, more often than not, exploit this for harassing her and also for extracting much higher compensation than is justified.

There is another provision in the Qur'an which is often exploited by men in the most un-Qur'anic way, i.e., the provision for polygyny. A man has been permitted to take upto four wives. But this is far from being a general provision for man. It is permitted only in exceptional situation and subject to stringent conditions. Many, *'ulama* feel that since this verse was revealed after the battle of Uhud, in which ten per cent of male Muslim population was wiped out leaving many orphans and widows, provision up to four wives was made to help these widows and orphans. The relevant verse is as follows:

> "And if you fear you cannot do justice to orphans, marry such women as seem good to you, two, or three, or four, but if you fear that you will not do justice, then (marry) only one or that which your right hands possess. This is more proper that you

may not do injustice." (4:3)

Thus, it will be seen that there is so much emphasis on justice. Holy Qur'an has exercised enough caution in this respect. Again in 4:129 Holy Qur"an makes men aware of difficulty in exercising justice between spouses. It says:

> "And you cannot do justice between wives, even though you wish (it), but be not disinclined (from one) with total disincliation, so that you leave her in suspense. And if you are reconciled and keep your duty, surely Allah is ever forgiving, Merciful.

"Thus Holy Qur'an makes it cleat that equal justice is not possible and one should not leave the first wife in suspense by marrying the other. The early' *ulama* also discussed what is meant by justice and generally they emphasised equity in maintenance of all four wives. But some felt it included equal love for all wives and since it is not possible as rightly emphasised in 4:129, the intention of the Qur'an is to promote monogamy. Also, the verses on polygamy should be read along with other verses of the Qur'an on husband-wife relationship to uderstand the real spirit of the Qur'anic approach to this question.

In 21:30 Allah says, "He put between you love and compassion." Thus, the relationship between husband and wife is basically of love and compassion. Then how just relationship can exclude love between the two. Also Holy Qur'an says: "They are a garment for you and you are garment for them." Thus, if the verses on polygamy are read in conjunction with these two verses it becomes very clear that equal love and dignity in husband-wife relationship is a must. *Libas* (garment) stands for human dignity. And since equal love with all wives is not possible and human dignity cannot be upheld without love and compassion multiple marriages are not encouraged by the Qur'an. Thus, polygyny is an exception, not a rule.

The women's question needs to be tackled with new sensitivity and freshness of approach. It is not true to say that what the medieval theologians thought on this question is immutable and divine. After all the '*ulama* are human beings, howsoever learned they may be and what is more important to emphasize is that they were product of their own time. What they thought on women's question reflected ethos of their period. The real vision of the Qur'an unflods itself with passage of time. The Qur'an really envisions equality of sexes and there is enough in the Qur'anic verses to draw this conclusion. Thus the verses 2:228 and 33:35 declare sexual equality in no uncertain terms. Yet in medieval ages these verses were by and large neglected or understood very differently. The time has come to unfold the real message of the Qur'an in this respect. Islam has treated women with great sense of dignity. True Muslims, therefore, should not allow an impression being created that Islam treats women unjustly.

It is not the intention of Islam to confine women to home and entrust her with the responsibility of minding household work and bringing up children alone. Nowhere is stated either in the Qur'an or any of the *hadith* that household work is her sole responsibility. It is, at best, a shared responsibility. In *Fatawa 'Alamgiri* compiled during the reign of Aurangzeb 'Alamgir, the Moghul emperor, we see that maintenance is defined by the *'ulama* to include cooked food, sewn clothes and a separate house to live in. Thus, a husband cannot insist that his wife cook food and serve him; on the contrary it is his duty to serve cooked food to his wife as part of maintenance. Minding children should also be a shared responsibility between the two. No *faqih,* i.e., Islamic jurist can insist that man should not share household responsibility with his wife and that it is wife's function alone. Even the concept of *qawwam* in 4:34 has undergone great change. The earlier commentators and theologians thought it meant either 'ruler' or controller of household affairs' 'caretaker of the family' while wife was his subordinate. The modern scholars maintain that this verse does not entitle man to dominate over woman but indicates his function of earning and maintaining family. It is only a functional concept and does not show any inherent superiority over woman. Even a scholar like Maulana Azad maintains this and says that in those days it was man who earned (the word *qawwam* is an exaggerated form of *qama* which means to stand and since one who earns stands too much is called *qawwam*) and spent on his wife and children and looked after them, he has been described as *qawwam* by the Qur'an. Maulana, therefore, argues that if wife earns and shares the expenses incurred on the family she will also be called *qawwam* as she also performs the same function as her husband does. There may also be cases in which wife earns and husband does not. In that case she will be *qawwam* and husband will not. And there are many families where the wife is the sole bread earner.

Thus, whichever angle we look the women's problem from, she is not the looser or unequal from the Qur'anic standpoint. We should not impose our own thinking and explanations on the Qur'an. It is too much to think that what we feel is the real intention of the Qur'an. Thus, for example, many people justify polygyny by saying that since woman gives birth to child and man cannot go near her for several months and she goes through the menstrual periods, man needs to have more than one wife. It is purely an un-Qur'anic approach and an explanation never intended by the Qur'an. Such explanations reflect sexual obsession. In fact the verse 24:33 says:

> "Let those who do not find the wherewithal for marriage keep themselve chaste, until Allah gives them means out of His grace."

Thus, Allah requires that man remain chaste until he finds means to marry even one wife. Sexual obsession is obviously discouraged. Secondly, such explanations reduce a women to be a mere sexual object, not a companion to be loved and respected as the Qur'an requires. Allah has created *mawaddah and rahmah* (love and compassion) between the two and not mere sexual instinct. Sexual instinct is more for propagation of species than mere pleasure. Even most orthodox, *'ulama* would agree on this point. In fact, most of the Muslims take another wife more for sexual reasons than otherwise. This defeats the very purpose of treating women with love and dignity and as a companion. One must thoroughly revise the whole outlook on polygamy. Today women are much more educated and much more aware and hence would consider it below dignity to live with a co-wife and share her husband's attention and love with her.

As hinted above the question of Islamic identity *vis-a-vis* the West is being treated in terms of women's rights in Islamic world. Why only women should bear the entire brunt of the question of Islamic identity. Her clothes, her *hijab*, her role in the society is seen as part of Islamic identity, whereas man does not have to face any such restriction. He can continue to wear western dress and adopt new ways of life in the modern society without in any way violating the Islamic norms. Wearing western dress is even seen as more dignified as far as men are concerned. But if women takes to a different dress, Islamic norm is violated. The Qur'anic verses with such interpretations as to restrict her role are invoked. All will agree that thrust of the Qur'anic argument is that women dress modestly. She should not expose her sexual charms. This is also in a particular Arab context. The Arab women used to stand in public places and attract men's attention by displaying their charms, wearing anklets and thumping their feet to attract men's attention. Also, they would bare their body as much as they could. It is these vulgarities the Qur'an wanted to stop. It is also important to note that Qur'an never took away her right to *zeenah,* i.e., to adorn herself. She can be allowed to display her charms before her husband and those close relatives whom she does not marry *(mahram)*.

Thus the Qur'anic verse 4:31 gives the description of those before whom she can display her charms and adornment. This verse begins with the words which are quite significant. "And say to the believing women that they lower their gaze and restrain their sexual passions and do not display their adornment except what appears thereof".

The words "except what appears thereof" are quite significant. This clearly implies that certain parts of her body can remain open. There is almost a consensus among orthodox, *'ulama* also that the face and hands can remain open and that she can apply collyrium to her eyes (which is part of adornment) and wear rings in her fingers and bangles in her hands and these parts can remain open. We also find in *hadith* (Abu Daud 31:30) according to which the Prophet (PBUH) himself is reported to have told Asma, his wife, A 'isha's sister, when she appeared before him in thin clothes, through which parts of her body could be seen: "O Asma', when woman attains her puberty it is not proper that any part of her body should be seen except this, and he pointed to his face and hands". This settles conclusively that Islam never enjoined the veil for covering of the face.

The following verse 24:30 also makes it clear what is the real intention in observing modesty. It says,

> "Say to the believing men that they lower their gaze and restrain their sexual passions. That is purer for them. Surely Allah is Aware of what they do."

Thus it will be seen that it is not only the duty of woman to restrain herself from displaying her sexual charms but also of man to lower his gaze and restrain his sexual passions. In fact, both men and women have to observe a moral code. It is also to be noted that the concept of modesty is culturally conditioned. There cannot be a universally valid concept. What is considered modest in one culture may not be necessarily so in another culture. Western way of dressing for women (except ultra-modern and fashion oriented, which is promoted by the profit motives of the cosmetic industry) has its own dignity and modesty. All western women do not dress in ultra-modern and exotically fashionable ways. Such way of dressing is not only vulgar but is based on an idea of exploitation of women.

What early commentators have prescribed for women to wear is based on their own culturally conditioned notions. The Arabs have their own notions of what is *zeenah* (adornment), what is sexually charming and exciting and what constitutes modesty and modest way of dressing. Thus, what is binding on us is that women should refrain from displaying their sexual charms publicly and restrain their sexual passions and not necessarily wearing what Arab women wore and not to go by their concept of what constitutes modesty. We must distinguish between what is fundamental in the Qur'an and what is instrumental to achieve it in the society. What is fundamental is alone binding on the believers, not what is instrumental in a particular society to achieve what is fundamental. While observing chastity and restraining sexual passions is a fundamental requirement and binding on all believers wearing *hijab* or a particular type of dress prescribed by earlier commentators of the Qur'an is not binding. One must make distinction between the two. *Hijab*, if it means hiding or covering the face is certainly not what is prescribed by the Qur'an. It is a totally wrong notion that the Qur'an prescribes *hijab*.

It is also a culturally conditioned notion that women should not venture out except in prescribed fields. It is neither proved from the Qur'an nor from the *sunnah* (Prophet's sayings and doings). The women during the Holy Prophet's (PBUH) time used to take part in all acts including the battle field, and not only for tending the wounded. Their role was much more than that of nurses. The case of Umm 'Umarah (RA) is well known among them. In the battle of 'Uhud it was she who protected the Prophet (PBUH) from being harmed by the *kuffar* (unbelievers of Mecca, who were trying to kill him) Umm, 'Umarah took sword in her hand and attacked the man who tried to come near the Prophet (PBUH) and pierced sword into his body. She was, therefore, popularly known as 'woman of Uhud'. The Prophet (PBUH) also had great regard for her and always used to inquire after her health. We also have the instance of Ghazalah, a Kharijite woman who was known for her bravery and who, in battle, challenged Yusuf bin Hajjaj, the Umayyad governor who was feared even by all Arabs. He was a great tyrant.

Thus, we see that women took active part in combating situations and proved their might. Why should then women be restricted from taking part in military or police service, if they want? Hazrat 'Umar (RA) had appointed a woman as the chief inspector of markets in his time. In *Aghani* we read stories of highly skilled poets, musicians and lovers of art who were women. They were greatly respected. Some of these women were women of highest achievements in the diverse fields in life. Zubeda, the wife of Abbasid Caliph Harun al-Rashid was a highly skilled administrator. She was often consulted before major policy decisions were taken. It was she who built a network of canal which immensely benefited the people. Thus, it must be seen in those days there were no restrictions on woman, the like of which are being imposed today. It is again culturally mediated restrictions rather than prescriptions by the Qur'an or *hadith*.

Feudal culture put severe restrictions on women and confined her role to household affairs only. She was made to observe strict *purdah*. All that is changing now but still there is a lot of resistance to change. Cultural prejudices are not easy to fight. Thus, it is feudal cultural sensitivities which are restricting her role. Muslim women should fight these restrictions and try to excel in any field of their choice. The Muslim community cannot progress if their women remain confined to the house. Early marriage is also culturally determined rather than being a religious requirement. Child marriages or pre-puberty marriages should be ruled out. Islam, while permitting child marriage due to cultural reasons, had given her what is known as *khiyar al-bulugh* (option of puberty), i.e., she could annul the marriage on achieving puberty, if she did not approve of the same. Thus, child marriage is discouraged by Islam.

Empowerment of Muslim women is not possible until she overcomes all such restrictions imposed on her by the feudal society. She must acquire modern skills in order to excel in all these fields. In fact, What Islam has already given her by way of rights is being given to her now by the modern society. She should overthrow her restrictive role and fight for her Islamic rights and this struggle for Islamic rights will empower her.

Asghar Ali Engineer

List of Contributors

(1) **Asghar Ali Engineer**—Noted Islamic Scholar and Director, Institute of Islamic Studies and Chair, Centre for Study of Society and Secularism.

(2) **Prof. Imtiaz Ahmad**—Professor of Political Science, JNU, Delhi.

(3) **Gitanjali Ganguli**—Activist for Women's Rights.

(4) **Justice Saroj Saxena**—Retired Judge, M.P. High Court.

(5) **Munira Singaporia**—Research Scholar, USA.

(6) **Sheikh Rahim Mondal**—Sociologist : Will let you know Later.

(7) **Sabiha Husain**—Lecturer in Jamia Millia Islamia, Delhi.

(8) **Neelofar Akhtar**—Advocate, Mumbai High Court.

(9) **Dr. K.S. Durrany**—Social Activist, Delhi Holding Doctorate in Comparative Religion.

(10) **Diane D'Souza**—Henry Martyn Institute of Islamic Studies, Hyderabad.

(11) **Dr. Yoginder Sikand**—Research Scholar doing Post-doctoral Research in London University.

(12) **Abu Saleh Shariff**—Noted Statistician, New Delhi.

(13) **Dr. Malika Mistry**—Lecturer in Nes Wadia College, Pune.

(14) **Dr. Mandakini Pant**—Reader in Sociology, University of Rajasthan, Jaipur.

(15) **Dr. Ramla Baxamusa**—Retired Lecturer in Women's Studies, Bombay.

(16) **Dr. Muniza Rafiq Khan**—Lecturer in Sociology, Varanasi, U.P.

(17) **Hamida Naeem:** Lecturer in English, Kashmir University.

1
Islam, Women and Gender Justice

Asghar Ali Engineer

It is generally thought that Islam treats women unfairly and gender justice is not possible within Islamic law known as the Shari'ah law. This assertion is partly true and partly untrue. True as far as the existing Shari'ah laws are concerned. Untrue, as the existing laws were codified during 2nd and 3rd centuries of Islam when the general perspective of women's rights was quite different from today's perspective. The Qur'anic verses which are quite fundamental to the Islamic law, were interpreted so as to be in conformity with the views about gender rights prevailing then.

It is important to note that scriptural injunctions are always mediated through prevailing social ethos, it being more fundamental to frame laws based on scriptures as scriptures both reflect the given situation and also transcend it. There cannot be any scripture—revealed or otherwise—which is uni-dimensional, i.e., it reflects only a given situation. Every scripture tries to go beyond what is given and it faces stiff opposition from those who loose out if the transcendental perspectives are spelled out and enforced. The scriptures condemn prevailing social malaise and provide a new vision. Those who benefit from the new vision embrace the new faith. Those who loose oppose it tooth and nail. But, the vested interests and those who want to perpetuate the old order have their own strategies. Soon they find ways and means to hijack new religion to their own benefit. This is done in number of ways:

(i) They capture political power and religion becomes part of political establishment and looses its initial revolutionary thrust as it is appropriated by the ruling classes;

(ii) They convert religion itself into an establishment and a power-structure develops around it. Religion is then used more for distribution of favours than for spiritual enrichment;

(iii) Intellectual resources are used to restore *status quo ante* and this is done chiefly by interpreting the scriptures in a way which will rob it of its transcendental thrust.

Thus a theology is developed which is supportive of *status quo*. One must distinguish between what scriptural pronouncements are and how theology is woven around it. Scriptural pronouncements are divinely inspired and hence transcendental while theological formulations are human and hence often contradict divine intentions. Scriptural pronouncements are an option for the weaker sections whereas theological formulations are weapons in the hands of powerful interests. It is therefore necessary that theological formulations be continuously challenged by scriptural pronouncements. One must strive to build up creative tension between theological and the scriptural. While scripture remains immutable with its transcendental spirit, theology must change facing new challenges and newly emergent situations.

Those who oppose any change in theological formulations and Shari'ah laws are those who chose their dominant position and the priesthood who monopolise theology and religion for them is instrumental in promoting their interests rather than spiritual source of inner enrichment. The priesthood, monopolising theology, project it as divine and immutable. The run of the mill faithfuls' understanding of religion is mediated through the priesthood and hence they are made to believe that theology as formulated by them or their predecessors is divine and hence immutable. Any change will amount to changing the divine will.

In Islam, it is common belief that the shari'ah is divine and hence immutable. Whenever any measures for gender justice are proposed one meets with this stock argument. It is important to note that shari'ah, though undoubtedly based on the Holy Qur'an, is a human endeavour to understand the divine will. It is an approach to, rather than divine will itself. The priesthood, i.e., the community of *'ulama* projects it as a divine end itself and hence refuse to admit any change. 'The Shari'ah is divine' has become a commonly accepted position. Thus what was thought of women's rights during the early period of Islamic history has come to be the final and immutable. Even to think of, much less changing it, is, interfering with the divine, and hence an unpardonable sin.

As pointed out above, there is big gap between the scriptural, i.e., the Qur'anic pronouncements, and, Shari'ah formulations. While the Qur'anic pronouncements are purely transcendental in spirit, the Shari'ah formulations have been influenced by human situation as well as human thinking on all related issues. Women were in subordinate position in the patriarchal societies and this subordinate relationship came to be reflected in the Shari'ah laws relating to her rights. The transcendental divine spirit was conveniently ignored and the prevailing situation was rationalised through contextual Qur'anic pronouncements. As pointed out above, there is always a creative tension between what is and what ought to be in scriptures. However, this tension is often resolved in favour of the prevalent rather than the emergent and prevalent is eternalised by rationalising certain divine pronouncements.

On the Methodology of Creating Islamic Legal Structure

If we want to effect necessary change in the Shari'ah laws, it is important to understand the methodology of creating of Islamic legal structure. The Islamic legal corpus is known as Shari'ah. As Shari'ah is, after all, a human approach to divine will as reflected through the scripture, i.e., the holy Qur'an, it is not uniform but has several variants. In the Sunni Islam itself there are four different schools of jurisprudence, i.e., Hanafi, Shafi'i, Hanbali and Maliki. Besides these schools there is what is known as the Zahiri school. Also, there are several schools in the Shi'ah Islam as well. The Ja'fari or the Ithna 'Ashari School, the Isma'ili school and the Zaidi school.

The Sunni Islam bases Shari'ah—besides the Qur'an—on *Sunna* (i.e. the sayings and doings of the Holy Prophet), *qiyas* (analogy) and finally *ijma* '(consensus). However, except the Qur'an, the remaining three sources, i.e., *Sunna, qiyas and ijma'* are controversial. Some *ahadith* (sayings of the Prophet) are acceptable by some while they are rejected by others. Some *ahadith* are considered weak *(da'if)* and some of doubtful origin and some outright forgeries. Also, *qiyas*, analogical reasoning varies from jurist to jurist. There is controversy about *ijma'* as well. The crucial question is whose *ijma'*? Of the jurists and the 'Ulama or of the entire community? Also, has *ijma'* ever been possible? Have all 'Ulama, let alone the entire community, ever develped consensus on any issue? There are hardly any instances of this nature in the history of Islamic jurisprudence. Thus it will be seen that except the Qur'an which is divine and there are no textual differences about it, the three other fundamental sources, i.e., *Sunna*, *qiyas* and *ijma'* are human and hence controversial. It is also important to point out here that about the Prophet's pronouncements, i.e., *ahadith* there is controversy whether they be considered as divine or human. The *Ahl-e-Hadith* (i.e. the followers of Hadith) consider hadith as divine like the Qur'an while many others do not give it that status and consider it as human and hence not eternal.

The Shi'i jurisprudence (Shari'ah) is based on the Qur'an and the pronouncements of the Prophet as reported by Imams, i.e., the male descendants of the Prophet's daughter Hazrat Fatima and her husband 'Ali. The Qur'an as interpreted by these Imams is considered as the only right interpretation, every other interpretation is considered as mere conjecture or opinion *(ra'i)*. And *tafsir bi'r ra'i* (i.e. Qur'anic interpretation or exegesis through human opinion) is rejected outright in the Shi'a Islam. But there is controversy in the Shi'ah Islam as to who is rightfully appointed Imam. The Ithna 'Asharis (twelvers), the Isma 'ilis (also referred to as seveners), Zaidis, the Qaramitas and the Alavids, all mutually differ on this issue. All these sects have Imams of their own and consider others as not rightfully appointed and hence have no legitimacy. Also, the juridical pronouncements of these Imams differ from each other even on matters of principles, at times.

Thus had it been immutable the Shari'ah would not have differed from one school to the other and from sect to sect. The Qur'an, being divine, does not differ and is immutable. It admits of no change. However, its interpretation differs from sect to sect and from one school to the other. Thus the Qur'an is divine and its interpretations are human and what is human admits of change. The Shari'ah, being based on human interpretations of divine word, can, and does admit change. What was thought to be just in respect of women's rights in medieval ages, is no longer so. The idea of justice also changes with changing consciousness and what is just in one age may not necessarily be just in the other. We will throw more light on this aspect little later. It is in fact very important aspect as far as the Qur'anic concept of law is concerned.

One of the important sources of the Shari'ah law is *hadith* or *Sunna*. As pointed out above, this too is not above controversy. There are two types of controversies about this seminal source of Islamic law:

(1) whether *hadith* is divine or human, and

(2) whether it is authentic, weak or forged.

The Qur'an is unanimously accepted as divine and there is no controversy about it. Also, its contents are also accepted with unanimity and without any controversy. No one maintains that this or that verse of the Qur'an is unauthentic, or added later, or of doubtful origin. But it is not so as far as *hadith* literature is concerned. There are several *ahadith* which are controversial. Either they are considered of doubtful origin or weak or outright forgery. It is said that Imam Abu Hanifa, the founder of the Hanafi School of law, accepted only 17 *ahadith* as true and authentic and yet he used many more while giving his juridical opinions.

There are Muslims who maintain that *ahadith* are divine like the Qur'an. They believe that the Qur'anic verse:

"Nor does he speak out of desire, it is naught but revelation that is revealed" (53:3-4) applies to the Prophet's all pronouncements including his *ahadith.* These Muslims believe that *ahadith* too, are divine and hence above any human controversy. Thus this source of Shari'ah also becomes equally divine for them. However, there is no unanimity about it. Not only that *hadith* is not believed to be divine by large sections of Muslims, it is not above controversy as to its origin. Imam Bukhari, one of the greatest collectors of *ahadith*, is said to have collected more than six hundred thousand *ahadith* of which he accepted only four thousand and rejected others as of doubtful origin or outright forgeries. This clearly shows how some interested people were producing *hadith* literature to serve their own ends. Unfortunately, many of these *ahadith* went into juridical formulations in general, and about women, in particular. These formulations reflect the prejudices and dominant thinking of the time rather than the Qur'anic principles. These formulations, therefore, cannot be treated above change.

Also, there is yet another problem about *hadith* literature. And this problem remains, even if *hadith* literature is treated as divine and immutable. The Qur'an which is unanimously held to be divine by all Muslims contain many pronouncements which are directly related to the then prevailing Arab social structure. These pronouncements also reflect the social norms or social problems as they existed then. These pronouncements cannot be of universal application in other societies and cultures. We would like to cite examples. There was a practice called *zihar* among Arabs. It is mentioned in 33:4 and 58:2-3. It was a practice among Arabs to declare their wives like their mothers and abandon them. Thus in verse 33:4 the Qur'an says:

> "Allah has not made for any man two hearts within him, nor has He made your wives whom you desert by Zihar, your mother..."

Edward William Lane defines Zihar in his Arabic-English Lexicon as husband telling his wife thou art to me as the back of my mother. In verse 2 of Chapter 58 the Qur'an says.

"Those of you who put away their wives by calling them their mothers—they are not their mothers. None are their mothers save those who give them birth, and they utter indeed a hateful word and a lie..." And in verse 3 of the same chapter it is said, "And those who put away their wives by calling them their mothers, then go back on that which they said, must free a captive before they touch one another. To this you are exhorted..."

From above two verses we come to know that Arabs used to desert their wives calling them like the back of their mothers and some used to go back on that vow and would like to touch their wives again. The Qur'an prescribed that they free a captive (i.e. a slave) before breaking their vow. Now this practice was unique to the Arab society of that time. We do not find such practices in other societies. Also, today there is no institution of slavery, it has already been abolished. If an Arab today pronounces Zihar on his wife and wants to take back his vow there are no slaves available to free. Thus, such verses in the Qur'an should be treated as contextual, i.e., revealed in the context of that society and are no more valid as social practices have changed. Similarly, the institution of slavery is no more. There are several pronouncements about slaves and slavery in the holy Qur'an but they are no longer applicable as the institution itself does not exist any more. But in Shari'ah as formulated in the 2nd and 3rd century Hijrah (Islamic Calendar) these practices prevailed and hence elaborate laws were made by the jurists based on Qur'an or *hadith*. But they are totally irrelevant today. Thus the proposition that Shari'ah laws are immutable is not maintainable.

The Qur'anic verses thus should be divided into two categories namely (1) contextual and (2) normative. The normative pronouncements of the Qur'an are eternal and while rethinking issues in Islamic Shari'ah, particularly pertaining to women's rights the normative pronouncements will have precedence over the contextual. But during the early centuries, contextual often had precedence over normative and it was quite 'normal' then. And hence these formulations became widely acceptable in that society. These laws were thought to be normative then and hence struck deeper roots in society as well as in hearts and minds of the people as well and came to acquire status of immutability with the passage of time.

Thus, even if *hadith* is accepted as divine its contextuality will have to be kept in mind. It is also said, and rightly so, that the Prophet explained the Qur'anic verses through his words and deeds and who knew the meaning and import of the Qur'anic verses better than the Prophet. Quite true. But the question of contextuality remains. The holy Prophet, while dealing with the given society, could not have gone beyond its context in explaining and practising the Qur'anic pronouncements. Again it can best be illustrated with an example of women's status in that society. While explaining the cause of revelation of the Qur'anic verse 4:34, all classical commentators like Tabari, Fakhruddin Razi and others maintain that the Prophet allowed a woman (daughter of his companion) right to retaliate against her husband who had unjustly slapped her but, in view of the prevailing social ethos it laid to unrest among the men and Qur'an reversed the Prophet's decision. This once again shows that the question of contextuality is very important and highly relevant in all judicial pronouncements be they those of the Prophet or other Islamic jurists.

Another example in this respect is that of *milk-e-yamin,* i.e., legitimising sexual relations with a slave girl. There is near unanimity among the Islamic jurists that it is permissible to have sexual relations with slave girls and that the Prophet himself had such relations with a Coptic Christian slave girl. The modernists and some other commentators of course challenge this formulation and maintain that the Prophet had married her. But Maulana Maududi, one of the contemporary Islamic thinkers and founder of the Jam'at-e-Islami, maintains in his commentary on the Qur'an (*Tafhim al Qur'an*) that the Prophet had relations with the slave-girl without marrying her. Most of the eminent medieval jurists concur with this. But if this view that sexual relations with a slave-girl is permissible is accepted, the contemporary society would not approve of it. Thus, the Prophet's Sunna cannot be seen out of its social context.

There were four great jurists in Sunni Islam who founded four different schools of jurisprudence. All four differ from each other on many issues. Much has been written on causes of these differences. But the modern scholars maintain that one important reason was their differing social situations. Imam Hanbal and Imam Malik lived in Madina and thus were quite close to social ethos of that society in which the Prophet himself lived. They were closer in their juridical formulations to what the Prophet said and did in that society. Imam Shafi'i and Imam Abu Hanifa, on the other hand, lived in Egypt and Iraq respectively which were confluences of many cultures and thus were unorthodox in their methodology in arriving at juridical opinions. While Imam Malik and Hanbal mainly relied on *Hadith*, Imam Sahfi'i and Abu Hanifa used *qiyas* and *ijma* 'more liberally, apart from *Hadith*. Thus, while the former two Imam's formulations were closer to Arab practices in Mecca and Madina, the latter two Imam's formulations had been largely influenced by other practices as well. This clearly shows that Shari'ah is influenced by human situations and can incorporate situational changes. The Arab '*adat* (the Arab customary law) also became integral part of the Shari'ah law. Thus, the then prevailing opinions about women in the Arab society greatly influenced the Shari'ah laws pertaining to women. The Arab *'adat* cannot certainly be considered divine injunctions and hence immutable. In fact the Arab *'adat* had great relevance as long as Islam was confined to the Arab society. But once it spread out to far off areas, the need to incorporate other practices also became equally important. And now the changed consciousness about women's rights can also not be ignored.

There is yet another problem about the hadith literature which is, as pointed out above, an important ingredient of Shari'ah. The *ahadith* were generally reported by the Prophet's companions. In this respect even the most authentically reported *ahadith* present different kinds of problems. Firstly, most of the *ahadith* reported by the companions were not the exact words of the Prophet but the overall meaning of what he said. There are hardly few *ahadith* which can be said to be the exact words of the Prophet. Secondly, the *hadith* literature also incorporates the reports about what the companions saw the Prophet doing. Thus, the Prophetic Sunna includes both what the Prophet said as well as reports about what he did in different situations.

Now among the Prophet's companions there were all kinds of people. There were companions who had sharp memory and good understanding and comprehension of the problems. There were companions who had very poor understanding of the complex issues and also there were companions who had poor memory. And there were companions who spent several years with the Prophet and there were companions who spent only a few hours with him, and even those who saw and heard him from a distance. All that these companions reported having heard from the Prophet became part of hadith corpus which then was used for formulating Shari'ah laws.

Not only that. There is yet another problem. The *ahadith* have been reported by people who heard it from the companions of the companions *(tab'i tabi'in)* and companions of the companions of the companions of the Prophet. Thus, there is whole chain of narrators known as *rijal* (the narrating men or women). The collectors of *ahadith* did try to develop the science of *rijal* (i.e. *'ilm al-rijal*) criteria to judge the honesty and integrity of the narrators. But this criterion judged the honesty and integrity of the narrators rather than his or her understanding, comprehension or intelligence. Moreover, there were often missing links. And also the cases wherein much was not known about one or more of the narrators in the chain. Many narrators were of totally different cultural backgrounds—some narrators being Arabs and others non-Arabs not properly acquainted with the Arab affairs. Also, many narrators had their own biases for or against women (also about other matters) and these biases definitely affected their narratives or reports.

It was for this reason that the Prophet had strictly prohibited his followers from compiling his sayings. He knew very well that his sayings may not be reported faithfully to future generations for various reasons. Also, he was fully aware of the fact that the future generations will insist on strictly following what reaches them as the sayings of

Allah's Messenger though they may be facing different circumstances. Even the first Caliph Hazrat Abu Bakr did not permit compilation of *ahadith* for similar reasons. Still people did compile these *ahadith* though much later. And by the time they were compiled, spurious ones had mixed up with authentic ones.

It will be thus seen that *hadith* literature, even if entirely authentic, presents several problems and it cannot be considered as highly reliable source of Islamic legislation. But the Islamic *juris corpus* is as much based on the problematic *hadith* literature as on the holy Qur'an. Still the 'Ulama project it as unquestionable divine and hence immutable. They refuse to admit any change even though sweeping changes are taking place in the social, cultural, economic and political circumstances. The doctrine of *taqlid* (mechanical imitation) is emphasised by the contemporary jurists in the world of Islam. They maintain that rethinking about the formulations of the great Imams is not permissible. In fact these formulations are treated as divine. Also, most of the 'Ulama do not even permit taking more favourable provisions for women from other schools of law. They insist that any one school should be followed in its entirety. Some 'Ulama of course permit such an approach. But they are fewer in numbers. Now more and more 'Ulama are coming around to permitting this approach which has given some relief to women. The Ottoman rulers had adopted this approach in nineteenth century itself. But still it is not widely accepted. *Taqlid* is the generally established rule. It is causing great deal of hardships to Muslim women everywhere.

The holy Prophet had anticipated the problems which will arise in future. He took care to leave some guidance in this respect. Firstly, he encouraged what is known as *ijtihad* (i.e. exerting oneself to solve newly arising problems if no precise guidance was available in the Qur'an and Prophet's Sunnah). The *hadith* regarding Ma'adh bin Jabal is well known about this. When the Prophet appointed Ma'adh as governor of the Yemen, he asked him how will he govern." According to the Qur'an", Ma'adh replied. "And if it is not in the Qur'an?" the Prophet asked him. According to the Prophet's "Sunna", replied

Ma'adh. And if he does not find anything of the sort in the Sunna also?, the Prophet inquired. "Then I will exert myself to solve the problem (*Ana ajtahedo*)". The Prophet patted his back in approval. Also, the Prophet is reported to have said that even if one makes mistake in doing *ijtihad* he/she will earn one merit and if one does not err he/she will earn two merits. The Prophet did this to encourage Muslims to solve problems which were likely to arise in future.

From this, many modernists argue that one must resort to *ijtihad* to solve new problems and issues including women's issues. However, the orthodox 'Ulama argue that the gates of *ijtihad* were closed long ago and also that now there are no qualified persons to do *ijtihad*. They feel the great Imams and some of their followers had the requisite qualification and none today has such impressive merits. Some 'Ulama do feel the need for *ijtihad* but they too stop short of resorting to it for fear of consequences. Some who did, faced the wrath of the fellow jurists and were even ostracised. The debate is raging in the Islamic world for and against *ijtihad*. And when it comes to women's issues and rights, the resistance to change and rethinking is much greater in the male-dominated Islamic world.

Dr Muhammad Iqbal, a noted Urdu poet and thinker from India (d. 1938) was greatly in favour of *ijtihad*. He wrote in his *Reconstruction of Religious Thought in Islam* :

> "The ultimate spiritual basis of all life, as conceived by Islam, is eternal and reveals itself in variety and change. A society based on such a conception of reality must reconcile, in its life, the categories of permanence and change. But eternal principles when they are understood to exclude all possibilities of change which, according to the Qur'an, is one of the greatest 'signs' of God, tend to immobilise what is essentially mobile in its nature." (pp. 147-48).

Iqbal states in the above book very boldly,

> "The only alternative open to us, then, is to tear off from the hard crust which has immobilised an essentially dynamic outlook on life, and to rediscover the original verities of freedom,

equality, and solidarity with a view to rebuild our moral, social and political ideas out of their original simplicity and universality."(pp.156). Iqbal thus maintains that *ijtihad* is necessary to rebuild the law of Shari'ah in the light of modern thought and experience.

Ijtihad, I would like to emphasise here, is even more necessary today in respect of Shari'ah laws pertaining to women. It is highly regrettable that the Shari'ah law is almost inoperative in many other respects (like property and contract laws, criminal laws, financial transactions, etc.) but when it comes to women's issues, the Shari'ah laws are sought to be strictly applied. In several Muslim majority and minority countries, modern secular laws are applied in respect of all other things except laws pertaining to marriage, divorce, maintenance, inheritance etc. i.e. in the sphere of what is called personal laws. The greatest resistance, in the name of Shari'ah, is manifested by men when it comes to according better status to women. In this respect the Shari'ah becomes sacred and immutable and arouses great passions. The Islamic world, if it has to understand the dynamic spirit of Qur'an, and enact it in real life, will have to enact changes in the Shari'ah laws and accord women an equal status. In fact time has come to put the Qur'anic vision of sexual equality in practice.

As pointed out earlier, there are verses in the Qur'an which have contextual significance. These verses formed the legal foundations of Islamic law in that age. But these were not the verses having impress of permanence and principles. There are certainly the verses which lay down norms and principles. Today the Islamic legislation should be based on these verses. Before we examine these verses, we would like to set out certain values which are fundamental to the Islamic teachings. Any legislation which ignores these fundamental values could be anything but Islamic. It is necessary to understand that the classical jurists though did not ignore these fundamental values but the application of these values was constrained by the social ethos of the age. The Prophet's traditions also had to take these constraints into account.

The most fundamental values in Islam, as expounded by the Qur'an are justice, benevolence and compassion. The Qur'anic terminology for these values is *'adl, ihsan* and *rahmah*. The Qur'an talks of these values in imperative category. The Qur'anic verse 16:90 testifies to this: And surely Allah enjoins justice and benevolence (to others). Thus it will be seen that justice is very central to the Islamic value system—as central as love to the Christian ethics. No legislation in Islam which ignores this value can be valid.

It is this concern for justice which makes the Qur'an show deep concern for the weaker sections of society. Thus the verse 28:5 expresses this concern for them and says:

"And we desire to bestow a favour upon those who were deemed weak in the land, and to make them the leaders, and to make them the heirs."

The Qur'an desires to bestow the mantle of leadership on this earth upon the weak. The Islamic jurisprudence has to imbibe this spirit towards the weaker sections of society. And, women certainly belong to this category as far as the patriarchal society is concerned.

It is important to note that the values like justice and compassion cannot be applied independent of the age. In the medieval period the understanding of the concept of justice was very different from what it is today. Our era is a democratic era and justice in our era cannot be deemed to have been done if equality of all humans irrespective of sex, race and creed, is not ensured. Discrimination between one and other human being on any ground, including the sexual one, will be taken as injustice. But in medieval ages these discriminations were thought to be quite natural and non-violative of the concept of justice. Even slavery was thought to be natural and in keeping with the principles of justice. In fact, if a slave ran away from the master it was thought to be an unjust act. Today, let alone slavery, even bonded labour or child labour is considered as grossly violative of justice. Thus, the concept of justice greatly varies in a democratic era from that of feudal one. And yet justice as a value remains important in both the ages. The expression of the concept of justice in a particular era is not fundamental but justice *per se*. However, in religious traditions, including in those of Islam, more important is the expression of justice in a particular age than the notion of justice itself. It is because of this the expression of justice in the *hadith* literature is more important than the notion of justice as fundamental value in the Qur'an. What was thought to be just during the classical period of Islam is thought to be just even today. And not only that the orthodox think the expression of the notion of justice today is violative of divine will. It is this attitude which impedes change in Islamic legislation so as to accord women equality with men.

However, one finds in the Qur'an full support for sexual equality in several verses. The Qur'an was certainly mindful of what was just in that era when it was revealed and what ought to be just in the transcendental sense. When the Prophet permitted a Muslim wife retaliation against her husband as a measure of justice, the Qur'an over ruled him and permitted a measure of conditional male domination, though conditionality of justice was stipulated (see the verse 4:34). It would have been thought to be unjust if the Qur'an had permitted the wife to retaliate against her husband and it would not have found acceptability in that society.

However, the Qur'an also did not intend to eternalise the then acceptable notion of justice. The dynamics of 'is' and 'ought' or interaction between history and eternity informs the whole spirit of Qur'an. Unfortunately the orthodox miss this very spirit while reading the Qur'an from their own perspective. The verse 33:35 is much more fundamental in this respect as it clearly accords women equality with men in all respects. While 4:34 is informed by the spirit of that era, the verse 33:34 deals with the eternal dimensions. The orthodox, however, do not wish to go beyond the divine injunction expressed in 4:34. They have frozen their minds in the classical age of Islam. What was temporal has become permanent for them and what is permanent is just brushed aside as of no consequence.

The Qur'an must be re-read and re-interpreted in today's context as the classical jurists read and interpreted it in their own context. No reformation is possible without such re-reading and re-interpreting the Qur'anic verses. The real intention of the Qur'an—that of sexual equality—comes through several verses. Those verses need to be re-emphasised. The verse 2:228 ("And women have rights similar to those against them in a just manner") is quite definitive in this respect. It hardly needs any comment. Maulana Muhammad Ali, a noted Pakistani commentator says commenting on the above verse: "The rights of women against their husbands are here stated to be similar to those which the husbands have against their wives. The statement must, no doubt, have caused a stir in a society which never recognised any rights for the woman. The change in this respect was really a revolutionising one, for the Arabs hitherto regarded women as mere chattels. Women were given a position equal in all respects to that of men, for they were declared to have rights similar to those which were exercised against them. This declaration brought about a revolution not only in Arabia but in the whole world, for the quality of rights of women with those of men was never previously recognized by any nation or any reformer. The woman could no longer be discarded at the will of her 'lord', but she could either claim equality as a wife or demand a divorce." (Maulana Muhammad Ali, 1973, p. 97).

However, much of this spirit of justice and equality was lost when the Islamic doctors legislated under the influence of their own social ethos. The Qur'anic categorical imperatives were ignored, as pointed out before, in favour of those verses which were of the nature of concession to the age. There are many instances of this, polygamy, being one. Firstly, it was a permissive measure in some circumstances (large number of war widows and orphans to be taken care of as many men perished fighting in the battle of Uhud) with great emphasis on justice to all the wives (their number not exceeding four). It was great advance over the pre-Islamic practice of marrying unlimited number and without any obligation towards the wives.

Secondly, the verse on polygamy (4:3) is followed by the verse 4:1 which emphasises sexual equality in the words that ...

"Lord Who created you from a single being (*min nafsin*

wahidatin) and created its mate of the same (kind) and spread from these two many men and women..."

And the verse 4:2 which talks of justice for orphans and widows. Then polygamy is permitted provided one marries widows and orphans (and not any women) and there also justice with all wives is a must failing which one must marry only one. No one before had insisted on such conditionalities for plurality of wives. Thirdly, the verse 4:129 states that even if you desire you cannot do justice between wives and ends by saying that do not leave the one with total disinclination and incline towards the other leaving the first in suspense. If the verses 4:3 and 4:129 are read together, polygamy is as good as not permissible. But the jurists, in order to avoid implications of reading the two verses together resorted to various explanations and took help of *hadith* to keep possibility of polygamy open. And, much worse, in practising it, conditionality for justice was hardly enforced. In today's conditions, polygamy should be done away with in order to implement the Qur'anic conditionality. Abolition of polygamy will serve the end of justice far better than its practice today. The arguments that men are more sexual or that in case there are more women than men, it will be better to permit polygamous marriages to avoid immoral relations, etc. are all attempts at human rationalisation than divine intention. These arguments do not hold much water as there may be excess of women over men in one country and excess of men over women in another. And prostitution and immoral sex thrived even when men could marry any number of wives and also keep slave girls without limit.

Also, normatively speaking the Qur'an has conceded all rights to women which were available earlier only to men. She could exercise her right to divorce her husband as men could divorce her at will. The Prophet permitted a woman called Jamila to divorce her husband—against his will and without consulting him—just because she did not approve of his looks. While the verse 2:229 permits her to liberate herself from an unsatisfactory marriage by suitable compensation to husband (i.e. returning the dower amount), the verse

4:35 gives her right to appoint an arbiter of her own to settle the marital dispute or agree to divorce. Also, the Qur'an requires of men to keep their wives in goodly manner and to leave them, if necessary, in a benevolent manner. And the verse 4:19 lays down that women could not be inherited or taken as wives against their will. Men are also exhorted in this verse not to take a portion of what they have given to their wives and to treat them kindly. It was also emphasised in 9:71 that believing men and believing women are each others friends and they (both men and women) enjoin good and forbid evil. Thus, both enjoy equal obligations and from this verse jurists like Abu Hanifa have concluded that woman can become Qadi, i.e., judge as it is her obligation also to enjoin good and forbid evil.

It is argued from the verse 4:11 that a daughter inherits half that of son and hence man is superior. Some modernists also argue on the basis of this verse that it is injustice to a daughter as she has been given half that of son and hence it is bias against female sex. It is simply not true. From one perspective one can say it was a cautious reform in favour of daughters. In pre-Islamic society, daughters did not inherit at all and now they were given right to inherit half that of son. From another perspective it could be argued that it was not bias against daughters that they were given half that of son but daughters were duly compensated by *mehr* (dower amount at the time of marriage) whereas sons had to loose out by paying dower to their wives. And the wives do not have to spend anything by way of maintenance as it is enjoined upon the husbands to maintain their wives. Also, a woman inherited as wife and mother too. Moreover she did not contribute to family wealth in those days by way of earning but now she does and her portion could be increased in view of the changed conditions. Thus the Qur'an has done no injustice to her in matters of inheritance also.

Another question is of *hijab* (veil). There is no injunction in the Qur'an that she veil her face. The verse 24:31 only lays down that women should not display their adornment and fineries publicly and that they should cover their breasts (tribal women in those days used to leave their breasts uncovered) and that they should not strike her feet with anklets in public so as to draw attention to their adornments. In this verse both men and women have been asked to lower their gaze (4:30-31) and to restrain their sexual passions. As for what constitutes adornment and what should be displayed and what should be not, there are sharp differences of opinion. These differences are human and every commentator has his views. But Tabari, the noted classical commentator has summarised the views of many eminent jurists in his *Jami 'al-Bayan*. According to him adornment means:

(1) adornment of dress or the clothes that a woman wears, in other words, she is not required to cover the clothes she wears;

(2) it means the adornment which the woman is not required to cover, such as collyrium, rings, bracelets and her face;

(3) the exception (*illa ma zahara minha*) relates to a woman's clothing and her face.

These were opinions of the theologians of those days. Today the sensibilities in this respect are very different and the scope of the exception can be made much wider subject to, and that is real intention behind it, to restain sexual passion and protect ones chastity. To prevent extra-marital sex is the responsibility of both men and women and not of women alone, as per the Qur'an. Also, both should avoid wearing sexually stimulating dress. They should wear dignified dress. Covering of face by women is not required in the Qur'an at all. It was cultural practice of some post-Islamic societies. The Qur'an also does not require women to be confined to homes. On the contrary they could earn and what they earned was theirs alone as per 4:32 (And for women is the benefit of what they earn). The cultural practices like confining women to home were sought to be legitimised later by inventing suitable *ahadith* or by far fetched interpretations of the Qur'an.

In conclusion it should be said that if one goes by those verses of the Qur'an which belong to the normative category or which are of the nature of laying down principles and givers of value, men and women should enjoy equal rights in every respect. It would be necessary to re-read and re-interpret many verses which were used for centuries to subjugate women in Muslim societies. This subjugation was more cultural and patriarchal than Islamic or Qur'anic. The whole *corpus juris* of Islam relating to women needs to be seriously re-thought on the basis of Qur'an.

2

Should the Muslim Practice of Triple Divorce be Banned: Pros and Cons

Imtiaz Ahmed

Modernist legislation does not, generally speaking, arise out of genuine public demand. There exist the two well-defined groups of the 'ulema', who are for the greater part traditionalists, and of the modernists, many of whom are modern lawyers. Modernist legislation is imposed by a government whenever the modernists have succeeded in gaining its sympathy and the government feels strong enough to overcome resistance of the traditionalists. Modernist Islamic legislation therefore often appears somewhat haphazard and arbitrary.*

This brief paper focuses on the issue of Muslim practice of triple divorce which has been a subject of much heated controversy in recent years. It is brief because this seminar has an activist rather than an academic thrust and no useful purpose will be served by engaging in a detailed discussion of the subject from an academic viewpoint. The aim instead is to draw such insights as a serious academic exercise would suggest so that a basis for initiating practical action by those who are concerned with the broader issue of amelioration of the status of women can be worked out. This is precisely what this paper attempts.

*Joseph Sachacht, *An Introduction to Islamic Law*, Oxford, The Clarendon Press, 1964, p.105.

For charting out a practical course of intervention in respect of Muslim divorce practices, it is necessary to clear a few cobwebs that have so far clouded discussion and action. For the sake of brevity, I should like to limit myself to three such cobwebs which to my mind need to be cleared for the sake of clarity as well as for realistically appraising the nature of the problems that the Muslim practice of triple divorce raises for women.

Comparison of Position of Hindu and Muslim Women

First there is a strong tendency in the way discussion on this subject has so far gone on to implicitly make a comparison with Hindu women. This is a part of a larger proclivity of Muslims to always look at their own situation against Hindus as if the social and economic histories and political economies of both communities were similar, if not the same. This proclivity is regretable enough in itself as it immediately has the effect of changing the terms of the discourse and leads to a focus which deflects away from the problems which Muslims claim they face. Applied to Muslim women, this tendency has the effect of setting Muslim women apart and creating the belief and impression that the problem Muslim women face is unique and distinct. Whether this is indeed the case cannot be presumed on impressions. It would have to be demonstrated empirically.

Let me illustrate this point. There is general recognition that a Muslim Woman's position as compared to men in the family is unequal. This recognition cannot be the basis of presuming that this is different from the unequal nature of the relationship which Hindu women have with men in the family. If comparison is really the aim, then one would have to systematically explore what is the precise nature, intensity and manifestation of the unequal relations of Muslim women within the family and then go across and look at the nature, intensity and manifestations of the unequal relations of Hindu women within the family. Only through such thorough and controlled processes of research can similarities and differences between Muslim and Hindu women can be established. Such studies do not exist at present.

There has been much social research on Muslim women in recent decades. Its quality may be questionable at times, but it nevertheless has succeeded in producing considerable empirical evidence that is quite enlightening. Even so, on the point of comparison with Hindu women this research continues to be remarkably deficient. Practically all the studies that I am familiar with (exceptions are few and far between) have looked at Muslim women in isolation from the wider society of which Muslim women are also a part. One consequence of this has been that comparison with Hindu women is implicitly made without actually exploring this comparableness as a part of the research exercise. If comparison is to be made, then we would require different kinds of studies that build this comparableness in the very process of drawing up the research design.

There is one sense in which the contrast between Muslim and Hindu women can be presumed. This is that the religious values and laws relating to women are divergent and contrasting. On the one hand, textual Hindu values relating to women are far more gender discrimatory than textual Islamic values, though at base both traditional systems subordinate women. Under both systems a woman is supposed to stand in relation to man in the same position as man stands in relation to the total social system. Again, after enactment of Hindu Code Bill women can be said to have been given rights which are not yet legally available to Muslim women. However, it remains open whether these differences of textual values and legal priviledges make for actual differences in the social standing of Hindu and Muslim women within the family.

One of the points conclusively established by social research on Muslims in India is continuing influence of Indian cultural ethos in the life of Indian Muslims. Even though every Muslim in India (and this holds for Muslims everywhere) claims adherence to the Qur'an (and therefore to the Islamic *sharia'h*), the truth is that on many aspects his attitudes and behaviour deviate from textual religious values and norms because of the continuing hold of cultural orientations and practices that enjoy legitimacy in the Indian environment. For example, textual Islamic values emphasise equality of all believers but social practices on this point diverge substantially. Again, textual values sanction divorce, but a stigma attaches to divorce and a divorced women among Muslims. This is largely a result of the hold of indigenous (one may well say Hindu) values on Muslims.

Of course, one is not arguing that the negative attitudes towards divorce and divorced women are uniform throughout the community either among Hindus or among Muslims. Among Hindus themselves such attitudes operate most forcefully among the higher castes whose lifestyles are supposed to reflect a deeper imprint of textual religious values. There is otherwise a great deal of variation across caste communities and classes. Among lower castes negative attitudes towards divorce and divorced women are greatly attenuated. This picture is not particularly different among Muslims. Among higher castes and social classes of Muslims divorce is frowned upon. Among intermediate and lower castes and social classes of Muslims such attitudes are absent. The point one is making is that both textual religious values and legal enactment are a poor guide to establishing points of comparison across religious communities.

This has a direct relevance to the terms of the debate over whether triple divorce is a problem for Muslim women. The case for intervention on this count cannot be made to rest on the premise that Muslim women are more disadvantaged in this respect than Hindu women. This is how the case has often been presented. My point is that building the case in this manner is self-defeating for several reasons. For one thing, we do not have any comparative data to show that Muslim women are any differently placed than Hindu women when it comes to divorce. Even the differences that exist between the two communities in terms of textual values of formal legal codes are of little significance in this respect because such sociological evidence as we possess suggests that despite differences on these counts there are remarkable similarities between them when it comes to social practices. Therefore, if a case for any intervention for change in Muslim divorce practice has to be made at all, it should be specifically made to rest on a logic which is internal to the community. It should not be made to rest on the logic that Muslim women are any more or less disadvantaged than their counterparts in other religious communities.

Second, there is need to be clear about the rationale for any change that may be contemplated. Usually, those who have argued in favour of intervention on this count have couched their position in terms of the concept of gender justice as articulated in modern democratic and liberal theories. This presumes that any religious or cultural tradition that does not believe in absolute equality of men and women and does not accord them absolutely equal rights in every sphere of life lacks a concept of gender justice. This is a problematic construction that has the potential to obfuscate any possibilities of change. After all, within all traditions and religious or cultural communities, opinions are divided between those who would want to adhere to relatively conservative interpretations and those who would want to explore the possibilities for more broadbased interpretations to advance the general good. The arguments of both sections of opinion are within the tradition and the disputation is really over matters of interpretation. On the other hand, when the case for intervention is anchored to a framework which lies outside the tradition, the terms of the discourse are at once transformed. The question then is transposition of the values of one tradition by the value premises of another. When this happens the basis for dialogue easily breaks down and a hardening of attitude takes place. The liberal and democratic framework recognises no space to a tradition that is not consonant with its values. The other tradition sees no reasons to interact and respond where autonomy of its own values is not even conceded. It becomes a question of the tradition either surviving through open resistance or being vanquished by another tradition.

Many may be inclined to argue that this mode posing the interaction between the liberal-democratic and religious-cultural traditions is somewhat exaggerated. They would contend that what one is anticipating is not a complete displacement of one tradition or its value premises by another, but rather for a degree of cultural acculturation where one tradition takes from the liberal-democratic tradition what it lacks without jeopardising its own viability. This line of reasoning ignores two significant dimensions. First, acculturation is a process that is definitely shaped and governed by a relationship of power. Under the circumstances, any anticipation that a transposition of values can take place through a process of acculturation misses the point that all traditions, whether religious and cultural or liberal-democratic, carry a conception of their own worth on which they can compromise only under duress and that too not without putting up stiff resistance. Acculturation or adoption of values of liberal-democratic values by traditions whose value premises are different is inherently problematic. Second, where this acculturation is pressed, whether by the pressures generated by liberal-democratic values from outside or by advocates of change from within, the response is either defensive or apologetic such as we have often seen when countries have struggled against colonial domination where the pressure for acculturation was probably the heaviest.

Concept of Gender Justice

There is need to recognise that a conception of gender justice is not unique to the liberal-democractic tradition. Other traditions too have conception of gender justice, except that their conceptions may not be quite consonant with the conception of gender justice in the liberal-democratic tradition. Consider, for example, the case of Islam though much of what I say about Islam would hold equally for other religious traditions whether eastern or western. One can say that Islam does not have a conception of gender justice, but when one is saying this what is the criterion on which one is basing one's judgement. Is one basing it on an evaluation of the Islamic tradition in terms of the value-premises of the liberal-democratic tradition? Or, is one basing it on the evaluation of Islam on its own value premises? My own view is that when we assert that Islam lacks a conception of gender justice what we are really saying is that judged against the yardsticks provided by liberal-democratic theories Islam cannot be said to contain a concept of gender justice. This is not the same thing as saying that Islam does not have a concept of gender justice. My own view is that Islam too has a conception of gender justice which differs significantly from the liberal-democratic conception of gender justice. Under the Islamic conception of gender justice, men and women are not seen as equal nor are they actually conceded absolutely equal rights and privileges (as in the liberal-democratic tradition), but a great deal of emphasis is placed upon treating women with consideration and ensuring justice to them. This conception may not entirely accord with the liberal-democratic conception justice, but then insisting that conceptions of gender justice in other traditions must necessarily subscribe to that conception is tantamount to denying autonomy to other traditions and their conceptions of the good life. This is a predicament that much of multicultural theory and practice is trying painfully to come to terms with.

Strategies for Protagonists of Change

My own view is that from a practical point of view there are two possible courses open to those who are trying to bring about change in traditional societies where the conceptions of good life have an intrinsic integrity of their own and are contemporaneously at variance with the liberal-democratic values. One course is to attempt to displace the conceptions of the tradition by those from liberal-democratic values by insisting that the fundamental integrity of the tradition must be broken up, particularly if it has no place for liberal-democratic kind of values, by transplanting the liberal-democratic values on to the tradition. The other course can be to take the tradition as an integral whole and to work towards enlarging the traditional conception of good life to subserve contemporary ends. If the first course is adopted, one is forced to take an outsider position *vis-a-vis* the tradition and one is likely to end up fighting the battle for change on a hostile terrain. I dare say that this precisely has been happening with the efforts of those who have been struggling for bringing about social change in traditional societies, including Muslim societies. On the other hand, if the second course is followed, one has the advantage of struggling for change from within the tradition and the terrain is neither hostile nor entirely foreign. One of the advantages of this strategy is that it is perfectly in line with the tradition of dialogue and contestation over the meaning of the *sharia'h* which has been a feature of Muslim societies right after the death of the Prophet.

The protagonists of change must have a clear conception both of the modality for change and the terrain over which they would like to fight. If the modality is one of displacement of what are intrinsically Muslim conceptions of gender justice by a liberal-democratic conception of gender justice, the resistance would be bitter and the chances of making headway are bound to be limited, especially in a situation where Muslims are in a minority and their worries are centred on the preservation of their distinctiveness in a supposedly unfriendly cultural environment. If the modality is one of enlarging women's rights and priviledges by working within the Islamic conception of gender justice, there is at least hope that one would enlist wider support and carry a section of the traditionalist opinion along. The thrust in the latter case would be to harp upon the possibilities which the values of the tradition allow and whom subsequent interplay of conservatism or vested interests has tended to restrict. For some of us modernists those values may be archaic and outmoded, but for the vast majority of Muslims they continue to remain sacrosanct and worth-pursuing. For this reason at least, if for no other, caution would require us to highlight the deviations from the proclaimed values as a basis for working towards change rather than collide headlong with the traditional value-premises relating to gender merely on the ground that they do no accord with liberal-democratic value premises.

Finally, there is need to be clear about the change that is desired. At the present time, the protagonists of change are divided along a series of different lines and different courses of change. Some of them are likely to be satisfied if a marriage contract is designed that can ensure that a Muslim woman is not shortcharged. Others are inclined to demand that the provision for triple divorce is abrogated as it is this legal provision that is the cause of real misery for women. Still others would like that a system of registration of Muslim marriages is adpted or a uniform law of marriage and divorce is enacted so that all women are entitled to the same privileges and rights without any discrimination on the ground of religion and culture. These differences of opinion seem, in my view, to emanate from a lack of knowledge of the real sources of hardships for Muslim women in the event of divorce and the conception one carries of marriage stability as a value in itself. Such differences of viewpoints and strategies are likely to confuse the nature of the precise intervention that is called for dealing with the situation prevailing on the ground. It also overlooks the point that there has to be a degree of balance between the need for marriage stability and the option for dissolution of marriage in any society.

Divorce Laws and Legislations

Civilised opinion has been veering around to the point that a system of divorce should not be such as to make marriage itself into an oppressive bond. Nor should it make divorce so easy that one can get out of the marriage bond with ease. It should make it possible for marriage stability to subsist, but at the same time it should provide for dissolution of a marriage where spouses legitimately feel that they cannot live together for whatever reasons. In other words, the system of divorce should not be such as to allow for a free interplay of caprice and flimsiness. For instance, the jurisprudence that the Supreme Court in this country has been evolving is that legitimate divorce should be easily allowed, but capricious and flimsy divorce should be discouraged. It is against this kind of evolving jurisprudence that our conception of Muslim divorce should be formulated. Unless this is done, there is danger that we may find ourselves advocating a system of divorce that renders a divorce extremely difficult and complicated so mush so that it may turn out to be oppressive for even those genuine cases where dissolution of marriage may seem to be the only way out for the spouses to exist in mutual social and mental health and harmony.

Characteristics

On the face of it, the Islamic law of divorce would appear to be remarkably modern. There elements make it easily comparable to the laws considered modern. On a comparative view of divorce laws across the different societies, it appears that in order to qualify as modern a divorce law should have at least three characterstics. First, it should allow for divorce, though there are significant differences across the world in the degrees of ease with which divorce in the different societies is allowed. Traditionally, divorce laws in different religious traditions disallowed divorce altogether. Under Hindu law, at least the part of the law that governed marriage practices of higher castes, divorce was not permissable at all. Virtually the same was the case with the Christian law before the rise of Protestantism. Catholic law laid down that a validly contracted marriage could not be dissolved and divorce was therefore disallowed. This doctrine underlay the ideology and law of marriage in Europe for centuries and the history of divorce since the sixteenth century has been, for the most part, a rejection of the Catholic position. On the contrary, Islamic position on divorce was from the beginning more reasonable. While divorce was openly condemned as the most despised by God, provision for divorce was made. Conditions under which divorces could be allowed as well as the procedure to give legal effect to a divorce were clearly laid down.

Second, a modern divorce law is supposed to vest the initiative to decide whether the marriage should be sustained or whether it would be better in the interest of the spouses to dissolve it should vest in the spouses rather than an external authority. If we trace the development of divorce laws in different countries in Europe and America, it is clear that the change has been in two significant directions. On the one hand, the trend has been to shift the responsibility for defining marriage breakdown. Historically, a divorce was defined as a legal solution only in those unions where one of the partners had been the victim of a matrimonial offense and sought to free himself from the contract on these grounds. The guilty party could not sue for divorce on a unilateral basis and could hence was kept in marital bondage at other legal partners' discretion. The great difficulties faced in legally disengaging oneself from marriage impressed upon the individual the seriousness of the marriage vows. Even if it was normally easy for individuals to embark upon the contract, these obstacles acted as a disincentive to their harbouring ideas of easily breaking it. This position has changed.

Moreover, the church and the state established the criteria for acceptable behaviour in marriage by limiting the grounds on which a separation or divorce might be obtained. On the other hand, the trend has been in a direction away from the imperative of apportioning or attributing blame to either spouse. Modern divorce legislations simply recognises that a marriage can break down in such a way that it is 'irremediable', 'irreconcilable', or 'irretrievable'. The law does not require information on the reasons for the breakdown of the marriages but simply evidence of it. The evidence required by most of these laws is that the couple has lived apart for a certain number of years. Legislations passed in recent years in most European countries enable couples to terminate unions on the ground that their marriage have broken down and are quite beyond repair. Therefore, no-fault divorce without the necessity of the divorce court having to go into the reasons for the breakdown of marriage is the second significant characteristics of modern divorce law.

Judged against this criterion, Islamic law is again remarkably modern. For one thing, it allows no-fault divorce; a marriage can be ended on the ground that it does not work, and there is no necessity to allocate blame and retribution between the two partners. Second, it places the power to pass judgement on the viability of a conjugal relationship within the control of the individual husbands and wives. It does not vest this power into any outside agency and the role assigned in traditional Muslim practice to the Qazi is merely that of seeing that divorce has followed the procedure laid down in law and not to adjudicate on or pass judgement on the viability of a conjugal relationship. This in itself may help to make the process of marital breakdown a more dignified and less punitive experience, although there are many dimensions to this experience only some of which are directly attributable to wider social institutions such as the law and the sanctions that it exerts on the individual. Finally, Islamic law allows for reconciliation between the spouses even after the process of divorce has been initiated. The Quran repeatedly exhorts reconciliation between estranged spouses.

The third characteristic of a modern law of divorce is that it should be fair and just towards both partners. On the face of it the Muslim practice of triple divorce which vests a unilateral right upon the husband to pronounce a summary divorce upon his wife by simply stating three times at one sitting that he is divorcing her would appear to be, and has been found by the courts in the country, to be repugnant to the principle of equity, justice and good conscience, but in order to deal with this question one has the recognise a distinction between what may be described as the revealed injunctions in the Quran and those injunctions that came to be subsequently articulated in varied ways in the jurisprudences enunciated by the different schools of Muslim law. As far as can be ascertained from a careful reading of the Quran, which Muslims consider to be the primary and most authoritative source of canonical law, this practice did not originally constitute a part of the body of rule that were supposed to govern divorce among Muslims. It came to be permitted only subsequently as the relatively liberal principles of early Islam came to be compromised to accommodate deviations from the prescribed principle. This happened not only in the sphere of divorce but in a variety of other spheres of life as well.

Variations—Quranic Law Vs Muslim Personal Law

There is a powerful line of reasoning among Muslims that does not fight shy of asserting with uncanny aggressiveness that Islam offers a complete blueprint for life for all times and cannot be changed. If the revealed text was quite as explicit as average Muslims commonly believe is truly the case, there would indeed have been no basis for this kind of variation to prevail. Yet, the fact of the situation is that such variation currently exists, leading to a curious situation that one can talk in the same breadth, as it were, of a Quranic law and a Muslim Personal Law. The two are not necessarily consonant, not at least on many points in respect of divorce practices. Formal Muslim scholarship has not been successful in dealing and coming to terms with this dichotomy, which continues to previl even today, and is to a considerable extent unresolvable because the revealed injunctions are either self-contradictory (one revealed injunction cancels out another) or are not sufficiently precise so as to rule out conflicting interpretions. This has resulted in an unhappy and uncomfortable situation where, despite each school of Islamic law claiming to derive its auhority from the Quran, interprets it differently in a way that a diversity of forms and formal procedures is allowed to prevail in respect of divorce practices among different Muslim communities. The accretion and subsequent rationalisation of the practice of triple divorce principle should be instructive by itself for Muslims in that it goes to show, contrary to the conviction which Muslims commonly espouse, that they are adhering to what had been originally revealed to them through the Quran. On the contrary, what this demonstrates is that what Muslims today hold to be the original body of formal rules and prescriptions, has been changing historically in response to social developments through accretion of deviations in supercession of the originally enunciated Quranic principles and rules.

Popular Muslim belief is likely to view such an assertion as blasphemous, or at least as a gross misrepresentation of the truly Islamic spirit, but that is not so because the dichotomy is not real and does not exist in reality, it is so because average Muslims do not have a sufficiently deep understanding of the Quran and have generally constituted their beliefs about what the Quran prescribes on the basis of what they are told by those who claim to have a degree of knowledge of the Quran. No useful purpose will be served by going into the question as to how informed or reliable their own understanding is. What needs to be noted is that those claiming access to and command over the revealed injunctions choose to press and pass on what according to their belief and interpretation is the message and prescription of the Quran. As a consequence an average Muslim grows up believing that what his preacher *(moulvi, pesh imam, or alim)* has taught him is the true message of Islam. He at no point seeks to match what his preacher has told him with what the Quranic text itself enunciates in reality either because he has no access to the latter or lacks the authourity to challenge institutionalised scholastic opinion which is supposed to be the virtual monopoly of the trained clerics (*alims* in the first instance and by extension *moulvis and pesh imams* who constitute the agencies directly responsible for dissemination of Islamic beliefs and values to common mass of Muslims). For this obvious reason, which links up with the larger and deeper question of how an average Muslim is socialised into Islamic beliefs and values in the first place, the variation between what we described as Quranic law and Muslim Personal Law is able to prevail widely among Muslims in India.

Advocacy for Change

Of course, this situation is not without its positive dimensions. One positive consequence flowing out of it is that a basis is created for dialogue and debate and for public opinion to be mobilised in favour of reform of social practices that are considered to be either oppressive or unfair towards those adversely affected by an aspect of the legal code as it is sought to be imposed by those claiming institutionalised standing to be the sole arbiters of either Quranic injunctions or Muslim Personal Law. For over a century, there has been repeated public pressure for changes in divorce practices and issues arising out of it. The first time such public pressure resulted in modification of the law relating to divorce was with respect to the period for which a woman whose husband had disappeared and whose whereabouts were not known had to wait before she could contract another marriage. Under Hanafi law which governs the large majority of Muslim in the Indian subcontinent, she was required to wait for a period of ninety-nine years before she could contemplate contracting a second marriage. Obviously, the practice was severely oppressive and public pressure was mobilised to change the legal position in accordance with the considerably liberal Quranic position adopted by other schools of Muslim Personal Law. Again, over the past several decades public pressure has been building up in favour of a modification of the Muslim practice of triple divorce (unilateral repudiation of marriage at one sitting by the husband without any formal social intervention) which Hanafi law allows as legally tenable and binding on the wife and her kinsmen. The proponents of change rely upon the Quranic injunctions as against the Hanafi law to buttress their claim for a change in this procedure for divorce.

One direction along which change is currently advocated is that the practice of triple divorce whereby a Muslim husband enjoys a unilateral right to divorce his wife at will should be banned. This is a direction of change to which even traditionalist opinion is willy-nilly veering around and there have been several indications of their inclination in its favour. The All India Fiqh Conference, an organisation of Muslim theologians and experts of Muslim jurisprudence, adopted a resolution a few years ago that the practice of triple divorce did not receive sanction from the Quran and could be abrogated. Even leaders of the recognised body of Muslim clerics, the Jamiat-ul-Ulema-i-Hind, has come to concede that the practice of triple divorce, though legal in terms of law, amounts to a sin. Pressed hard by organised public opinion and all-to-frequent judicial pronouncements precipitated by the growing tendency of Muslim women to establish their rights and seek justice through the courts in the face of the refusal by the community to respond to their urge for being treated fairly, which the traditionalists see as an external interference in the integrity of Muslim Personal Law, the traditionalist may well be willing to be persuaded to placing a formal ban on the practice of triple divorce. Their real problem is that they would not like to appear to be greatly enthusiastic to initiate this change on their own and would like to continue to pretend indifference as long as it is convenient.

Implications of Abolishing Triple Divorce

There is need to be clear about two things before we start raising the pitch of the campaign for abolition of triple divorce so that the traditionalist reluctance caves in. The first is whether this is, and indeed should be the agenda of the protagonists of change in Muslim divorce law, or wheather it has actually been forced on them by other forces. The experience of being divorced unilaterally is a new experience for women of the middle classes, but for women of the poor classes this has always been a familiar experience so much so that divorced women are virtually coming to constitute a distinct category of the poor among Muslims. What women are saying is that they are dependent upon their spouses and role of the housewife is often their sole source of livelihood. Therefore, when their husbands exercise the rights of unilateral divorce they should not get away without fulfilling their liabilities towards them.

This comes out very clearly from the large number of cases that Muslim women are beginning to bring to the courts for adjudication. They are not asking for their divorce be annulled so that they are taken back by their husbands. Nor are they necessarily arguing that the Muslim practice of triple divorce should be abolished. At best, where that issue has been agitated at all, as indeed it has been in the case of Zeenat Fatema Rashid, the argument has been that triple divorce has to adhere to a formally prescribed procedure under which the husband must pronounce divorce on three different occasions separated each time by a month after a reconciliation council consisting of a representative each of the wife and the husband has concluded that the couple cannot live together and this procedure was violated in their case. What they are asking for is that, if their husbands choose to divorce them unilaterally, they should at least have the assurance that they can subsist at the level of poverty which their married life provided. In other words, the husband should be liable to pay their dower and provide them maintenance so that they are at least assured of a level of subsistence commensurate with their husband's social standing. If the protagonists of change in Muslim divorce law settle for a ban on the practice of triple divorce, the agenda that most of the women who are seeking rights of sheer economic survival through the courts, and many more who would like to but are prevented from doing so by the high costs of litigation, would die a natural death.

The second aspect that needs careful consideration is whether merely banning the practice of triple divorce would necessarily prevent marriages from breaking up and would not make the situation of women worse. Unfortunately, little sociological research exists at present on divorce practices among Muslims in this country. However, from a few studies that are available it is clear that triple divorce is not the only modality that husbands necessarily rely upon to divorce their wives. Quite frequently, because triple divorce renders them liable to settle the dower amount (which too is not particularly large in the majority of cases) and return the dowry, they resort to a skillful and ingenious use of the stratagem of *khula* 'form of divorce to disengage themselves from a marriage which they want to break. They would cast away the wife and coerce her to ask for a divorce at their own initiative so that they are able to escape the liability of paying her dower, returning her dowry and providing her maintenance. If the practice of triple divorce is outlawed, this would not by itself reduce the incidence of divorce because the world has yet to find a way of forcing an alienated spouse to persist in a marriage which has broken down. If the option of formally dissolving the marriage is closed to him, he would normally desert his wife or run away. In the case of Muslims, the *khula* 'form of divorce offers an alternative route to an alienated husband to abandon his wife. If the practice of divorce is outlawed, the chances are that an increasing number of husbands would start using that stratagem to get rid of the wives they are already determined to leave. Needless to add, the *khula* 'form of divorce would hardly be a better alternative as it would deprive women of whatever little claims they can have on their husbands and would make them liable to the suffering of waiting a long time before they are freed.

There are other ways in which a simple ban on the practice of triple divorce may worsen the situation of Muslim women. As is well known, divorce is not an isolated legal event that is unrelated to other personal, familial, and social actions and circumstances, but is the final stage of a marital process. In crude and schematic terms the main stages of the process are marriage, marriage breakdown, the decision by one or both spouses to terminate the marriage, and finally its legal dissolution by divorce. Needless to say, all marriages go through this process all at once. Usually, some go to the point of breakdown without any manifestation of it in legal terms, the spouses living apart independently without the intervention or imprimatur of the law. Evidence suggests that where wives experience break down, they sometimes decide to terminate the marriage later on and eventually go in for divorce by asking their husbands to pronounce triple divorce. This kind of divorce is described in the Islamic scheme of things as *khula* 'but the modality it relies upon is that of pronouncement of triple divorce by the husband. If the practice of triple divorce is simply abolished this relatively hassle-free mode of termination of the marital relationship would cease to be available to women whose marriages terminate socially and who wish to dissolve them legally. The only option open to them would be to take recourse to the courts which besides being expensive, are a source of considerable harassment, so much so, that even in societies where legal processes are quick and smooth women have been found to hesitate initiating legal action for divorce for the inconvenience and costs that this entails.

One obvious legal implication of imposing a simple ban on the practice of triple divorce would be that the power to pass judgement on the viability of a conjugal relationship which is at present placed within the control of the individual husbands and wives and would pass on to some external authority, be it the divorce court judge or an institution that might be created within the framework of the community (which I would not feel very comfortable with at any rate, because the patriarchal ethos widely prevalent in the community would then have a backdoor to enter and act to the detriment of women). Since the use of the triple divorce procedure is widespread among Muslim men of the lower social strata, the chances are that they would simply desert their wives to fend for themselves or to bring in a case if they wanted the marital relationship to be formally terminated. Or, if they decide to move the authority empowered to dissolve a marriage their wives would be obliged to spend on litigator required to contest the husband's intention where the outcome is in any case uncertain. This will bring in elements of adversarial procedure into the divorce process and will make it less dignified and more punitive.

To sum up, it is clear that simply banning the Muslim practice of triple divorce does not hold out a great deal of promise for the amelioration of the situation of Muslim women, particularly those poor women with children, who are directly affected by this practice and are coming to constitute a distinct, economically disadvantaged group within the Muslim community. The protagonists of change in Muslim law of divorce should go beyond the triple divorce procedure to demand enactment of a Muslim Matrimonial Causes Act that simultaneously seeks to arrest the problems of rising incidence of divorce and growing pauperisation of an increasing number of women and children among Muslims. Limitations of time prevent me from dilating on what such a law should contain, but it is clear that ensuring that a woman gets the rights, economic and social, that Islam accords her as well as maintenance where she does not remarry (which possibility is greatly restricted in Indian Muslim society for several reasons) shall have to constitute an integral part of any such legislation. Muslim traditionalists have resisted addressing these issues because they think that this will compromise the integrity of Muslim Personal Law. This integrity is already being compromised as an increasing number of Muslim women are taking their matrimonial disputes and claims outside the community domain on to the public sphere. Many more would do so only if they had the necessary resources to engaged in litigation. Preservation of the cultural identity of the community is a poor excuse for failure to address the problem of break down of social organisation that is beginning to beset the community.

3

The Discourse Around Muslim Personal Law

Gitanjali Gangoli

In India, personal laws of different communities have been framed as markers of identity, more so, in the case of the Muslim community. This remains a shifting marker, and creates a set of images, both in the self image of different members of the Muslim community, and in the perception of the state, different political parties, and individuals. In this study, I explore the contours of the debate through the entry points of legislative debates, judicial pronouncements and the media. I would also look at the varied ways in which the discourse has impacted the lives of Muslim women. Some moments of historical significance relevant to this study are: the constituent assembly debates in the 1950s, the Lok Sabha debates in the 1970s on issues of adoption, maintenance and marriage; the cases filed by Shahnaz Shaikh (1983) and Shah Bano (1985), followed by the law passed by Parliament, i.e., the Muslim Women (Protection of Rights upon Divorce) Act, 1986; the debates on triple *talaq* (1993), and polygamy (1995) after Supreme Court judgements on these issues.

It has been suggested that identity formation takes place in moments of crisis. While in the most part, identity with a group may not be strong, it can become intense when there is a perceived or real threat to the interests of the group.[1] Some moments of crisis for the members of the Muslim community in India are the partition of India in 1947; communal riots; the demolition of the Babri Masjid in December 1992. I would suggest that personal laws played a prominent role in shaping the identity of the Muslim community and the Hindu community. However, I try to demonstrate through this chapter that identity formation notwithstanding, neither community is monolithic in its responses to various crisis.

The first section takes a look at legislative debates around Muslim Personal Law (henceforth MPL) between 1937-55. Prior to independence, two major laws were passed that aimed at codifying the Shariat, i.e., the Shariat Act, 1937, and The Dissolution of Muslim Marriages Act, 1939. This section also looks at the debates around Uniform Civil Code (henceforth UCC) in the years following independence. Section II examines the legislative debates in 1976 around amendments to the Special Marriage act, 1955, where mainstream attitudes to Muslim law become apparent. Section II also looks at two proposed bills on adoption in 1972, and in 1980. Section III studies judicial interpretations on various aspects of MPL. The last section examines the initiatives and the responses of feminists to these issues in Bombay and elsewhere.

SECTION I

Legislative Initiatives: Muslim Personal Law, 1937-55

In the 1930s, the process of codifying Muslim personal law was initiated at the behest of members of the community. Two legislations, that is, the Shariat Act, 1937, and the Dissolution of Muslim Marriages Act, 1939 were passed. The purpose of these acts was to apply the MPL to Muslim men and women who were governed by customary laws. In the perception of those initiating these laws, these were progressive steps, giving Muslim women rights denied to them under customary law. Here, it may be relevant to point out that the term 'customary law' has never been defined in the legislature. It is taken to mean conventions and usage adhered to by people for a long period of time.

"The bill aims at securing uniformity of law among Muslims in

> all their social and personal relations. By doing so, it also recognizes and does justice to the claims of women of inheriting family property who, under customary law, are debarred from succeeding to the same.[2]

The Shariat Act brought all Indian Muslims under the Shariat laws in matters related to inheritance, divorce, marriage and guardianship. The 1939 Act extended to all Muslim women rights of divorce that had been restricted to Hanafi Muslims.[3] During this period, the codification of MPL was seen as a step that inspired other communities to follow suit. As Justice Ranade stated:

> "If we, (i.e. Hindus), abjure government help under all circumstances, we must perforce fall back, behind Parsees, Mohomeddans and Christians, who have freely availed themselves of such help in recasting their social arrangements."[4]

However, the reality of partition, communal riots and independence led to a shift in the perception of Muslims as being pioneering in the area of codification of law. In the decade following independence, the leaders aimed to focus on reform of Hindu law. The Hindu code bill, drafted in the 1940s, faced tremendous opposition both within and outside parliament. The bill was divided into four separate parts, and passed as The Hindu Marriage Act, 1955; The Hindu Minority and Guardianship Act, 1956; The Hindu Adoption and Maintenance Act, 1956 and The Hindu Succession Act, 1955. These laws have long been presented as model laws, that initiated in Indian society progress and enlightenment. This is not the place to support or dispute these claims, which has been done elsewhere[5], but I would like to point out that these set of laws have created an exclusionist, yet inclusive legal code for Hindus. It includes in its scope, Buddhists, Sikhs and Jains. It includes anyone who is not a Muslim, Parsee, Christian or Jew. Scholars have suggested that this legal description of a Hindu, in relation with the four religions excluded from it, means that these religions become its legal 'other'.[6]

The Hindu Marriage Act, as lawyers have pointed out, offers very limited rights to divorce. It also includes the 'right to conjugal rights', which militates against the rights of women, and legitimises marital rape. As lawyer Kirti Singh describes the act:

> "Another novel feature of this act was that it made women equally liable with men as far as payment of maintenance... was concerned. Among the Members of Parliament who objected to this clause were: B.K. Ray, Renu Chakravarty and Sucheta Kripalani. They pointed out that the provision was highly unjust to women since women did not have an equal right to property... Renu Chakravarty... declared, give us equal laws of inheritance and we shall be prepared to give you that alimony."[7]

The move to give equal property rights to Hindu women was however met with stiff resistance. The Hindu Succession Act, 1956 gave a daughter a share in the ancestral property, but did not make her an equal share holder with her brother. Even this limited reform was met with opposition. Members argued that it would destroy Hindu society, and create discord between brothers and sisters. It was further argued that the government should pass a uniform civil code, and until that was done. Hindu laws should not be tampered with.[8]

For many conservative Hindus, the demand for a UCC was a way to put off reforms in Hindu laws. The Hindu code bill was projected as a communal step. It was argued that the Hindu code bill was 'absolutely unnecessary' and that 'it goes against the principle of having a common civil code'.[9] Many members of the constituent assembly pushed for a UCC, on the grounds that it would facilitate national integration; others opposed it on the grounds that it would jeopardize the cultural identity of minorities, especially Muslims. This was perhaps a historic moment when the debate around UCC become petrified into a debate around individual rights, citizenship and national integration on the one hand, and minority rights, and cultural diversity on the other. The following statement by K T Shah in 1949 encapsulates this dilemma: "Rights of minorities are not of the individual, but of the group."[10]

The general sense of unease with ideas held paramount till date and perhaps impressive perceptiveness is apparent in the following excerpt from a speech made by Jawaharlal Nehru in 1949.

> "Nationalism, of course, is a curious phenomenon, which at a certain stage in a country's history, gives life, growth, strength, a unity but it has the tendency to limit one...Culture, which is essentially good, becomes not only static, but aggressive and something that breeds conflict and hatred when looked at from a wrong point of view. How you are to find a balance, I don't know."[11]

Nehru here seems to equally critical of the limitations of nationalism, as of culture. He sees in both these phenomenon, something that is not immediately apparent. Meanwhile, sections of Muslims who had stayed back in India found it a bewildering experience. In 1950, a member of the Jamait-e-Ulema-e-Hind wrote an article in an Urdu newspaper, in which he warned Muslims that Hindus were basing their constitution on the laws of Manu.[12] Given the rhetoric of some members of the Constituent Assembly, this was perhaps not an entirely unreasonable fear. Yet, to attribute the failure of the Constituent Assembly to implement a UCC with the obstructiveness of Muslim members remains a common, though unfair trend. During the course of the Constituent Assembly debates, Shri R.K. Sidwe exhorted Muslims to give up their 'isolationist outlook on life' for the sake of national integration and unity.[13]

The UCC was, however, rejected by many non-Muslims as well, for various reasons. One is articulated in these words of Shri K.M. Munshi:

> "I know there are many among Hindus who do not like a Uniform Civil Code...they feel that the personal laws of inheritance, succession etc. are really a part of their religion."[14]

Raj Kumari Amrit Kaur, active in these debates, held to the view that a UCC could not lead to national integration. As she put it:

> "How would a uniform civil code be conducive to national unity when uniform laws for crimes, contracts, torts and constitutional rights could not promote it..."[15]

Even some of those who held strongly to the desirability of a UCC, stopped short of making this clause justifiable. K.M. Munshi and Krishna Swami Aiyyar, ardent supporters of a UCC, as a means of strengthening nationalism, voted against the inclusion of the clause as a fundamental right, and hence legally enforceable. Munshi had made a strong statement that the failure of the state to amend personal laws of different communities would lead to a denial of rights of women. Yet, he supported the placing of the clause in the section on Directive Principles of State Policy, a legally non-enforceable section.[16] Clearly then, the issue of opposing the UCC was more than that of Muslims obstructing it. What is clear is that the debate on the UCC was conducted mostly on the question of national integration, not of gender justice.

Between the mid 1950s to the mid 1970s, little or no debate took place on the issue of MPL in the legislature. The only effort to do so was in the 1960s, when a move was made to reform the MPL. It was dropped when Vice President, Zakir Hussain conveyed a sense of resentment on behalf of the entire community.[17] Some possible reasons for the silence on this issue could be the retreat of communal forces during this period, the gender indifference of the Left which seemed in ascendancy at that point and a greater focus on nation building in the specific Nehruvian mould.

In 1970, however, the All India Muslim Political Convention resolved, inter alia that:

> "This convention urges that a clear announcement be made at an early date by the central government that no attempt would be made to change the personal laws of any community, and especially that of Muslims."[18] The fears of at least one section of the Muslim commentators will seem puzzling in the absence of any serious or concerted proposal on the part of the legislature to reform or change MPL, or indeed any other personal law. Unless, of course, one contextualises it in the fear and insecurity that characterised Muslim politics following the partition and widespread communal riots. For many Muslims,

personal laws were perhaps already fixed as markers of their identity—a contentious ground for debate. The next section examines legislative debates in the period when Hindu communal forces were much more in the forefront, that is, the late 1970s and the 1980s.

SECTION II

Muslim Personal Law, Communalisation and Legislative Debates, 1976-95

Legislative debates during this period reveal a 'Hinduised' understanding of life and law, with in which Islamic tenets are seen at best as aberrant and different. The language and cultural imagery remains hinduised, sometimes even when used by non-Hindus, and for subjects that are 'secular'. During a debate for grants to the Ministry of Social and Women's Welfare, Shri E S M Fakir Mohommad said:

> "Sir, in India, we worship women as the universal Shakti; the world will not survive without women. We pay homage to our country in the name of Bharat Mata."[19]

Such imagery is apparent in the lengthy debates in the Lok Sabha in 1976, while debating the proposed amendments to the Hindu Marriage Act, 1955 (henceforth HMA) and the Special Marriage Act, 1954 (SMA). The 1976 amendment is known to bring the HMA 'on par' with the SMA, but what is disregarded is that the amendment gave to Hindu men their right to ancestral property provided they married another Hindu under the act.[20] This amendment to the SMA favouring Hindu men, and returning their 'ancestral rights' was passed without any debate or discussion.[21] The clause served the additional purpose of making marriages between Hindu men and non-Hindu women less attractive than marriages between Hindus, as the former would mean a loss of coparcenary rights for Hindu men.

The 1976 debates on the SMA and the HMA were full of allusions to marriage that fitted closely to brahmanical and Hindu perceptions of marriage. What is striking is that the allusions were made with relation to 'Indian' marriages. The following excerpt indicates this trend:

> "According to Indian culture and tradition, marriage is a sacred and eternal bond. When a man and a women enter into marriage, our culture and civilisation tells them that only death can separate the two."[22]

Some MPs quoted from the *Manu Smriti,* lamenting the collapse of the romanticised traditions of their mythised histories. One member spoke of the lack of fidelity in Indian society in these words:

> "It is no laughing matter. A soldier who goes to the battlefield or a person who comes to a big city to earn his living, do we expect all these people in the twentieth century to be Ramas? Ramas have different connotations in Bombay. ...Ramas today in Bombay are the domestic male servants...."[23]

The different connotation that Naik refers to here are based on some assumptions: that the north Indian Aryan Rama of mythology is now forced to share his illustrious name, though not his glory with domestic servants.

We can see a link, by no means tenuous, between these notions of society and marriage, and those carried out a decade later in the Lok Sabha prior to the passing of the infamous Muslim Woman (Protection of Rights Upon Marriage) Act, 1986.[24] In the 1986 debates, several MPs expressed a discomfort with some perceptions of Muslim marriages, so different from 'Hindu' marriages.

> "Now, the law of Muslims relating to marriage and divorce is this...Marriage is a matter of contract...it is not a sacrament at all. A woman is not married to a man till eternity, as it was with the Hindus and as it was with Catholics in the olden days... to the Muslims, divorce was very much known...a concept which possibly was revolutionary at that time and might have been considered so."[25]

Other MPs put far less carefully worded critique of Muslim law and society:

> "....a Muslim husband in this country enjoys the privilege of being able to discard his wife at any point of time, whenever he choses to do so, for reasons good and bad, indeed for no reason at all."[26]

One MP held it fitting to issue a warning to all Muslims to transform themselves:

> "I would like to warn the Muslims also. They have made divorce a very ordinary and easy thing. Recognize the need of the hour and change yourself."[27]

On a different level, Geeta Mukherjee put forward her understanding of Muslim divorce, in which she articulated a feminist understanding of the issue. As she pointed out:

> "When an Islamic marriage takes place, (the) woman's consent is necessary. But, please remember, at the time of divorce, the divorced woman's consent is not at all necessary."[28]

This nuanced understanding was, however, not taken up for serious debate, which focused only on simplistic assumptions of Muslim marriages, and society. At a general level, the assumption was that sacramental 'Hindu' marriages were superior to 'Muslim' marriages which were contractual.

There was only one recorded protest to the communalisation of the debates, a protest that was not acknowledged or responded to:

> "The Law Minister talks about Muslim representatives (in the Lok Sabha)...no one is a Hindu representative or a Muslim representative in this house.. He is communalising the whole issue."[29]

Like the issue of marriage and divorce, adoption too has been a somewhat contentious issue. Under existing provisions under personal law, only Hindus can formally adopt children under the Hindu Adoption and Maintenance Act, 1956. The personal laws of all the other religious communities do not allow formal adoption.[30] In order to redress this, attempts have been made in the Lok Sabha to pass bills on adoption that would be applicable to all communities, first in 1972, and in 1980.

Both these bills have not been passed, due to opposition from members representing different communities and groups: tribes in the North East, Parsees and Muslims. For different reasons, members of these communities have seen the adoption bills to be antithetical to their interests. The opposition of some Muslims is based on some related fears: one, that the bill is a way to introduce a UCC—and by extension, Hindu laws—through the backdoor. Second, that adoption is against the tenets of their religion. Significantly, the second fear is shared by some members of the Parsee community. The Minority Commission, delegated to look into this question in 1980 reported that many members of the Parsee commuity feared that if adoption was allowed, economic and religious right will be ensured including the right to use the fire temple. Members of the community demanded their exclusion from the proposed bill.[31]

The Minority Commission held that:

> "We do not think that we need to go into religious controversy. If there are persons who feel the need to adopt to be greater than the any supposed prohibition by their religious texts, they should be allowed to resort to the secular doctrine of adoption."[32]

Significantly, in spite of evidence to the contrary, it would seem from some available writing on the subject that only Muslims opposed the bill. According to Vasudha Dhagamwar, a supporter of the bill, and of the UCC, the uneasiness of the Parsees over the adoption issue was "qualitatively quite different from the stand of the unswerving opposition by the Muslim leaders."[33] I would choose to disagree with this formulation. For, the Parsees interviewed by the Minority Commission held that they desired exclusion from the bill on the same grounds as Muslims.

In Bombay, in 1995, the ruling Shiv Sena-BJP combine introduced a bill on adoption which was passed without debate by the state assembly and council, but however did not pass muster with the central government. The President of India refused to sign the bill on the ground that it was too contentious.[34] The 1995 bill itself was framed in close consultation with social organisations working on adoption.

What was contentious about the bill was that the bill itself was framed with the desirability of the UCC being a vital part of its rhetoric. The bill begins with these words.

> "Whereas article 44 enshrined in the constitution of India, which is one of the Directive Principles of State Policy provides that the State shall endeavor to secure for the citizens Uniform Civil Code through- out the territory of India;

And Whereas the Uniform Civil Code has become the need of the hour;

And Whereas, the government of Maharashtra feels it necessary to make a beginning for introduction of Uniform Civil Code in the state by introducing enactment of uniform civil law of adoption and for matters concerned therewith, as a first step towards achieving the goal of Uniform Civil Code in the State of Maharashtra."[35]

The adoption bill states in bald terms the intentions of the state government, i.e., to introduce a UCC. The timing of the bill, three years following anti Muslim riots led by the Shiv Sena in Bombay, and a few months after the election of the Shiv Sena-BJP combine in the state assembly election, gives one cause for concern. It can perhaps be argued that the communalisation of the issue of adoption is most apparent in the Maharashtra bill.

The next section looks at judicial interpretation on issues of civil law.

SECTION III

Judicial Interpretations and Muslim Personal Law

Judges have responded to, and contributed to the public debates on MPL and UCC, through various cases on maintenance, divorce, polygamy, guardianship and inheritance.

The issue of maintenance to divorced Muslim women was politicised in the mid 1980s following a Supreme Court case regarding a divorced Muslim woman's right of maintenance under Section 125 Cr P C. [36] The details of the case are as follows. Shah Bano filed for maintenance in the Court of Judicial Magistrate after she was thrown out of her house after thirty years of Marriage. Following this, she was divorced by her husband who maintained that he had paid her *meher* (dower) and was not obliged to pay her any more maintenance under MPL. The Magistrate awarded maintenance to the effect of Rs. 25 a month, this sum was enhanced to Rs. 179.20 on appeal to the High Court. The husband appealed to the Supreme Court, stating that he was not obliged to pay her maintenance following the divorce under MPL.

The Supreme Court judgment on the surface took a valid legal stand, that Section 125 Cr PC was a part of the criminal law of the country, hence was applicable to all Indians. What was contentious was the statements on Islamic law made during the judgment. Sir William Lane was cited as saying that the fatal point in Islam was its degradation of women. The statement made in 1843 was held relevant in the mid 1980s. The judge went on to say:

> "It is a matter of regret that Article 44 of our constitution has remained a dead letter...a common civil code will help the cause of national integration by removing disparate loyalties to laws that have conflicting ideologies."[37]

The judgment raised a furore at various levels. As a sociologist pointed out:

> "The (Shah Bano) case... raised the entire question of the relationship between on the one hand, secular law, as promulgated and implemented by the institutions of the state, and on the other, the rights of minorities and the rights of women."[38]

A question that seems relevant is the political context within which the controversy grew. This was certainly not the first judgment that had held that Muslim divorcees have the right to maintenance under Section 125 Cr. PC. Another Supreme Court judgment in 1979 had raised precisely the same point, but had not, unlike the Shah Bano case, opined on the limitations of MPL.[39] Among possible-reasons for the furore could be the communlised atmosphere of the mid 1980s, and the statements of the judges on MPL.

The judgment itself became an arena of conflict, with Hindu fundamentalist leaders hailing it as a positive step and Muslim leaders opposing it. Shah Bano, unable to bear the pressures exerted on her from within the community recanted in an open letter to Muslims. The letter, poignant in its helplessness, stated:

> "Maulana Mohommad Habib Yar Khan, Haji Abdul Gaffar Sahib and other respectable gentlemen of Indore came to me and explained the commands concerning nikaah, divorce, dower and maintenance in the light of the Quran and the hadith....Now, the Supreme Court of India has given the judgment on 23 April 1985 concerning maintenance of the divorced woman, which apparently is in my favour. But since the judgment is contrary to the Quran and the hadith and is an open interference in Muslim Personal Law, I, Shah Bano, being a Muslim, reject it and disassociate myself from every judgment that is contrary to the Shariat"[40].

The Rajiv Gandhi government gave in to the pressures exerted by the more orthodox in the community, passing the Muslim Women (Protection of Rights Upon Divorce) Act, 1986. The bill removed divorced Muslim women from the ambit of Section 125 Cr P C, choosing to focus on one time relief to divorced women. What is significant is that the voices of those members of the community who had taken a different stand on the judgment were ignored. A memorandum was submitted to the Prime Minister on February 26, 1986, signed by several members of the community, including teachers and advocates, the memorandum bemoaned the threat to the 'secular fabric' of the country posed by the controversy. The signatories distanced themselves from those members of the community who opposed the judgment and stated:

> "We believe that Muslim women have the right to maintenance—a right that they enjoy in several Muslim countries, through the rational and progressive interpretation of Islamic principles, as in Morocco, Iraq, Egypt, Turkey, Libya, Tunisia, Syria and Algeria...We emphasize the necessity of safeguarding the

interests of all sections of the minorities. That is why the demand to exclude Muslim women from the purview of section 125 Cr P C.,... would adversely affect both rights and interests of Muslim women."[41]

Following the enactment of the Muslim Women (Protection of Rights Upon Divorce) Act, 1986. Daniel Latifi and Sona Khan, Delhi based lawyers filed a writ petition in the Supreme Court. The petition stated that the Act was discriminatory "calculated to disrupt and divide the most exploited and vulnerable section of our people". It also stated that the Family Courts Act, 1984 exciuded Muslim women and aggravated this "situation of apartheid whereby the weakest section, namely the women of the minority community, would per se be prejudiced." The petition submitted that the act be struck down on various grounds, including that it violated the right to equality before the law and equal protection of the law guaranteed under the constitution, that it would encourage divorce and female infanticide, thus militating against "two of the causes to which the Holy Prophet of Islam dedicated a great part of his life"[42].

The petition is remarkable in that it combined religious and secular arguments to oppose the law that was passed.

The Muslim Women's Act was opposed at different levels. As an elderly school teacher pointed out, the contention that the 1986 act enjoyed majority support of the community was erroneous. "When they say this, they simply ignore the views of countless Muslim women, whose voices are muffled by their fathers, husbands and the mullahs"[43].

BJP however chose to read the debate in different ways. The party, responsible for violence against women in riots, chose to oppose the 1986 act on the grounds that it violated women's surrender to obscurantism and bigotry[44].

The BJP's 'politically correct' stand was offset by some virulent statements made by its allies, Shiv Sena in Bombay. Bal Thakaray, in a statement in 1985 had this to say:

"Communal minded Muslims have no place in this

country...Those who do not accept our constitution and our laws, should quit the country and go to Karachi or Lahore"[45].

It might be useful to look at the interpretations of the 1986 act, to see the impact that this law has had on women. Some of the judgments based on this act have tried to interpret it as liberally as possible, in order to provide a fair settlement for divorced Muslim women. Under Section 125 Cr PC, as we have seen the maintenance amount awarded was most often measly, in fact there is a ceiling of Rs.500[46]. In 1995, Justice TV Ramakrishnan of the Kerala High Court dismissed the petition of K Haji who pleaded that the maintenance amount of Rs. 30,000 as one time settlement after divorce granted to Amina, his ex-wife by the Session Court was illegal under the 1986 act. The act granted 'reasonable and fair provision' and maintenance during the period of iddat. Justice Ramakrishnan ruled that:

> "We are of the view that the Legislature has deliberately used the two provisions 'provisions' and 'maintenance' with the intention of expressing two different things or ideas...(Following the Shah Bano case), the revolt from a section of the Muslims was only against the continued liability (post-iddat) declared by the Supreme Court. There was no dispute regarding iddat maintenance. From the statement of Objects and reasons, it is evident that the Parliament has enacted the new legislation partly to contain the revolt...and to protect the rights of divorced women who may not have the necessary means of livelihood after the period of iddat. It is difficult to think that Parliament has, by enacting the Act, completely taken away the right of Muslim divorced women under Section 125 Cr PC...without making any provisions as a compensatory measure..."[47]

In an earlier case, the Gujarat High Court ruled that the 1986 act provided for fair settlement according to the financial status of the husband. Justice M B Shah ruled that:

> "...Under S 125 Cr PC, the maximum amount which a divorced women would get is only Rs. 500, even though her former husband is a rich person. Therefore to give her full protection or

benefit, this Act is enacted and her rights are specified... It has not only provided for free and fair provision and maintenance to the divorced woman and her minor children, but it has also specifically provided that she is entitled to get meher or dower amount from her former husband"[48].

Given the understanding of lawyers, activists and litigants that a one time settlement is better than monthly payments, the 1986 act does benefit Muslim women, but only if interpreted by a pro woman judge. In its very conception, however, it remains discriminatory, as it denies a section of women access to a secular law on the grounds of their religion.

Other judgments bring out anomalies of the act more clearly. While MPL allows for the mother to be the natural guardian of her children—a right denied to women of other communities—the act does not spell out the responsibilities of the father in providing child support following divorce. In a 1991 Calcutta High Court judgment, the judge criticised the act saying:

"The act of 1986 is remarkably silent as to the futures of the minor children who have crossed the age of two years...As no provision is made subsequent to that age in the Act of 1986, the mother as natural guardian of such unfortunate minor children shall have to fall back upon the all embracing and beneficial provisions of Section 125 Cr PC"[49].

Thus the judge found a way to circumvent the 1986 Act, and retrieve to the destitute woman her right to Section 125 Cr P C, but only in her role as mother.

"We are not concerned with the divorced wife, as she has rightly and justifiably not claimed any maintenance for herself in view of the provisions of the Act of 1986. But we are concerned with the fate of the minor children. Here, it is pleaded that the minor children are unable to maintain themselves, and not only that, the divorced wife is also unable to maintain them without any maintenance amount from her former husband."[50]

If the mid 1960s were taken over by legal debates on

maintenance and divorce, the legal issues that were taken up for debate in the 1990s were those of divorce under Muslim law and polygamy. The issue of talaq-e-bid'at, known more popularly as triple talaq, has been seen as the marker of Muslim identity by Hindu fundamentalists[51]. In 1993, Justice Tilhari of the Uttar Pradesh High Court struck down *talaq-e-bid'at* as invalid, but only after holding forth on the joys of marriage, the sorrows of divorce, and the 'plight' of a Muslim divorced woman:

> "The plight of a divorced woman can be realised...marriage is a status which creates vested rights and interest of cohabitation, succession and maintenance. It brings a bloom to the life. Divorce brings a plight of vagaries...and upheaval in the life of a woman...The Hindu Marriage Act introduced divorce and a divorced woman has been declared to be 'entitled to claim maintenance from her husband'. ...Under Muslim law, the plight of a woman divorced by her husband is more pathetic. It is the husband who has the free hand to divorce his wife... even orally, by declaring talaq thrice... the poor Muslim woman has been held to be entitled to maintenance for a limited period of three months and then left to the vagaries of fate"[52].

The judge then went on to declare triple talaq as unconstitutional, and being sinful under Islam, under the mandate of the Holy Quran. Justice Tilhari seems to share the commonly held perception that triple talaq is a common practice in Islam. The terms of the discourse within which the learned judge operates is to reiterate the 'superiority' of Hindu laws and cultural practices, and the centrality of marriage as an institution. As a political commentator pointed out soon after the judgment, Justice Tilhari was the judge whose sympathies with the right were abundantly clear when he had passed a judgment allowing 'darshan' (the right to worship) for Hindu pilgrims at the spot of the demolished Babri Masjid in 1992, where a make shift temple had been erected. Gautam Navlakha, commenting on the Judgement says:

> "While supporting the Tilhari Judgment, the left and feminist groups should take care to expose the pseudo campaigners of

Muslim women's rights, who remain silent about the plight of Hindu women. Is the judgment and the support thereof based on women's rights or on communal arguments of Muslim obduracy and backwardness?"[53]

Justice Kuldip Singh's judgment in a case on bigamy in 1995 raised similar issues. The case was about a Hindu man, who converted to Islam in order to solemnize a second marriage. The Supreme Court judgment speculated about MPL, comparing it unfavorably with Hindu law. Justice Singh advised the Parliament to enact a UCC so as to prevent cases such as these. He ruled that:

"The personal law of the Hindus, such as relating to marriage, succession and the like have a sacramental origin, in the same manner as in the case of the Muslims or the Christians. The Hindus, along with Sikhs, Buddhists and Jains have forsaken their sentiments in the cause of national unity and integration, some other communities would not, though the constitution enjoins the establishment of a common civil code for the whole of India"[54].

Justice Singh held that a common civil code would prevent errant men from converting to Islam in order to escape the provisions of their personal laws, which would penalize them for bigamy. The stated purpose of the proposed common laws was therefore, to 'save' Hindu marriage, not to empower Muslim women from the ill effects of polygamy. At another level, the judgment reflects the patriarchal agenda of preserving, and glorifying marriage at all costs.

"Marriage is the very foundation of a civilised society. Marriage is an institution in the maintenance of which the public at large is deeply interested. It is the foundation of the family, and in turn of the society without which no society can exist" [55].

It can be argued that the Hindu Marriage Act, 1955, while disallowing polygamous marriages, has not been very effective in doing so. Judges have recognised as valid, only a marriage ceremony that includes the saptapadi, leaving out a range of customary practices. Hindu men have used this clause with impunity, to deny the wives—first or second—rights due to them. In a 1994 case, the marriage between Gulab Singh and Surjit Kaur, performed through local rites, was invalidated in the Supreme Court. Surjit Kaur was married before, which was held against her by the learned judge, who held, "merely because there was distribution of sugar or gur, that would not constitute a valid marriage. Surjit Kaur was in the habit of changing husbands frequently...the bare fact that the man and the woman (have been) living together as husband and wife does not, at any rate give them the status of husband and wife, even though they may hold themselves out before the society and the society treats them as such"[56].

Such judgments have prompted feminist lawyers to argue that the loopholes in the HMA allow Hindu men "to escape the criminal consequences of a bigamous marriage, and from the economic responsibility towards the second wife."[57] What is significant is that under the HMA, 1955, the second wife, being denied legal status, is not entitled to maintenance, while under MPL, this is not the situation.

Not surprisingly, these aspects have not been taken up in the 1995 judgment on bigamy. Even less surprising is that this judgment, like the Shah Bano and the Tilhari judgments before it have been appropriated by Hindu communal forces. A bill initiated by the Shiv Sena-BJP combine in Maharashtra in 1995 to prevent bigamous marriage quotes approvingly from it in its statement of objects and reasons.[58] While the moderate rightist forces may want to prevent Muslim men from marrying more than once, the more extreme right displays an envy for the Muslim man's legal right to marry more than once. Swami Muktanand Saraswati, a member of the VHP held, "There are no (equal) laws regarding marriage. Today, a Hindu man can marry only one women, while a Muslim man can have five wives. If a man wants to have 25 wives, let him."[59]

It might be relevant to point out that the limits of legal and judicial discourse on the UCC become apparent when one recognises that there is hardly ever any discussion or debate on the areas of MPL that might be considered progressive in MPL, that is, the proviso on inheritance. A Muslim woman has the right to parental property. A married woman inherits her husband's property in its entirety in the absence of children, otherwise she shares it with her children. Unlike in Hindu Succession law, there is no concept of coparcenary rights, nor can Muslim women be cut off from the property completely through the provision of a will.[60]

The judgments and debates that have focused on MPL, however, look mostly at the anomalies within it. The focus remains on the 'obscurantism' of MPL. Debate on the UCC become limited to 'prove' that the Muslim community is stagnant and resistant to reform, and to the urgency for a UCC for 'nationalist' purposes. The more militant believe that a UCC should be forced on a reluctant population. Chief Justice Lodha, in a public meeting stated:

"More fantastic is the belief that a common civil code should not be forced upon the Muslim, that they should agree to it voluntarily. As if the imams will let them."[61] At a more 'modarate' level, it has been argued by Hindu communalists that the fear of the minorities that a UCC would mean the implementation of a Hindu code was unfounded. A statement by L K Advani, the BJP President in 1995 is meant to allay the fears of the minorities:

"When the BJP talks of a Uniform Civil Code, it does not contemplate imposing the Hindu Law on the country. Our party manifesto has clearly stated that the BJP would ask the Law Commission to examine the Hindu Law, the Muslim Law, the Christian Law, and the Parsee Law and cull out the modern, progressive, equitable ingredients of these laws and on that basis, draw up a Common Civil Code. If some of the laws relating to the Hindus today have to go on that account, they have to go. For example, the Hindu Undivided Family may have to go. Whatever has to be done, has to be done for all."[62]

The next section will focus on the responses of the women's movement to articulations such as these, and more specifically, on the entire issue of the communalisation of Muslim Personal Law.

SECTION IV

Muslim Personal Law and Women : Initiatives and Responses

In the 1950s, the role of the women legislators and the All India Women's Conference in the debates around personal laws has been well documented.[63] The feminist movement since the 1970s have been sporadically, though meaningfully engaged in the debates around personal laws. In 1974, the Status of Women report commissioned by the Indian government to a group of feminists, studied, among other things, the range of personal laws applicable to women. Regarding MPL, the report recognises that while Muslim women have the right to divorce under some provisions, Muslim men clearly enjoy more power, as they have the right to unilateral divorce. The report simultaneously recognises the limitations of legal reform, and the need for legal change.

> "Legislation alone can not eliminate rigid traditionalism, with its desire to preserve the status quo....(however) legislation is the only instrument which can bring the Muslim divorce law into line with not only the needs of society, but with the prevailing laws in other Muslim countries."[64]

The status of women report recommended the elimination of unilateral right of divorce for Muslim men, and the extension of maintenance for Muslim women. The report recognised the superiority of MPL over the personal laws of other communities in the area of inheritance rights for women.

> "Muslim law makes no distinction between movable and immovable property, and the rights of a female heir, unlike a widow or daughter has always been recognised, and they have inherited absolutely (unlike the old Hindu law)."[65]

The authors of the report conclude that there is an urgent need to implement a UCC. What is noteworthy is that they too base this demand on the grounds of national integration, not entirely on gender parity. The report reads:

> "The absence of a Uniform Civil Code is an incongruity that can not be justified with all the emphasis that is placed on secularism, science and modernisation. The continuance of various personal laws which accept discrimination between men and women violate the fundamental rights and the preamble....and is against the spirit of national integration and secularism."[66]

In the early 1980s, Muslim law was not frontally the topic for debate. A bulletin brought out by a civil liberties group in 1982 notes that there were few seminars and discussions on reforms in Muslim personal law were no longer popular and the explanation proffered was that there was a feeling that this was not the right time to raise it.[67]

In October 1983, the issue of MPL was raised legally by Shahnaz Shaikh, a 24 year old Muslim woman, who was actively involved in the women's movement in Bombay, and a member of Women's Centre and Forum Against Oppression of Women. Shahnaz Shaikh was married to Abdul Rab Ravish in 1981. Abdul Rab Ravish was 17 years older than her, and had displayed great mental and physical cruelty to her during the course of their marriage. He divorced her orally in September 1983, and threw her out of the house without giving her the meher set at Rs.12,000 at the time of marriage. In her petition filed against the Union of India and Abdul Rab Ravish as the second respondent, Shahnaz stated that she was not claiming any relief from her ex-husband. The petition stated:

> "The Petitioner says that she does not blame the Respondent No.2 for whatever has happened to the Petitioner as the Petitioner feels that the Respondent No.2 behaved in the manner he has done only because the existing personal law is so much loaded in his favour."[68]

Shahnaz laid the responsibility for her oppression on the state. She pointed out in her petition that although there were enough provisions in the Constitution, the Union of India had not enacted fair laws for Muslim women. The petition stated:

> "...Respondent No.1 has not deemed it proper or necessary to

make any laws to ensure social justice for Muslim women and have restricted themselves to law making only for Hindus, Christians and for Scheduled Castes and Tribes. The Petitioner says that the Respondent No. 1 is fully aware that Muslim women constitute over 4 crores in number and are a weaker section of the Indian society. A careful and unbiased research into the various provisions of law affecting Muslim women would easily reveal the need for social reform and balancing legislation."[69]

Shahnaz went on to dismiss the excuse put forward by political leaders that it had been left to the leaders of the Muslim community to initiate reform within the community As the petition pointed out that:

"The Petitioner says that by their default in this regard. Respondent No. 1 has allowed the beneficiaries of a socially unbalanced law to continue superiority over Muslim women at their option."[70]

The petition felt that Islamic faith and legal provisions needed to be separated, as one could be a believer and yet not believe in the validity of MPL. Due to practices like triple talaq and polygamy, Islam, instead of being revered as one of the greatest religions of the world, was being subjected to derision and abuse. The petition went on to submit that as a Muslim woman, she had been discriminated against by the State by a delirection of its duty to make laws applicable to all Indians. She pleaded that practices such as purdah, polygamy, and unilateral talaq were unconstitutional, and "not essential for the practice of Islam", hence the court rule that these practices be struck down as "unconstitutional, null and void, inoperative and of no effect"[71]

Shahnaz's petition made her famous and she was attacked and targeted by Muslim fundamentalists, pushing her into hiding. In addition, she found to her dismay that her lawyer was a member of the RSS, and wanted to use her case for Hindu communal purposes. The Shah Bano controversy that followed further revealed the polarisation of the issue of reform. Shahnaz's sharp and valid criticism of the Indian state was completely taken over by the debates of communal forces. Meanwhile, she also found herself isolated within the women's movement.

> "We debated the UCC a lot, but even within the women's movement, I felt my minority status, felt that this is Hindu feminism. They were all very nice people, but they were not trying to understand me."[72]

Shahnaz's isolation within the movement and her community led her to withdraw her petition. In a shift in perception, she felt that change in MPL should come from within the community, as appeals to the state vitiated the debate. In 1987, she started a collective primarily meant for Muslim women, called Awaaz-e-Niswaan (The voice of women):

> "On the UCC, we felt that we should frame if differently, call it women's code and that's what we have been calling it from day one in Awaaz-e-Niswaan...that's how we avoid the religious framework."[73]

However her conviction that work needs to be done within the community did not detract from her belief that Islam has its limitations as far as women's rights are concerned:

> "When I started reading the Quran for my petition, I became interested in some of the progressive things it was saying for women...I liked those, but then in the same Quran, there are other things that are very oppressive."[74]

Asghar Ali Engineer, a Bombay based Islamic Scholar and a Bohra reformer, however looks at Islam in a very different, perhaps less nuanced way. His perception is that the Quran provides almost unlimited scope for reform, and that the Quranic injunction that "women have rights similar to those of men" is unambiguous. Any anomalies that have crept into law are the result of mis-representation.[75] This view has informed the efforts of a Bombay based group called the Nikaahnama Group, made up of Muslim women who identify themselves with the women's movement. The group has worked out a model *nikaahnama*, a marriage contract, on the basis of which women can claim rights to matrimonial property, and some safeguards from unilateral divorce and polygamy. The *nikaahnama* states that maintenance at divorce be given to women according to the financial status of the man, and that if unilateral divorce does take place, the woman is entitled to an enhanced *meher* (dower). It also states that the permission of the first wife be taken if the man wants to contract a second marriage, and in the case of subsequent marriages, the permission of all the wives be taken.[76]

At one level, this prism does have its positive aspects, as it could potentially enable women to evolve a feminist understanding of practices and laws, alienating the men in the community. The flip side is that the terms of the debate become restricted to the ones set by the community, and the texts under study. To elaborate, the model Nikaahnama has no provisions for women who do not enter into marriage. Besides, the provisions to 'regulated' polygamy which the *nikaahnama* sets out are found inadequate and unjust from a feminist viewpoint. A feminist argued that women in oppressive marriages have no choice but to accept various indignities at the hands of their husband, and 'regulated polygamy' will not ensure the rights of women. "The responsibility to prevent polygamous marriages cannot be placed at the doors of women, who are already vulnerable. As a conception, regulated polygamy is unfair unless it is accompanied by regulated polyandry."[77] Another issue is that the experience of the group has been that even these limited reforms, clearly unacceptable to many feminists, are not taken seriously by the religious leaders.[78]

It has been argued that customs like polygamy and triple tala are not very common among Muslims, hence they do not pose a major issue for women within the community. The implication is that these are issues blown out of proportion by political parties. However, this can be questioned by some studies based on the experiences of women. Efforts by the Bombay based Women's Research and Action Group, the India chapter of the international network, Women Living Under Muslim Laws, have been to conduct studies in different parts of India to research the condition within which Muslim women live, and their attitudes to Muslim laws. A part of the study in Baroda questions the generalised feeling that Muslim women are impervious to change. The report states that while polygamy is not really common among Muslims, it does acquire a threatening meaning for women situated within the community. As the report states:

> "Most of the 388 women seemed to say,' we do not want it, whether it is common or not. 81.7% were unambiguous and clear that they wanted abolition of polygamy, an indication that they felt threatened by it. Polygamy makes their position within marriage insecure, for they do not really think their husbands can treat two or more women on par, nor are women willing to be put in competition with another woman for their husband's affections."[79]

Within the women's movement, there have been some criticisms of the 'reform from within' position. One of the more sophisticated articulation of this point of view is that this form of legal pluralism is based on the primordial identity of community, and is thus antithetical to feminism.

> "I believe that a feminism which is based on a critique of biologism and on the sexual division of labour rests, definitionally, on the right to chosen political affiliation and privileged social identities... above birth bound ones, it can not first uncritically with primordialism. Primordial claims can not be a feminist principle, because they are a principle of irrevocable distention, and will divide women by region, caste, religion and race."[80]

The argument glosses ovér the context within which women live their lives, suggesting that an allegiance to feminism, defined in rather rigid, monolithic terms, means an automatic break with all that is defined as 'primordial', that is region, caste, religion and race. We have seen that women within minority situations, in this case, Muslim women try to balance their feminist politics, and their religious identity. There is an effort, apparent in efforts like the Nikaahnama Group to change both. Nor do women like Shahnaz Shaikh 'first uncritically with community ties. Besides, as the Women's Research and Action Group study reveals, attachment to religious identity does not necessarily preclude a feminist orientation.

There are, therefore within the women's movement, multiple perceptions to the issue of reform. On the one hand, are the efforts of groups like Awaaz-e-Niswaan and the Nikaahnama Group who work on internal reform. Then, there are the perceptions that the debate should be articulated only in terms of women's rights, a view shared by Sangari, and the Bombay based members of the Forum Against Oppression of Women:

> "We believe that... a religionwise categorization (of personal laws) tends to become inward looking, and leads to the logic of internal reforms. It also detracts from the inadequacies and discrimination that all women face and share in common."[81]

The All India Democratic Women's Association (AIDWA), attached to the CPIM, takes a somewhat different position on the issue. In a convention held in December 1995, they suggest that the debate for a UCC and personal law reform has to be taken out of the realm of communal propaganda. This can be done by separating religion from politics. The convention demanded a legal ban on the use of religion for electoral purposes. Regarding the question of law, the Convention asserts that:

> "The Convention asserts a step by step approach to strengthen the common legal ground for women of all communities by bringing in legislations in specific spheres with immediate effect. This will provide benefit to all Indian women, as well as strengthen their unity. At the same time, the existing personal laws of all communities need drastic reform to make them more equal."[82]

AIDWA resolved to push for changes in areas that affect all women: that is, the issues of matrimonial property, registration of marriages, domestic violence. Simultaneously, they support the push for reforms within different communities.

A Delhi based group, Working Group for Women's Rights, in 1995, worked out a position that is conceptually different from that of the ways in which family laws are perceived so far. They suggest the preparation of a comprehensive package of legislation that would embody gender justice, including equal family laws, as well as equal laws in employment. This package would be available to all men and women in the country, yet they can choose allegiance to personal laws in moments of legal dispute, or at any other point. The suggestion is:

> "All those who are born as or become citizens of India would come under the purview of this framework of common laws...All citizens would also have the right to choose at any point in their lives to be governed by personal laws if they so desire. The choice to be governed by personal law has to be a conscious decision by an individual citizen. If such a choice is not made, the new gender just legislation would be applied. In keeping with our conceptual framework of gender just laws as the rights of citizens, we believe that citizens, who have chosen personal laws should be able to revoke their choice and move back to the common laws at a moment of legal conflict."[83]

The suggestions made by the two women's organisations do mark a conceptual shift in the impasse between internal reform and common laws. While the AIDWA position aims at careful reform in which reform of 'non controversial' areas be accompanied by reforms of personal laws, the WGWR position stakes a more direct claim to women's rights by aiming at a comprehensive package of gender just laws. A concession is made to the pressures that women may face by allowing the option of choosing personal laws at any point. WGWR's efforts are not unlike that made by Shahnaz Shaikh in 1983 that is, to make an unresponsive state open to the oppression of women as citizens of the country-except that here, woman (and men) are given the option of choosing personal law. The effort is to make available to women a set of laws that are non communalised, in other words to take the debate away from communal forces. What is significant is that in both these efforts, the focus is not only on personal laws, but on other areas of law—-criminal law, employment and labour law—that are perhaps as misogynist and unequal as personal law.

An issue not always explored in the discourse around MPL is that of another kind of denial of rights. In family courts, set up in the mid 1980s at the behest of the IWM to expediate civil matters pertaining to family laws, Muslim women have been kept out of the perview of the court.[84] In other words, for matters including economic settlements, Muslim women have to go to the High Court, involving a process that is longer and more cumbersome than approaching the Family Courts. This is an issue that the women's movement has not taken up. I suggest that the focus on law within the movement has often left out the problems inherent in the denial of justice when it comes to the implementation of some of these laws. As we have seen, this is apparent in the practice of several laws civil and criminal.

REFERENCES

1. For elaboration of this theme, see Sudhir Kakar, *The Colours of Violence*. Viking Penguin Books India, New Delhi, 1995, esp. Preface: vii-x.

2. M.H.M. Abdullah, member of the Legislative Assembly cited in Kamran Arif, *The Evolution of Muslim Family Law in India*. Unpublished Paper, 1994.

3. Kirti Singh, "Women's Rights and the Reform of Personal Laws," in Gyanendra Pandey, ed., *Hindus and Others. The Question of Identity in India Today*. Viking Penguin Books India, New Delhi, 1993: 177-197, esp. 177-79.

4. Justice Ranade, quoted in Shahida Lateef, *Muslim Women in India, Political and Private Realities*. Kali for Woman, New Delhi, 1994:56.

5. Madhu Kishwar, "Codified Hindu Law. Myth and Reality". *Economic and Political Weekly*. August 13, 1994: 2145-2161; gives a detailed analyses of the debates during the drafting and

the development of the 'Hindu code bill'.

6. Kumkum Sangari, Politics of Diversity. Religious Communities and Multiple Patriarchies. *Economic and Political Weekly.* December 23, 1995: 3787-3810, esp. 3798-9.

7. Kirti Singh, *op.cit.,* 186.

8. *Ibid.,* 187-88.

9. Thakur Das Bhargava, quoted in Madhu Kishwar, Codified Hindu Law. Myth and Reality. *op.cit.,* 2152.

10. K.T. Shah in B Shiva Rao, *Framing of the Indian Constitution. Select Documents.* Volume 11. Indian Institute of Public Administration, New Delhi, 1967:39.

11. Jawaharlal Nehru, Speches. 1949-53. Volume II. *The Publication Department,* Government of India, 361.

12. Quoted in M.A. Karandikar, *Islam in India's Transition to Modernity.* Orient Longman, New Delhi, 1987.

13. Quoted in Vasudha Dhagamwar. *Towards a Uniform Civil Code.* Indian Law Institute, New Delhi, 1989: 28.

14. Constituent Assembly Debates. Appendixed in Vasudha Dhagamwar, *op.cit.,* 127.

15. Quoted in G.S. Bhargava, Towards a Common Civil Code. *Mainstream.,* March 6, 1983: 11-13.

16. Vasudha Dhagamwar, *op.cit.*

17. Karandikar, *op.cit.,* 180.

18. *Ibid.*

19. *Lok Sabha Debates.* May 5th, 1985: 239.

20. This right had been denied to them under the act in 1954, when it had been ruled that any person marrying under this act would be governed by the Indian Succession Act, 1925.

21. *Lok Sabha Debates.* May 20, 1976: 160-166; May 21, 1976: 8-90, May 24, 1976: 8-38.

22. *Lok Sabha Debates.* May 21, 1976: 85. Shri Chandra Shailani. Translated from Hindi.

23. *Ibid.* 76. Shri B.V. Naik.

24. Chapter V. *Legislative Debates in 1986: The State and 'Women's Issues'* looks at the debates in greater details. Here, I focus on only specific aspects of the debates.

25. *Lok Sabha Debates.* May 5, 1986: 315. Shri A.K. Sen.

26. *Ibid.* 334. Shri H.A. Dora.

27. *Ibid.* 471. Smt. Vidyavati Chaturvedi.

28. *Ibid.* 424. Smt. Geeta Mukherjee.

29. *Ibid.* 318. Shri Saifuddin Chaudhry.

30. Multiple Action Research Group and Women and Child Development, Human Resource Ministry, *Hamare Kanoon.* Volume IV, New Delhi, 1992:, 7-20.

31. *Recommendations of the Minority Commission on the demand from a section of the Parsees for exclusion of the Parsee community from the purview of the Adoption Bill., 1980.*

32. *Ibid.*

33. Dhagamwar, *op.cit.* 28.

34. Adoption, being a topic on the concurrent list, needs presidential assent before it can be amended by any state.

35. *L.A. Bill No. XXXI of 1995.* A Bill to provide for adoption of child and for matters connected therewith.

36. Mohommed Ahmed Khan V.Shah Bano Begum and Others. AIR 1985. SC 945. Section 125 Cr P.C. is a part of criminal law, the purpose of the section being that to prevent destitution. Under this

section, the 'destitute' person was entitled to relief to the maximum amount of Rs. 500.

37. *Ibid.*

38. Veena Das, *Critical Events.* Oxford University Press. New Delhi, 1995: 93.

39. Bai Tahira V Ali Hussen Fissalli Chothia and Another. AIR 1979. SC 362.

40. Shah Bano, Open Letter to Muslims. *Inquillab.* November 13, 1985. Translated from Urdu.

41. Memorandum by Committee for Protection of Rights of Muslim Women, reprinted in Asghar Ali Engineer, ed., *The Shah Bano Controversy:* Orient Longman, Hyderabad, 1987: 217-221.

42. In The Supreme Court of India. Public Interest Jurisdiction. Writ Petition No. 868 of 1986. In the Matter of the Muslim Women Protection of Rights upon Divorce Act, 1986.

43. Sahiba Rahman, quoted in Rohini Hensmen, *Oppression Within Oppression. The Dilemma of Muslim Women in India.* Working Paper No.1. October 1987. Women Living Under Muslim Law.

44. Statement by BJP National Executive in a meeting in Chandigarh, 1986.

45. Quoted in *Loksatta*. December 12,1985. Translated from Hindi.

46. See for instance, Shahzadi Begum V.Mohommad Abdul Gaffar. 1981. Cri L J. 1532, where a maintenance order of Rs. 75 was awarded under Section 12 Cr P.C.

47. K. Haji V. Amina II (1995) DMC 260.

48. Arab Ahemadhia Abdulla V. Arab Bail Mohmuna Saiyadbhai. AIR 1988 Gujarat 141.

49. Mohommad Murtaza V. Kauser Parveen. 1991. Cri L. J. 3202.

50. *Ibid.*

51. Talaq-e-bid'at essentially means a form of divorce where a husband can divorce his wife by uttering 'Talaq' (divorce) thrice in a single sitting.
52. Rahmatullah V. State of UP, Khatoonisa V. State of UP. Judgment dated April 4th, 1993.
53. Gautam Navlakha, Triple Talaq: Posturing at Women's Expenses. *Economic and Political Weekly*. May 21, 1994: 1264.
54. Sarla Mudgal and Others V. the Union of India and Others, II 1995. DMC 351 (SC).
55. *Ibid.*
56. Surjit Kaur V. Gulab Singh and Others. 1994. (1) UJ (SC) 223.
57. Flavia Agnes, Hindu Men, Monogamy and Uniform Civil Code. *Economic and Political Weekly*. December 16, 1995: 3238-3242, esp. 3238.
58. LA Bill Number XXXII of 1995. Maharashtra Legislative Secretariat. *A Bill to provide for the prevention of bigamous marriages in the State of Maharashtra.*
59. Quoted in Saffron Brigade. *Frontline*. January 6, 1993.
60. Multiple Action Research Group and Women and Child Development, Human Resource Ministry, *Hamare Kanoon*. Volume V. New Delhi 1992.
61. Quoted in Mani Shankar Aiyyar. "Uniform Civil Code. A Primer for the Village Idiot". *Sunday*. August 20, 1995: 15-18.
62. L.K. Advani, quoted in Madhu Deolekar, *India Needs a Common Civil Code*. Vivek Vyaspeeth, Mumbai, June 1995.
63. Kirti Singh in Gyanendra Pandey, *op. cit.*, Vasudha Dhagamwar, *op. cit.*
64. *Towards Equality. Report on the Status of Women*. Government of India. 1974: 121-22.

65. *Ibid.*, 140.

66. *Ibid.*

67. Kamila Tyabji, Muslim women and the Uniform Civil Code. *PUCL Bulletin.* September 1982: 25.

68. Shahnaz Shaikh V. The Union of India and Adbul Rab Kavish. Civil Writ Petition No. 32 of 1983. In the matter of Article 32 of the Constitution of India and in the matter of Article 14, 15, 25 and 26 of the Constitution of India and in the matter of the Muslim Personal Law. In the Supreme Court of India. Civil Original Jurisdiction: 3.

69. *Ibid.*, 3-4.

70. *Ibid.*, 4.

71. *Ibid.*, 6-10.

72. Shahnaz Shaikh, interviewed in Ritu Menon. The Personal and the Political in Kamala Bhasin. Ritu Menon and Nighat Saead Khan. *Against All Odds.* South Asian Women's Forum, Kali for Women and ISIS 1994 : 173-182, esp. 174.

73. *Ibid.*

74. *Ibid.*, 186.

75. Asghar Ali Engineer, Women and Muslim Law. Presentation at Consultation on Gender Just Laws. Organised by Forum Against Oppression of Women, Lawyers' Collective and Human Rights Law Network, Bombay. June 5-8th, 1996.

76. Oral Presentation by Vahida Nainar and Nahida Sheikh at Seminar on Reforms in Law. Organised by Women's Centre, Bombay. March 1996.

77. Rohini Hensmen at *ibid.*

78. Vahida Nainar and Nahida Sheikh at *ibid.*

79. Bina Srinivasan, *A Cry For Change, A Report on Muslim Personal*

Law and their Implications for Women in Baroda. Women's Research and Action Group. Bombay 1994: 31.

80. Kumkum Sangari, *op.cit.* 3239.

81. Nandita Gandhi and Nandita Shah, *The Issues at Stake. Theory and Practice in the Contemporary Women's Movement in India.* Kali for Women, New Delhi, 1992: 229.

82. All India Democratic Women's Association, *National Convention. Equal Rights Equal Laws.* December 9 and 10th, 1995.

83. Working Group for Women's Rights. New Delhi. Statement in Uniform Civil Code. A Debate. *Alternatives/Vikalp.* Volume V. No. 3. 1996: 90-91.

84. I owe this point to Flavia Agnes. The Family Courts Act, 1984 was followed by The Maharashtra Family Courts Rules, 1987.

4

Legal Rights of Maintenance and Guardianship of Muslim Woman

Justice Sarojini Saxena

Legal rights of Muslim women are well defined in Muslim Law. Even then they have been interpreted by various High Courts as well as by the Apex Court. In this study, I shall try to give a brief resume of those decisions.

Women's rights of inheritance, polygamy, triple *talaq*, divorce, maintenance and ban on entry into Mosques has enraged women activists in India as well as in Muslim countries. In Muslim Law, a divorced woman is entitled to get maintenance from her husband during the period of Iddat (3 lunar months). In *Shah Bano's* judgment (*Mohd. Ahmed Khan Vs. Shah Bano Begum* AIR 1985 SC 945), the Apex Court decided to uphold divorced Muslim woman's claim to get maintenance from her husband under Sec. 125 of the Cr. P.C. In that case, their Lordships held that after divorce during Iddat period the husband is liable to pay maintenance to his wife under Muslim Law, but after the period of Iddat if she is unable to maintain herself then she can file a petition under Sec. 125 Cr. P.C. against her husband for getting maintenance for herself till she remarries and certainly as provided under Sec. 125 of the Code. In that judgment, the Apex Court held that to this extent Sec. 125 of the Code overrides personal law. The Apex Court held:

"The true position is that, if the divorced wife is able to maintain herself, the husband's liability to provide maintenance for her ceases with the expiration of the period of iddat. If she is unable to maintain herself, she is entitled to take recourse to Sec. 125. Therefore, it cannot be said that there is conflict between the provisions of Sec. 125 and those of the Muslim Personal Law on the question of Muslim husband's obligation to provide maintenance for a divorced wife who is unable to maintain herself."

In Shah Bano's case, the Apex Court approved its earlier decisions given in *Bai Tahira Vs. Ali Hussain,* AIR 1979 SC 362 and *Fazlunbi Vs. K. Khader Vali,* AIR 1980 S.C. 1730. Their Lordships also held that Mehr is not the amount payable by the husband to the wife on divorce. Their Lordships have quoted the decision given by Privy Council in *Hamira Bibi Vs. Zubaida Bibi,* AIR 1916 P.C. 46 at page 48, wherein Privy Council held that:

"Dower is an essential incident under the Mussulman law to the status of marriage, to such an extent that is to say that when it is unspecified at the time the marriage is contracted, the law declares that it must be adjusted on definite principles."

Their Lordships of the Privy Council further held that it is either prompt dower payable before the wife can be called upon to enter the conjugal domicile, the other deferred payable on the dissolution of the contract by the death of either of the parties or by divorce. This statement of law was adopted in another decision of Privy Council in *Sabir Husain Vs. Farzand Hasan* AIR 1930 P.C. 80 at page 83. It is specifically observed that Mr. Syed Ameer Ali was a party to the decision in Hamira Bibi while Sir Shadi Lal was a party to the decision in Syed Sabir Hussain. This judgment of Shah Bano created furore in the Muslim community and it culminated in passing of the Act, i.e., Muslim Women (Protection of Rights on Divorce) Act, 1986. Its Sec. 3 provides that notwithstanding anything contained in any other law for the time being in force, the divorced woman shall be entitle to a reasonable and fair provision and maintenance to be made and paid to her within the iddat period by her former husband. Its sub-sec. (2)

lays down that where a reasonable and fair provision and maintenance has not been made and paid, she may file an application before a Magistrate for an order of payment of such provision and maintenance. While deciding such an application under sub-sec. (3), the Magistrate may, if he is satisfied that her husband having sufficient means has failed or neglected to make or pay her within the iddat period a reasonable and fair provision and maintenance for her, make an order directing the husband to pay such reasonable and fair provision and maintenance to the divorced woman, as he may determine as fit and proper having regard to the needs of the divorced woman, standard of life enjoyed by her during her marriage and the means of her former husband.

Sec. 4 of the Act further provided that notwithstanding anything contained in the foregoing provision of this Act or in any other law for the time being in force, where a Magistrate is satisfied that a divorced woman has not remarried and is not able to maintain herself and is desirous of obtaining maintenance for post- iddat period, the Magistrate may direct payment to be made to her by her children, parents, other relatives or Wakf Board in that sequence. Sec. 5 of the Act gives a right to both the parties to give an option to be governed by S. 125 to 128 of the Code when their application under S. 3 (2) of the Act is pending for disposal. Sec. 7 of the Act lays down that every application by a divorced woman under S. 125 or 127 of the Code pending on the date of commencement of this Act shall be disposed off by the Magistrate in accordance with the provisions of this Act, but subject to the provision of S.5. All these provisions of this Act, in short Muslim Women Act, are interpreted by various High Courts.

In *Peer Mohd. Vs. Hasinabee* (1995 JLJ 110), it is held that husband gave divorce to his wife after fixation of maintenance by the trial court u/s. 125 of the Code. Divorce was not given during proceedings before trial court, hence divorce at revisional stage makes no change. Provisions of Muslim Women Act do not govern the case. In *Abdul Rashid Vs. Smt. Farida's* (1994 MPLJ 583) judgment, relying on Apex Court's decision M.P. High Court has reiterated that

Sec. 125 of the Code is a secular provision. It applies to all persons belonging to all religions and has no relationship with personal law of parties. Right to maintenance u/s. 125 of the Code is not taken away by Muslim Women Act. On divorce Muslim woman's application will be governed by the said Act from date of divorce. Husband is liable to maintain her during iddat period only and not thereafter. Every application under Sec. 125 of the Code made before or after divorce would be governed by 1986 Act. Under Sec. 4 of this Act, a divorced woman can obtain maintenance for post-iddat period from her children parents, other relatives and State Wakf Board if there is any, if she avails this remedy.

In *Abida Begam Vs. Shafi Mohammad* (1996 MPLJ Note 14) Sec. 125 of the Code and Sec. 3 (2) and Secs. 5 & 7 of the Muslim Women Act are again interpreted by a single Bench of M.P. High Court. In that case, maintenance was granted under Sec. 125 of the Code to wife and daughter prior to coming into force of Muslim Women Act. It is held that such order would continue to remain valid and enforceable even after commencement of Muslim Women Act. Sessions Judge's order in revision setting aside maintenance order on the ground that provisions of Sec. 125 Cr. P.C. ceased to govern parties in view of their failure to exercise option under Sec.5 of the Act was erroneous. It is clarified that Secs. 125 to 128 of the Code would be applicable to the proceedings filed under Sec. 3(2) of the Act, if the parties to the proceedings, on the first date of hearing, exercise their options in that regard either jointly or separately. It is difficult to hold that the provisions of the Act would apply to proceedings, already concluded u/s. 125 of the Code. The provisions contained in Sec. 125 are beneficial provisions incorporated in the Code for safeguarding the interest of deserted/divorced hapless women, who are unable to maintain themselves. As is apparent from the nomenclature of the 1986 Act., this Act was enacted by the legislature with a view to protect the rights of divorced Muslim Women. Keeping the above object of enacting these provisions in mind, the correct interpretation of Sec.7 of the Act would be to hold that the orders passed by the

Magistrate under the provisions of Sec. 125 of the Code prior to the coming into force of the Act, would continue to remain valid and enforceable even after the commencement of the Act. Any other interpretation would frustrate the very purpose of enacting the 1986 Act.

In *Julekha Bi Vs. Mohammad Fazal,* reported in 1999 (2) MPLJ 64, a single Judge of M.P. High Court has interpreted the implications of Sec. 125 of the Code and of Sec. 3 of Muslim Women Act. In that case, order of maintenance was passed in favour of Muslim wife under Sec. 125 of the Code. Thereafter, husband gave divorce to his wife. When wife enforced the order of maintenance, the husband opposed it on the ground of subsequent divorce High Court held that divorced wife is not entitled to get maintenance from her husband after the period of iddat.

Provisions of Sec. 3(1)(a) and Sec. 125 of the Code were interpreted by a Full Bench of Andhra Pradesh High Court in *Usman Khan Rahamani Vs. Fathimunnisa Begum,* 1990 CRI.L.J. 1364. The Full Bench held that:

> "Muslim woman shall be entitled to a reasonable and fair maintenance within the iddat period to be made and paid by her former husband. It is equally clear that the reasonable and fair provision and maintenance has to be made and paid by the husband within the period of iddat, which has been defined under S.2(b) of the Act. There is nothing in the section which can be read to mean that the husband is liable to make reasonable and fair provision and maintenance beyond the period of iddat."

Interpreting the words "within" occurring in Sec. 3(1) (a) of the Act. the Full Bench held "it clearly means that there is an obligation on the part of the husband to provide fair and reasonable maintenance to his divorced wife within the period of iddat and for the period of iddat only." It cannot be interpreted that this liability of the husband extends beyond the period of iddat. To take a contrary view would result in complete negation of the principles envisaged under S. 3(1)(a) of the

Act of 1986 and defeat the very purpose of the Act. S.4. casts liability on the relatives or the Wakf Board to pay maintenance to the divorced woman if the divorced woman has not remarried or is unable to maintain herself after the iddat period. Their Lordships also held that the word 'Provision' and 'maintenance' in Sec. 3(1)(a) convey same meaning. They cannot be read as meaning two different things. Liability of husband to pay maintenance as well as to make reasonable provision are confined only to the period of iddat. This was the view of Justice Ramanujulu and Justice Sardar Ali Khan of this Bench.

Justice Bhaskar Rao gave a minority view disagreeing only on this point that a reasonable and fair provision and maintenance to be made and paid do not convey the same meaning. The Muslim woman's right to claim maintenance after iddat period under Sec. 125 of the Code was crystallized by Shah Bano's judgment. Which came into controversy and under a threat of erosion. In this background of protection, the resultant provisions are S.3 (1)(a) and S.5 of the Act, the former casting a liability on the husband to make a reasonable and fair provision even for the period beyond the iddat apart from payment of maintenance within the iddat period and the latter giving the option to the parties to be governed by S. 125 to 128 of the Code if it is simply a question of payment of maintenance for the iddat period that is truely intended by Sec. 3 (1)(a) and nothing more, neither the Legislature would have wasted its breath by incorporating the liability of making a provision reasonable and fair, apart from paying maintenance, in Sec. 3(1)(a), nor would it have allowed Sec. 5 to remain otiose in the statute since no Muslim former husband with minimum commonsense would opt for governance by the provisions of Secs. 125 to 128 of the Code of Criminal Procedure in the absence of any corresponding or balancing liability cast on him by one or other provision in the statute. It is equally important to note that S.4 of the Act significantly omits the word 'provision' from the term "a reasonable and fair provision and maintenance".

The words in Sec. 3(1)(a) "within the iddat period" lay stress on the urgency of making or paying and they cannot be read as confining the liability to the limited period of iddat, save in so far as maintenance is concerned the Muslim Law is settled on that aspect. Interpreting the distinct liability of making a reasonable and fair provision as having been confined to the period of iddat would not only render the very S.5 on the statute otiose but also defeat the specific purpose of casting that liability on the former husband by S.3(1)(a) in contradistinction from S.4 whereunder the liability of either the relatives or the Wakf Board is only to pay maintenance and there is absolutely no liability to make any provision under S.4 of the Act. The learned minority judge also relied on (1988) 3 Crimes 147—a decision of Kerala High Court in *Ali Vs. Sufaira,* which the majority view distinguished.

The minority judge after quoting the definition of 'provision' and 'maintenance' from Webster's Third New International Dictionary, observed that the word 'provision' means, an amount set apart to meet a known liability, the amount of which cannot be decided with accuracy. The known liability under Sec. 3(1)(a) of a husband is to provide for the future of the divorced Muslim woman. Thus, according to the minority view 'provision' and 'maintenance' cannot be read together in a compendious form.

The majority view also referred to *Md. Yunus Vs. Bibi Pheakani* (1987) 2 Crimes 241, a judgment by single Judge of Patna High Court; *Abid Ali Vs Mst Raisa Begum,* 1988 (1) Raj L.R.- a Division Bench judgment of Rajasthan High Court wherein it is held that the husband is liable to make provision as well as to pay maintenance only during the period of iddat. They dissented from the judgment of Gujarat High Court reported in *A.A. Abdulla Vs. A.B. Mohmuna Saivabhai.* AIR 1988 Guj. 141 wherein the learned single Judge took the view that "a divorced Muslim woman is entitled to maintenance after contemplating her future needs and the maintenance is not limited only upto iddat period. The phrase used in S.3(1)(a) of the Act of 1986 is "reasonable and fair provision and maintenance to be made and paid to her" indicates that the Parliament intended to see that the divorced woman gets sufficient means of livelihood after the divorce and that she does not become destiture or is not thrown on the streets without a roof over her head and her children." The learned Judge observed that the word 'provision' itself indicates that something is provided in advance for meeting some needs." A similar view was taken by Punjab & Haryana High Court in *Hazran Vs.Abdul Rehman,* 1989 Cri LJ 1519, wherein their Lordships held that order of maintenance u/s, 125, is not affected by the Muslim Women Act.

In *A. Abdul Gafoor Vs. A.U. Pathumma Beevi,* 1988 Cri. L.J. 1224, Single Judge of Kerala High Court held that after the enactment of Muslim Women Act divorced Muslim wife cannot invoke S. 127 of the Code seeking enhancement of her maintenance.

Recently (June, 2000) in a landmark judgment, Calcutta High Court has ruled that divorced Muslim women will get maintenance allowance till they remarry. Justice Basudev Panigrahi decided the revision petition filed by a divorced Muslim woman Sahkila Parvin. Deserted by her husband Haidar Ali in 1993, Shakila filed a petition seeking maintenance allowance against her husband. Despite service of the copy of the petition, the husband did not respond. On 15th July, the trial court granted maintenance allowance of Rs. 800/- for a customary three months iddat and mehr of Rs 2,500- to Shakila. Shakila assailed the said order by filing revision before the Calcutta High Court. While deciding her revision petition, Justice Panigrahi held the trial court had wrongly construed the provisions of S.3 of the Muslim Women Act and held that the expression such as "all reasonable and fair provisions and maintenance to be made and paid to her" should be construed liberally. His Lordship observed that the Supreme Court had unequivocally held that the provisions of Sec. 125 of the Code overrode the personal law and it necessitated the enactment of the Muslim Women Act in Parliament in 1986. Referring to 1994 judgment of a Division Bench of Allahabad High Court, Justice Panigrahi said, "according to the provisions of Sec. 125(3) of the Act, the right to receive maintenance allowance cannot be restricted to the period of iddat only in case of a divorced woman.

Bombay High Court has also recently interpreted the provisions of Sec. 125 of the Code and those of the Muslim Women Act. They held that divorced Muslim women cannot apply for maintenance under the Code and will have to do so only under the Muslim Women Act. A Full-Bench of Justice Ajit Shah, Justice Ranjana Desai and Justice J.A. Patil maintained that all pending applications under Sec. 125 of Cr. P.C. filed by divorced Muslim women after the commencement of Muslim Women Act will be treated as applications under the Muslim Women Act and accordingly disposed off. The basic issue before the Court was the interpretation of Sec. 3 of the Muslim Women Act, as there was controversy over the extent of liability of paying maintenance to women who have been divorced. Earlier Muslim divorcees could claim maintenance under Sec. 125 of the Code. This apparently clashed with Sec.3(1)(a) of Muslim Women Act, which provided that reasonable and fair maintenance should be paid during iddat i.e. three months after divorce. Various views have been taken by different courts on the extent to which payments can be made to a Muslim divorcee. With this judgment, the full bench has in fact resolved the dichotomy stating that Cr. P.C. can be covered under Muslim Women Act. The full bench ordered that all applications filed u/s. 125 of the Code by divorced Muslim women shall be disposed off by Magistrate in accordance with the provisions of Muslim Women Act. The full bench also clarified that while a Muslim husband's liability u/s.3 of Muslim Women Act to make a reasonable and fair maintenance is only restricted to iddat period he has to make reasonable and fair provisions for her within iddat which should take care for the rest of her life or till she incurs any disability under the Muslim Women Act. If the husband cannot arrange the full amount the Magistrate may direct monthly payment even beyond the *iddat* period, subject to fixing an amount. They also held that orders passed u/s. 125 of the Code prior to the commencement of Muslim Women Act are executable under Sec. 128 of the Code and are binding on both the parties.

The other connected question for consideration is whether Muslim Women Act has in any way affected Muslim divorcee's right to claim maintenance for her children residing with her *Gaffur Vs. Smt. Salma,* 1993 JLJ 39, propounds that:

> "Under Sec.125 of the Cr. P.C., Muslim father is liable to maintain his children. Divorced wife would not release him from liability. Under Muslim Women Act additional protection has been provided for maintenance of childern. It has not taken away the right of children to be maintained by their father even if he has divorced his wife".

In *Noor Saba Khatoon Vs. Mohd. Quasim,* (1997) 6 S.C.C. 233—The Apex Court considered the right of minor children staying with their divorced mother to claim maintenance under S.125 Cr. P.C. from their Muslim father having sufficient means till they attain majority or in case of females till they get married. The Apex Court has taken into consideration 3(1)(b) of Muslim Women Act, and observed that this provision provides additional maintenance to the divorced mother for maintaining her infant child for the fosterage period of two years from the date of birth of the child and is independent of the right of the minor children unable to maintain themselves to claim maintenance under S.125. That right is absolute under S.125 as well as under Muslim personal law. Benefit of S.125 is available irrespective of religion and it would be unreasonable, unfair and inequitable to deny this benefit to the children only on ground of their being born of Muslim parents.

Thus, we have seen that provisions of Muslim Women Act have been interpreted by various High Courts keeping in view the object with which this Act was enacted. To my knowledge, up till now no such case has reached the Apex Court, hence still Apex Court's interpretation of the provisions of Sec. 3 are awaited in the legal world. The very purpose of enacting this Act was to protect the rights of divorced Muslim women. The very name of the Act is indicative of the object with which this Act was enacted. When we compare Sections 3 & 4 it become apparent that Sec. 3(1)(a) makes husband liable for a reasonable and fair provision and maintenance to be made and paid to the divorced women within the *iddat* period, but u/s.4 when a divorced woman who has not remarried is unable to maintain herself after the *iddat* peiod, she is entitled to approach the Magistrate seeking order for the grant of maintenance to be passed against her children, parents, other relations and finally the Wakf Board in the same sequence. In Sec. 4 the words 'reasonable and fair provision' are not included. Sec. 4 is with regard to maintenance only. Thus, it becomes apparent that Parliament intended that the husband alone is liable to make a reasonable and fair provision for his divorced wife, but that is to be made within the period of *iddat*. The words 'reasonable and fair provision' themselves indicate that it is a provision for future, which cannot be exactly calculated and is to be assessed only on estimation. The yardsticks of this estimation are provided under sub-sec. (3) of S.3, which requires a Magistrate to consider the needs of the divorced woman, her standard of life enjoyed by her during her marriage and the means of her former husband before making such an order. The Magistrate has to take into consideration the same yardstick with regard to children, parents and other relations of the divorced women when he makes an order of payment of maintenance to such woman by these persons. Sec. 5 of the Act also gives an inkling into the mind of the Legislature that this fair and reasonable provision is not limited to the period of *iddat* only. Sec.5 provides that if on the first date of hearing of an application filed u/s. 3(2) of the Act the divorced woman and her former husband give an option jointly or separately that they would prefer to be governed by the provisions of Sec. 125 to 128 of the Code, the Magistrate shall dispose off such application accordingly. Sec. 127 of the Code is with regard to enhancement of maintenance already determined and ordered u/s. 125 of the code. If the intention of the Legislature was to limit the making or reasonable and fair provision within the period of *iddat* only, there was hardly any reason to include Sec.127 within the ambit of Sec. 5 of Muslim Women Act. Taking into consideration the phraseology used in all these Sections, the recent trend of various High Courts is that even after the period of *iddat* former husband is liable to make a reasonable and fair provision for his divorced wife, if she does not remarry.

The divorced Muslim Women's application for grant of

maintenance against Wakf Board straightaway also created problems because the Wakf Board objected that the liability to pay maintenance to a divorced woman trickles down to Wakf Board from the pinnacle of children, parents and then other relations, who are entitled to inherit property from such a divorced woman. Such objection was raised by Tamil Nadu Wakf Board in *Secretary, Tamil Nadu Wakf Board Vs Syed Fatima Nachi,* (1996) 4 SCC 616, wherein provisions of Sec. 4 of Muslim Women Act were interpreted by the Apex Court, it was held that:

> "State Wakf Board is liable to provide maintenance to a divorced woman, who is unable to maintain herself and has not remarried. Such divorced woman is not required to initiate proceedings in the first instance against her children, parents and relatives who have no means to pay her maintenance and obtain negative orders and then proceed against the State Wakf Board. She may direct her claim against the State Wakf Board in the first instance and in that proceeding she can plead and prove inability of her relatives to maintain her. If the State Wakf Board controverts that her relatives have enough means to pay maintenance they may be added as parties to the litigation. Under Sec. 4(1) prospective heirs of the divorced women are liable to pay her maintenance. It does not depend on the contingency that the divorced women has property which they would inherit. It looks incongruous though that a divorced woman having property would yet be unable to maintain herself. Seemingly, the phraseology has been employed to ascertain firstly such of those relatives who could have inherited her property, fictionally on the basis that she could be having property, and secondly as if she had died on the date when the need for identification arose. The speculative plea of any relative that he or she may not be available to be an heir on the date when the divorced woman would actually die, would either be here nor there."

In *Lily Thomas Vs. Union of India,* AIR 2000 S.C. 1850, a very intricate question of conversion into Islam for the sake of second marriage was passed before the Apex Court. In that case, Smt. Sushmita Ghosh filed a writ petition before the Apex Court alleging that she was married to Shri G.C. Ghosh on 10th May 1984 and they were enjoying happy conjugal life. Around 1st April, 1992 G.C.Ghosh told her that she should in her own interest agree for mutual divorce as he has converted to Islam and he may re-marry. G.C.Ghosh fixed his marriage with Miss Vanita Gupta, a divorcee with two children in the second week of July, 1992, G.C.Ghosh obtained a certificate issued by the office of Maulana Quar Mohammad Idris dated 17th June, 1992 certifying that G.C.Ghosh had embraced Islam.

She also asserted that her husband has converted to Islam solely for the purpose of re-marrying and has no real faith in Islam. He does not practice the Muslim rites has not changed his name or religion in official documents. Thereby she asserted that her fundamental right guaranteed under Art. 15(1) of the Constitution has been violated as she has been discriminated against by that part of Muslim Personal Law, which is enforced by the State Action by virtue of the Muslim Personal Law (Shariat) Act, 1937. She also filed a criminal complaint against her husband under Sec. 494 I.P.C. On inquiry it was found that G.C.Ghosh obtained his visa in 1995 describing himself as Gyan Chand Ghosh and religion Hindu. He signed marriage certificate also as G.C.Ghosh and not as Mohd. Carim Gazi. Even in the electoral roll, his name mentioned was Gyan Chand Ghosh and his wife's name as Vanita Ghosh.

The Apex Court considered this intricate legal issue when a Hindu renounces his religion and converts to another religion and marries second time, what would be the effect on his criminal liability. Their Lordships considered the provisions of Secs.5, 11, and 17 of the Hindu Marriage Act, 1955 and Sec. 494 I.P.C. and 198 Cr. P.C. The Apex Court observed:

> "Religion is a matter of faith stemming from the depth of the heart and mind. Religion is a belief which binds the spiritual nature of man to a supernatural being, it is an object of

conscentious devotion, faith and pietism..."

"If the person feigns to have adopted another religion just for some worldly gain or benefit, it would be religious bigotry. Looked at from this angle, a person who mockingly adopts another religion where plurality of marriage is permitted so as to renounce the previous marriage and desert the wife, he cannot be permitted to take advantage of his exploitation as religion is not a commodity to be exploited."

Their Lordships also held that "conversion or apostasy does not automatically dissolve a marriage already solemnized under the Hindu Marriage Act. They also took note of an earlier decision of Nagpur High Court rendered in *Gul Mohammad Vs. Emperor,* 1947 Nag. 121, wherein their Lordships of the High Court held that "conversion of a Hindu wife to Mahomedanism does not, ipso facto, dissolve the marriage with her Hindu husband." The Apex Court held that "mere conversion does not bring to an end the marital ties unless a decree for divorce on that ground is obtained from the Court."

About the offence of bigamy the Apex Court held that "the second marriage of a Hindu husband after conversion to Islam without having his first marriage dissolved under law, would be invalid. The second marriage would be void in terms of provision of S.494 I.P.C."

In this case the Apex Court has also considered that the concept of Muslim Law is based upon the edifice of Shariat, Muslim Law as traditionally interpreted and applied in India permits more than one marriage during the subsistence of one and another though capacity to do justice between cowives in law is condition precedent. Thus, even under Muslim Law plurality of marriages is not unconditionally conferred upon the husband. It would, therefore, be doing injustice to Islamic Law to urge that the convert is entitled to practice bigamy notwithstanding the continuance of his marriage under the law to which he belonged before conversion.

Rights of Guardianship

Rights of guardianship also at times create a problem mainly for the parents as well as for their minor children. This problem is further complicated if the father divorces his wife and wife remarries a stranger.

In *Rahima Khatoon Vs. Saburianessa,* AIR 1996 Gau. 33, the guardianship of person and property of minor daughter was also controversy. Mother of the said minor married another husband after death of her former husband. It was held that such a mother is not entitled to said guardianship of the person and property of the minor daughter. Paternal grand mother of minor was held proper for the grant of guardianship. If such mother either widow or divorcee remarries a stranger it further complicates the issue.

In *Ghulam Mohammed,* AIR 1942 Sind. 154, Chief Justice Davis observed.

> "Mother on remarriage to stranger loses only her preferential right to custody of her child which she otherwise possesses."
>
> His Lordships also observed that
>
> "It is not so much the remarriage itself which constitute the disqualification. The basis for disqualification is that if a woman marries a man not closely related to a child, the child may not be treated kindly."

In that case respondent mother had shown her grace by telling the High Court that if the father wants to meet Husna once in a week or so for two hours she has no objection, thus visiting rights were given to the father.

Zynad Bi Vs. Mohammad Ghouse, AIR 1952 Mad. 284 also lays down that the mother is entitled to the custody of her child despite the fact that she stayed separately from her husband, which was not a disqualification. In *Mir Mohamed Bahauddin Vs. Mujee Bunnisa Begum Sahiba,* AIR 1952 Mad. 280, it is held that if the mother marries a second husband, the custody of the child normally belongs to her former husband, particularly, if he is otherwise a fit and proper person to be appointed as guardian.

In *Mohammad Shafi Vs. Shamim Banno,* AIR 1979 Bom. 156, the learned single Judge has taken the view that the custody of the minor child in case of a boy until he attains the age of seven years and in case of a female until she attains puberty is with the wife. The right of the father to the custody of the child is deferred, and the primary right is in the mother and in the absence of the mother in other female heirs.

Khurshid Gauhar Vs. Siddiquinnissa. AIR 1986 All. 314 & *Hafizur Rahaman.* 1983 All WC 572—propounded that :

> "Mother is naturally not only more tender, but also better qualified to cherish a child during infancy, so that committing the care to her is of advantage to the child". Mohammedan Law is not taking any pedantic view of the matter. It does not lay down that in any circumstance and at any cost the mother would be disqualified for the custody of child, the moment she gets remarried. It can never be expected that any personal law would be so harsh as to ignore the welfare of the minor child. We have a similar situation of a case which the learned Author (Mulla's Principles of Mohammedan Law, 19th Edn.) has quoted from the Pakistani case, where the father gave up all claim to the custody of the child when the child was of tender age, and the mother, upon divorce, married a stranger and the minor was well looked after by the mother and where the minor being of the age of discretion refused to go to the father, the Court allowed the mother to retain custody of the child and rejected the father's application, the welfare of the minor being the prime consideration.

In *Zahirul Hassan Vs. State of U.P.* 1988 Cr. L.J. 230, Allahabad High Court has taken the view that:

> "The reason of the rule is that if a woman marries a person who is not closely related to the child, may not be treated kindly. It is otherwise, however, where the mother, for instance, marries her child's near relation because such man on remarriage is also expected to be kind to the child. But that is not absolute and it is open to the Court to appoint the mother as the guardian even if she has married a stranger, if the Court considers it to be in the interest of the minor."

In *Irfan Ahmed Shaikh Vs. Mumtaz,* AIR 1999 Bom. 25, the question of custody of minor child was under consideration. There was divorce between the parents. Mother remarried a stranger. The High Court held, that mother remarrying a stranger is not qualified to get custody on that count. But, treatment of child by stranger that is step-father is of paramount importance. There was absence of evidence of ill-treatment to child. Further, the child also refused to go with father but desired to live with mother and step-father. On these facts, custody of minor child was given to mother.

Thus, we have seen the underlying principles of Mohammedan Law on this aspect also revolve around the welfare of the child. There is no dogmatic insistence that the child must remain with the father even against the wishes of the child the moment the mother gets remarried to a stranger. That is to happen in normal condition. The Mohammedan Law has also provided for exceptional circumstances. It has never ignored the wishes of a minor child who is of the age of discretion like Husna in Irfan Ahmed's case.

The Muslim male still does not want to give up his right of polygamy and unilateral divorce. Keeping women in parda is common feature of some Muslim community. Many a social practice amongst Muslims are very retrograde and detrimental to the lives of women. Women's rights of inheritance, polygamy, triple *talaq,* divorce, maintenance and the ban on her entry into mosques shows the subordinate position of women in the community. There have been no major reform movements in the country improving the lot of women. Despite these adverse circumstances there have been efforts by scattered individuats to initiate the reform process among Muslim women. Recently, Kerala has initiated the practice of allowing Muslim women to enter and offer prayers in the mosque. The example of Kerala is now being emulated in Lucknow too. Many Muslim groups are also working on an ideal Nikahnama (marriage contract) which can protect the rights of women after marriage.

The Muslim scripture gives some ground to fight for better rights for women, though they are still far away from gender equality. The reform process in Muslim countries has begun by taking advantage of the scriptural version of religion. In Turkey and Tunisia, polygamy and unilateral divorce is not allowed and maintenance for a divorced woman is mandatory for three years. In Pakistan divorce is permissible only through an arbitration council and a man who takes a second wife without the consent of the first is liable to pay a fine of Rs. 10,000/- and or imprisonment upto three years (as Zeenat Shaukat Ali has stated in her interview in TOI 24.8.97). Recent court's judgment in Pakistan and Bangladesh have taken fairly progressive view in matters pertaining to women's rights in marriage.

5

Post-Divorce Problems and Social Support: A Study of Muslim Divorced Women of Maharashtra

Munira Siganporia

The divorce rate in India is rising due to recent social and legal developments. Divorce as an unhappy union is becoming more acceptable. There is ample evidence to show that divorce is becoming less of a social stigma and couples as well as society are accepting that marriages can breakdown. Parents have stopped forcing their daughters to go back to their husbands fearing suicide, murder or simply more physical abuse (Jain, 1987:21). Societal and caste/ community attitudes towards divorced women are also undergoing change and becoming more supportive.

Social Support

Social support (or social support network, natural support systems) is a term that everyone understands in a general sense. However its conceptualisation and definition have been very difficult, disparate and inconstant (Gottlieb, 1981; House, 1981). It can be said to include four basic types of aids: instrumental (material, financial, giving one's time); emotional (a sense of belonging and acceptance, trust, empathy and love); appraisal (feedback, affirmation), and informational (advice and suggestions) (House, 1981). Usually, social support networks are classified into two types: formal and informal networks. Formal networks are those that originate within the context of professional helping service (Richardson and Pfieffenberger, 1983: 222) such as professional counselling and legal services. Informal support networks can be dichotomised into voluntary and religious organisations. Unorganised informal support networks include family, friends, relatives, neighbours and teachers. The importance of informal social support networks has been widely recognised in India in the absence of formal social services. 'It encompasses all aspects of life: social, economic and political' (Gangrade, 1985:50). For an Indian, the family and the kinship group are the beginning and the end of his/her human universe. One's interdependence on the social network encourages a spirit of helping one another in crisis situations even at the cost of personal necessities and comforts. Social networks provide the necessary vitality for managing crisis situations in Indian families.

Since divorce is a particularly stressful life process, social support can buffer the negative consequences of marital disruption. In evaluating the role of the family as a source of social support it must be borne in mind that the divorced woman in India almost always returns to the family of her origin, either to her parents or sibling or to other relatives (Choudhary, 1988; Mehta, 1975; Pothen, 1986). The family provides housing, financial support, childcare and emotional support. Muslim divorced women likewise rely on their families for support, especially, financial support. According to Husain, ...so far as her maintenance is concerned, the husband is in no way responsible for it and she has to be maintained at her parents' place. The maintenance of the children is the responsibility of the husband but if he violates his responsibility or if children are retained or withheld by the divorced wife or her family, they ar naturally to be supported by them (1976: 156). In the case of Muslim women who observe purdah, in practice or in spirit, friends of the same sex are perhaps their only contact outside of the extended family. The friendship network can provide emotional support and information besides being the only source of socialising and leisure activities outside of the family. Support received from community sources such as women's organisations, self-help groups, neighbourhood councils would include referral, information about existing services, legal advice and education about rights. All over India, urban educated women have taken up cases of dowry deaths, sexual harassment, employment inequalities and maintenance after divorce. Many of them represent women who come to them for shelter and assistance in legal battles.

The Case of Muslim Women

There have been few prior systematic attempts to gather information about divorced Indian women and Muslim women in particular. Therefore, in order to find out about the social support available to Muslim women in the event of divorce or separation a group of 100 divorced Muslim women, 50 from those who had approached the Muslim Satyashodhak Mandal in Bombay and Pune and 50 from the community, were interviewed. The Muslim Satyasodhak Mandal was started about twenty years ago to bring about social change through education, training and self-sufficiency of Muslim women. The interviews generated data about the divorced women and their husbands' families, marriage (*mehr*, dower), divorce, (period of separation, type and procedure) and problems the women encountered as well as the coping assistance from their social support networks.

Thirty women in the sample belonged to the Shia sect and the rest to the Sunni sect. Eighty per cent of the women had very little education and belonged to the lower socio-economic class, with either no income or very little income (Rs.100-500). The most common type of work among those who were employed (58 per cent) was unskilled work. They were mostly employed to perform domestic chores, escort children to school or do packaging tasks at home. There were a few teachers, clerks/typists, tailors and executives. Most of them lived either in a *chawl* (60 per cent) or in a *zopadi* (twenty eight per cent). Fifty-eight women had one or more children. Except for six instances where the husband had custody, the children in the remaining cases were living with their mothers after the divorce. Forty marriages had lasted less than a year and in as many as 78 per cent marriages there were no attempts at reconciliation after the initial separation. The women usually returned to their parents home, living with other siblings and/or other relatives. There were only twelve women who lived alone or with their children.

The Time Factor

The length of time between separation and final divorce is an important indicator of the process of securing a divorce among the Muslims. Since the Muslims do not necessarily have to resort to any legal system for divorce, the time spent between separation and the final divorce could be as little as one month. However, in some instances where the woman applied for divorce the final settlement took more than five years. Thirty-five women applied to a priest or a marriage council for a divorce and three applied under the Dissolution of Marriage Act, 1939. In all the thirty-five cases, the divorce was granted only after the husband had agreed to the divorce. By comparison, out of the husbands who initiated the divorce proceedings, only nine applied to a priest and the wife agreed to the divorce. Seventeen husbands pronounced an oral divorce and twenty-eight sent the divorce papers (*talak-naama*) through the mail when the wife was visiting at her parent's home. All the Shias in the sample applied to their *jamat* or community council for divorce, ensuring some regulation of the divorce settlement.

Dowry, Maintenance and Mehr

The dowry Muslim brides usually receive is mostly gifts from family and friends (consisting of household articles, jewellery and clothes). Usually, the parents begin to plan and save for the dowry long before she is ready for marriage and at times even borrow money to provide for it. However, there is no guarantee within the legal system to ensure that the divorced woman can take back what is rightfully hers at the termination of marriage. Therefore, it is not surprising that only 35 women got back their dowry and 17 received some of it. Similarly, *mehr,* which is agreed upon in the *nikahnama* (marriage contract) and is supposed to be paid to the wife at the time of divorce (unless she initiates the divorce proceedings) was not received by 60 women. Usually, the mehr amount was negligible, but lack of payment of mehr is indicative of the ineffectiveness of this provisions in Muslim Personal Law. Seven women had been granted amounts ranging from Rs.100 to Rs.500 as maintenance. They were to receive it on a monthly basis. At the time of interview, only two women were still receiving the agreed amount. Four women received the money irregularly and one was paid only after the husband received a court order. Three women received a fixed amount of less than Rs.5000. Two were paid more than Rs.5000. One woman kept the house and was also given a fixed amount. She took the husband to court for maintenance and a home. She had three children and was living with her parents. After six year of no settlement in the court, she approached the local qazi who was able to bring together the husband's family and appeal on behalf of the woman and her children. The husband's family pressured the husband who had long since remarried into buying a room and giving a fixed amount as maintenance for the children. Ten women received maintenance for the *iddat* period of three months (up to Rs.2000) as per the *shari'at.*

In most cases where the women received any maintenance, the marriage council and Muslim Satyashodhak Mandal were the mediators. Twenty-one women mentioned that they had applied for maintenance after the divorce through the judicial process. Fourteen of them belonged to the Muslim Satyasodhak Mandal. It was not possible to determine the rate of success with the legal approach as most of the cases were still pending in courts at the time of interviews. While the association between their receiving maintenance and their sectarian or organisational affiliation was found to be statistically significant, it is important to be cautious in interpreting the role and importance of these councils as well as organisations like the Muslim Satyashodhak Mandal since the maintenance received in most cases was either a fixed amount of money or only for the *iddat* period. Even among those who were guaranteed maintenance on a monthly basis, only two women continued to receive money regularly.

Awareness of Rights Among Women

It is quite evident from the findings in this study that a husband has a greater choice and control in divorce strategy and outcome. Perhaps this situation is due, to some extent, to women's lack of knowledge about their rights under Muslim Personal Law. Considering publicity accorded to the *sharia't* in recent years by the media build up of the Shah Bano case and by Muslim community leaders, activists arid fundamentalists notwithstanding, the fact remains that women's knowledge about the provisions under the law is still very limited. The need for widespread education and information to women is evident from the response to the question on the extent of knowledge of *shari'at* as it relates to marriage, divorce, maintenance and custody of children. The women were asked about knowledge of Muslim Personal Law. The intent of this inquiry was to ascertain their knowledge base especifically relating to divorce procedure, issue of maintenance and custody of children. In spite of being personally affected by the *shari'at,* 43 women had no knowledge about the provisions of the law, while 45 were aware somewhat about their rights. Only 12 women had an extensive and comprehensive idea about provisions of the law. All of them had made a conscious effort to educate themselves due to their personal involvement with the law.

Financial and Socio-emotional Problems

The divorced women stated that they faced severe financial problems, not having money for food, medicines, clothing and other essentials for themselves and their families and not having money for the special diet, personal care and education of their children. The women mentioned that even when they were married, their husbands did not support the family. Many of them suffered from post-divorce depression, loneliness, insomnia, anxiety and fear about their future. Very often they did not have any leisure activities and could not afford to go to movies, on vacations or enjoy other social activities. However, most of them did not admit to feeling suicidal or suffering from acute mental illness/breakdown. Again, they stated that many times the reasons for the breakdown of the marriage included physical and mental abuse by the husband and the in-laws, husband's addictions and extra-marital affairs, all of which resulted in socio-emotional problems. All the women with children admitted that they faced problems of discipline, education and planning for the future of their children. Many said they had problems with childcare. One woman reported that due to lack of adequate childcare facilities, she had been forced to give up her job. Other women had to take their children with them, thereby resulting in school dropouts.

After divorce, the women faced mainly financial, socio-emotional and parent-child relationship problems. Almost all of them mentioned that housing was a major consideration in their decision to return to their parents/relatives home after the divorce. The answer to what causes a problem to be perceived as a problem after divorce is a combination of the marital relationship prior to divorce and the extent to which the women can rely on their own coping and availability of social support. In response to the question about the source of social support for the various problems, the women mostly mentioned their parents or relied on their own coping abilities. The most frequent source of support for food, housing, parent-child relationship problems and information on maintenance, divorce and guardianship was parents followed by self and siblings. Also, self was most cited as a source of support for many needed for personal care, clothes, education and any financial needs other than food. Friends were considered to be the most available source for leisure activities, e.g., going out for social gatherings, movies and religious events. However, 44 women stated that they did not have any leisure activities at all and so could not comment on the support sources. Interestingly, for socio-emotional needs (related to emotional problems like depression, loneliness, and suicidal problems) more women turned within themselves for courage to carry on with their lives. Many of them also had support from their mothers and siblings to deal with the post-divorce emotions. Thus, it appears that whenever the problem faced was not critical to survival, the women relied mostly on self support. If the women needed food, shelter or assistance with childcare, the parents were duty bound to support them. Except in a few extreme cases, the women did not have to deal with harassment from their social support systems. Perhaps this is an indication of the acceptance of divorce as an alternative to an unhappy marriage. But when harassment did occur, it was mostly by their father, brother or sister-in-law. Usually, they did not want her and her family to live with them.

Observations and Conclusions of Study

In conclusion, with reference to the role of social support, this study reconfirmed the importance of family support (parents, siblings and relatives) for divorced Muslim women in India. Besides, self-reliance has emerged as a very crucial source of support to divorced women. Many women affirmed that they continued to have financial and emotional problems and were worried about their future, the future of their children and specially about housing and being self-sufficient. These concerns are consistent with the fact that most women in India live with their families and housing is a constant problem in the cities. Also, women usually do not live independently and are not economically self-sufficient. Hence, the concern about their own future and the future of their children.

The majority of the divorced women were happy (88 per cent) that in spite of all the problems after the divorce, their marriage was over. Many of them felt that financial security through jobs, training and education would help women cope with problems after divorce. Besides, housing and family support were also considered important since most of them go back to their families after divorce. Thus, it is important to determine from the target population their needs and specific areas they would like assistance.

The thrust of women's welfare organisations, like the Muslim Satyashodhak Mandal, is towards providing legal aid to women to get their rightful due. Perhaps, this effort is the only tangible and concrete means of helping these women. Most of them have no jobs, their families are too poor to support them, and there is no financial assistance from government sources. However, it is clear from the findings of this study that women would rather have financial independence, jobs and education. Besides, the achievement through legal recourse is at best marginal since the maintenance and child support is usually inadequate.

Also, within the realm of social support, the study showed that there is a lot of reliance on self for coping with problems. The study of self as a coping mechanism, separate from other sources of social support, would yield valuable information on how to target limited resources in the most beneficial areas. Self-enhancement could be achieved through education, job opportunity and other avenues (social and leisure activities, participation in women's forums) for growth and support.

There is a great need for education and awareness among the Muslim women about their rights within Muslim Personal Law. Marriage councils and religious teachers/schools should include issues around family life, education, and societal obligations, as these are dependent to a large extent on the religious law in India. Most Muslims, even if they do not get any formal education, are exposed to religious teachings usually limited to reciting of the daily prayers and the reading of the Qur'an without any insight into the meaning of the Quranic injunction. Perhaps a better knowledge and understanding of the provision of the law and the injunctions of the Qur'an on the part of both men and women can significantly change the status of women and make them aware of women's rights and their obligations.

Clearly, the results of the study indicate that the women are not getting their rightful dues in matters of maintenance, dowry, *mehr* and child support even within the tenets of the existing Muslim law. Since the Muslims consider marriage a contract and there is always a *nikahnama* or marriage agreement at the time of the wedding ceremony, the *nikahnama* could be standardised to ensure that some of these issues become part of the marriage agreement. The *nikahnama* could state that the man cannot practice polygamy, and that the woman's right to divorce would be equal to that of the man and that *mehr* would be paid immediately after divorce. Since no uniform form of the *nikahnama* has been ordained in the Qur'an or the *shari'at,* such a step would not amount to changing or challenging divine law.

Also, the women should demand and insist upon getting their rightful due under Muslim Personal Law, The Dissolution of Marriage Acts and the recently passed Muslim Women's (Protection of Rights on Divorce) Act. Thus, they could demand that they get their *mehr,* maintenance for the *iddat* period and their dowry back when the husband wants a divorce. The passage of Muslim Women's (Protection of Rights on Divorce) Act has made it possible for the wife to be paid her *mehr,* dowry, maintenance for the iddat period and child support till the children are two years of age within a very short time. Thus, there is scope for justice within the constraints of Muslim law. The study shows that many women were subjected to physical and emotional abuse by their husbands and their families. Women are no longer willing to tolerate physical or mental cruelty and indignity and divorce is considered a relief and an end to an unfortunate relationship. But when the divorced woman returns to her family, she is totally dependent on her family and extended social support network to cope with the fears, anxieties and uncertainties about her and her children's future. The type and extent of support available from her support network will play a major part in alleviating her problems. Almost all women in India suffer from inequities that are a part of a wider socio-cultural complex and cannot be explained entirely in terms of legal codes or religious ethos. Therefore, the demand for reform or change should be a demand for sexual equality and to end sexual discrimination. Of equal importance is that women should come together as a group and demand rights so far denied to them. Education and economic independence would go a long way to improve the status of women. An expansion of women's roles beyond that of the mother and wife and increasing opportunities to learn, work and be productive will advance the status of women rapidly.

The major areas of need which can be addressed by social

welfare organisation/women's organisations are financial (for herself and her children) and socio-emotional (anxiety, depression, suicidal feelings, loneliness). Women can achieve a certain amount of financial independence with the help of training and job assistance. It is important to keep in mind the purdah (veil) system and familial restriction that usually prevent women from working outside of the home while planning job training. More home-bound, income-producing schemes like embroidery, tailoring teaching/tuitions, small-scale industries (like food-making, packaging) are not only ideal to set up with limited resources, but would also be more acceptable to the divorced women's family. She could balance her role as a mother if she has children and also fulfil her obligations as a member of the household, assisting with management of household chores.

The importance of women's organisations in providing a forum to share and assist women cannot be overemphasised. At present, these organisations focus more on women's right and how to achieve them. Therefore, their strategies vary from protests and resistance, consciousness-raising programmes through legal, religious and academic forums to campaigning the press, cinema and television. However, there is need for more individual and group counselling, assessment of psycho-social and family dynamics so that more women can be helped to cope with their problems. There should be provision for group, children and adolescent and family counselling and leisure activities, childcare, in addition to legal assistance and advice.

Finally, although efforts towards changes in the Muslim family and matrimonial laws should not be abandoned, it should also be kept in mind that mere changes in the law are not likely in themselves to result in a lasting solution. The question is how many people know the provisions of the law and can afford to take legal recourse? Therefore, it is important that along with legal reform there should be far-reaching social changes so that possibilities for women's collective action and bargaining power are enhanced.

REFERENCES

Choudhary, J. N., *Divorce in Indian Society,* Jaipur: Rupa.

Gangrade, K.D., 'Social Networks and Social Work', *Crisis Management in Indian Families,* New Delhi, Northern Book Centre.

Gottlieb, B.H. (ed). (1981), *Social Networks and Social Support,* Beverly Hills, Sage Publishing House.

J.S. (1981), *Work, Stress and Social Support,* Reading, MA: Addison Wesley Publishing Company.

Hussain, S.A. (1976), *Marriage Customs among Muslims in India,* New Delhi, Sterling Publishers.

Jain, M. (1987), 'Curious Role Reversal', *The Sunday,* June 24.

Mehta, R. (1975), *Divorced Hindu Woman,* New Delhi, Vikas Publishing House.

Pothen, S. (1986), *Divorce: Its Causes and Consequences in Society,* New Delhi, Shakti Books.

Richardson, R. and C. Pfieffenberger (1983), 'Social Support Networks in the Human Services', in J.K. Whittaker,

Garbarino J. and Associates (eds.) New York, Aldine Publishing Company.

6

Polygyny and Divorce in Muslim Society-Controversy and Reality

Sekh Rahim Mondal

Introduction

The practice and functioning of the two phenomena of socio-cultural importance like polygyny and divorce have been assessed in the background of Muslim social system. The author summarizes his observations firstly, on the various observations made in the Holy Quran and other religious texts based upon the findings of different prophets on these two specific issues, and secondly, he proceeds to highlight the actual happenings from the empirical data collected directly from the field. The study turns down so far prevailing notion of high incidence of polygyny and divorce among the Muslim community through the presentation of actual happenings and behaviour-patterns constituting the norms and traditions of the society concerned. Various causes behind the development of the misconception regarding the practice of polygyny and divorce have been put forward here and side by side with these the realistic situation has been presented.

Women's studies constitute the rising trend in contemporary social science research. Its basic objective is to study and collect information about women. There are many misconceptions in circulation regarding the status of women in Islam and these made the Muslim women's status rather ambiguous. Nature of permissibility of Polygyny and divorce in Islam and also in Muslim society are the issues that raised a good deal of controversy, specially in India.

Muslims are the largest minority in India. They constitute 12.12 per cent of India's total population, with a sex ratio of 927 females per 1000 male (Census, 1991). Modernization and change is the order of the day, but Muslims are found to lag behind. For various reasons Muslims are noted to be a impoverished, backward, tradition-bound but self-conscious people. Perhaps due to the influence of these and other factors, social reform has experienced a setback in Muslim society.

There is a prevailing notion that the incidences of polygyny and divorce are very high among Muslims and these cause serious problems to Muslim women's life. Such notion has not only affected the Muslim mind but also influenced the political and communal situation of the country. Therefore empirical assessment of the situation is considered essential.

The present study is an attempt to enquire the nature, extent and incidence of polygyny and divorce among Muslims in India, with special reference to West Bengal. Attempt will be made to assess critically the emergent problems related to these issues. Finally, some suggestions shall be made to improve the Muslim women's status as well as to resolve the emerged controversie on the said issues, particularly in India.

These findings have grown through empirical research on Muslim society. The facts presented have been collected both from secondary as well as from primary sources. The secondary data has been mostly drawn from published materials, while the primary data is gathered through field investigation among the Muslims in different places of West Bengal. Basic primary data were gathered through case studies from ten villages of ten different districts in West Bengal and those have been supplemented by observations and informations from other areas.

Polygyny and Divorce in Pre-Islamic Arab Society

In pre-Islamic Arab society women had no recognized place and they were in a state of subjugation. Marriage rules were highly flexible. Prepubertal child marriage was a common practice. Marriage by capture and purchase were also prevalent. Unrestricted polygyny was the order of the day. Polygyny was so prevalent that there was no rule regarding the number of wives that an Arab could keep at a time. Husbands were free to divorce their wives whenever they felt so. Often the women were divorced at the whim and pleasure of the husbands. Only the males had right to divorce their wives. Triple oral talaq in one sitting was a common form of divorce among the Arabs.

Thus, it may be assumed that the women in pre-Islamic Arab society used to suffer from several social injustices owing to unrestricted polygyny and unilateral form of divorce. But emergence of Islam and the social reform instituted by prophet Mohammad (PBUH) has a great irnpact on these systems (Ali, 1978; Ameer Ali, 1955; Qutb, 1968; Wolf, 1951).

Polygyny and Divorce in Islam

Islam dignified the status of women and raised it to a footing of equality with men. In Islam like men, women have a right to life, honour and property. The rights and responsibilities of women are equal to those of men, but they are not identical with them.

A woman in Islam has an independent status in marriage. Marriage could not be held without her consent. The contract of marriage gives the man no power over the woman's person, except what law defines and none whatever upon her personality and property. In Islam the institution of *mehr* (dowry) as an integral part of marriage, aims at empowering women with resources for safety and security.

Polygyny: Polygyny is permitted in Islam under special circumstances, with certain terms and conditions. The reasons behind sanction of polygyny in Islam was historical and circumstantial. In abnormal circumstances like war when large number of men were decimated and balance between the sexes was seriously shaken, on such an instance polygyny was permitted to overcome the social problems. Further, polygyny was one of the various measures to prevent illegal relationships or delinquent sexual behaviour. Polygyny was introduced as a form of marriage to meet the exigency of the situation. The rules of polygyny in Islam are said to have become established in response to certain pressing situation. In pre-Islamic Arab society polygyny was unlimited, but Islam imposed a restriction and limitation upon it up to four. But at the same time Qur'an states:

> "If you have a reason to fear that you will not deal fairly with the orphans, marry the woman who seem good to you, two, three, or four and if you fear that you can not do justice and equality with all, then you shall marry one" (Qur'an, 4:3).

Polygyny in Islam is conditional as Qur'an stipulates justice and equal treatment to all wives. The Islamic viewpoint in the context of monogamy vs. polygyny is quite clear. It is humanly impossible for man to love and treat all his wives equally as absolute justice in matters of feeling is impossible. Thus, polygyny is in no sense an essential or special feature of Islamic marriage system, in fact it recommended monogamy as the ideal form of marriage (Qur'an, 4: 129).

Thus, it is very clear that though Islam permits polygyny, yet it is neither prohibited, nor sanctioned without any reason. It permits polygyny, but it does not make it obligatory. It is neither an offence nor an injunction and nor even an article of faith. Moreover, in Islam, ploygyny is forbidden if it involved unlawful things or lead to unlawful consequences, such as injustice (Abdalati, 1975; Ahmed, 1982; Ali, 1955; Engineer, 1987; Lokhandwala, 1987; Mistry, 1993).

Divorce: Islam views marriage as a strong bond and a serious commitment. Marriage in Islam is not a temporary union but is meant for the entire span of life. Islam admits divorce only on certain grounds subject to certain formalities. It has made provisions for the dissolution of a marriage if it fails to serve its objectives. In Islam divorce is resorted to only when cohabition by husband and wife has become a most impossible and all efforts to reconcile them have failed. In the view of prophet Mohammad (PBUH), divorce is the most detestable in the sight of *Allah* of all permitted things and hold the notion that of all things *Allah* has made lawful for his believers, the most hateful to

Him is divorce.

Quran says: "O Prophet! when men divorce women, put away of their (legal) period and reckon the period and keep your duty to *Allah,* your lord....(Qur'an 65: 1-3). This Qur'anic verse states that if a woman is to be divorced, she should be divorced in kindness and not in anger and with a feeling of hurt. In such a context there is a need for two arbiters, one from wife's side and the other from husband's side. Islam does not confine the right of divorce to man only or to the woman alone, but to both the parties. Divorce encompasses many religio-legal aspects and is considered necessary and lawful only if reconciliation between the spouses is absolutely not possible.

Marriage is considered as a civil contract in Islam. For avoiding the evil consequences of unhappy marriage, a divorce is permitted. If no means of reconciliation are possible and divorce is the only way left to the spouses, the marriage may be dissolved according to Sunnah. In Muslim law, marriage may be dissolved in any one of the following ways:

Talaq

A *talaq* may be effected either orally or by written document *talaqnama*. Pronouncement of *talaq* may either be revocable (*talaq-ul-raja'i*) or irrevocable (*talaq-ul-ba'in*). In revocable *talaq* one does not dissolve the marriage until the period of *iddat* (seclusion) is over. While an irrevocable *talaq* may be effected in any one of the following ways:

Talaq-Ahsan

This form consists of one single pronouncement within the term of purity *(tuhr)* followed by abstention from sexual intercourse for the period of *iddat* (waiting period), which is of three months duration from the date of pronouncement, except in the case of pregnant wife. In that case waiting period is until the birth of the baby. This kind of divorce is revocable during the period of *iddat*.

Talaq-Hasan

In this form of divorce a man must make three pronouncements during three consecutive terms of ritual purity *(tuhrs)*, no biological relations having taken place in between these periods. At the pronouncement of divorce for the third time, the divorce becomes final and irrevocable. The wife should be maintained during these months. In this form of divorce there is a chance for the parties to reconcile before the third pronouncement of divorce. After the third and final pronouncement the wife can not remarry her former husband.

Khula' or Mubarat

This is the form of divorce by mutual consent of the husband and the wife without the intervention of the court. In *Khula'* the wife makes the proposal, while in *Mubarat* either spouse may make the proposal. *Khula'* bestows special rights to women to seek dissolution of marriage.

By Judicial Decree at the Suit of the Husband and Wife

Talaqul-Bida'

The forms of divorce that are not made in accordance with the Sunna is considered as *Talaqul-bida'*. These are developed historically under certain situations, thus got negative sanction from the society. They have of following forms:

Triple Declaration

In this form pronouncements are made at a time. The pronouncement is made either in a single sentence or in three sentences. This form of divorce is irrevocable. Triple oral *talaq* is a debatable issue. Some interpreters are of the opinion that pronouncement of triple *talaq* in one sitting is a pre-Islamic practice. The prophet (PBUH) was not happy with it as indicated by the Hadith. Once Prophet stood up in anger when he came to know that a person has divorced his wife by pronouncing triple *talaq* in one sitting. He even asked one of his disciples Abu Rukanah to take back his wife even after pronouncement of triple *talaq* in one sitting. The first Calipha Hazrat Abu Bakar also did not permit it and was prohibited until early period of Hazrat Umar, who enforced it again as a temporary measure in certain circumstances. Actually triple *talaq* in one sitting is not in keeping with Islamic spirit; thus it has rightly been described as a sinful form of divorce. This form of divorce is not lawful to Ahel-e-Hadith school, while for Hanafi school it is lawful.

Single Irrevocable Declaration

Pronouncement of divorce is made only once during the period of purity of the wife. It is disapproved by the Hanafi school.

Vow of Abstinence (Ila)

This is a type of irrevocable divorce, a husband takes vow of abstinence and swears not to have sexual relations with his wife from a maximum period of four months. If a reconciliation is made during this period, the vow is invalid, but if no reconciliation is made and the term expires, the marriage becomes irrevocably dissolved.

Zihar

It was very common during pre-Islamic days when a man specifically said to his wife: "thou art to me the back of my mother"

Maintenance of a divorcee is another controversial issue. In pre-Islamic Arab society nothing was given to a divorcee by way of maintenance. But Islam has given a divorcee the right to maintenance. Quran says: "the divorced women too shall have (a right to) maintenance in good by manner. This is the duty for all who are faithful to *Allah* (Qur'an, 2: 241). Actually Qur'an has not fixed any time-limit for maintenance. Neither the amount of maintenance nor the period has been mentioned and this lead to differential interpretations among the scholars and jurists on this issue. The common practice is that when divorce takes place, there is a waiting period called *iddat,* during which the divorcee has to be completely supported and maintained by her husband. But after third or final divorce, they are no longer obliged to one another. Further, in case of marriage getting dissolved by *talaq,* the wife is entitled to get the immediate payment of the whole unpaid *mehr,* but she loses her claim over it in case she goes for *Khula'* (Husain, 1976; Islahi, 1978; Yasmeen, 1989).

Islam and Dynamics of Muslim Law

Muslims governed themselves according to *Shariat* (Islamic

law). The chief sources of Shariat are Qur'an (words of the God) and Hadith (tradition of the Prophet) and later supported by *ijma* (consensus of opinions of jurists), *Qiyas* (analogical deductions of above three sources) and *ijtihad* (interpretation in a new situation).

The traditional Islamic law is not an uniform legal code. In course of history differences in the interpretation of Shariat by Ulama caused to generate various theological schools of Islamic jurisprudence. All these produced considerable diversity of doctrine and the laws. As a result, there eventually came into existence several schools of Sharia laws. Various laws arose not only due to controversy on juristic issues, but also due to external influences (theological, political and social) which conditioned the thought and approach of jurists.

Owing to diversities of Islamic laws there is no uniformity about rules relating to dissolution of marriage. For example, under Sunni law a *talaq* uttered once even under compulsion, influence and anger is valid. While under Shia law, an intention to divorce is a necessary element to make it valid. To the followers of Ahel-e-Hadith triple *talaq* in one sitting is illegal, while to Jamat-al-Ulama and Sunni Hanafi it is legal. There are even variant popular laws relating to *talaq* issue at regional and local levels, especially in rural areas, owing to self styled explanation of so-called traditional rules by the Mullahs and Maulavis. All these not only aggravated the *talaq* controversies, but make the issues more complex and critical.

Classical Islamic laws relating to polygyny and divorce are quite fair to women in some respects, but these have lost their original spirit in actual practice. Some Muslim men have often used it quite arbitrarily against women. Thus in practice power to divorce was primarily enjoyed by the husband. However, the passage of Sharia Act 1937 and the Dissolution of Muslim Marriage Act VIII of 1939, gives substantial relief to Muslim woman and who thereby acquired the right to divorce her husband on certain grounds. But it is sad to say that in spite of all such restrictions, Muslim men enjoy moral freedom when compared to women as far as divorce rule is concerned.

This is undoubtedly a problem of male domination in a patriarchal authoritarian Muslim social system (Engineer, 1991; Puri, 1987; Menon, 1981, etc.).

Polygyny and Divorce Among Muslims in India: Myth and Truth

Incidence of Polygyny and Divorce: A Review

There is a myth about polygynous character of Muslims and it is also very often projected that the Muslim population is increasing due to practice of polygyny among them. But empirical studies have shown that the proportions of polygynous marriages are very low among Muslims in India (Ahmed, 1976).

According to the report of the committee on status of women in India during the decades 1931-41, 1941-51 and 1951-61, the percentage of polygynous marriage among the Muslims were: 7.29%, 7.06%, and 4.30% respectively. While the corresponding figures among Hindus were: 6.79 per cent, 7.15 per cent and 5.06 per cent and among tribals the frequencies were 9.13 per cent and 17.98 per cent respectively. Thus it is clear that the incidence of polygyny is low among Muslims and there had been a gradual decrease of polygynous marriages among them.

A study was conducted by the Census Department, Govt. of India, 1961, on the practice of polygyny in the country. The study revealed that the incidence of polygynous marriages was the highest among Tribals (15.25 per cent), next came Buddhists (7.97 per cent), followed by Jains (6.72 per cent), Hindus (5.80 per cent) and Muslims (5.73 per cent). Thus it is seen that the incidence of polygyny was lowest among the Muslims (Census of India: 1971).

The incidence of polygynous marriages among Hindus and Muslims in different periods of time is presented in Table 1.

TABLE 1

Incidene of Polygynous Marriage Among Hindus and Muslims in Different Periods of Time

Period of Time	*Percentage of Polygyny among Hindus*	*Percentage of Polygyny among Muslims*
50 years ago (1911)	2.73	4.50
41-50 years ago (1921)	4.54	4.76
31-40 years ago (1931)	5.55	5.17
21-30 years ago (1941)	6.79	7.29
11-20 years ago (1951)	7.15	7.06
Last 10 years (1961)	5.06	4.31
All periods	5.8	5.73

Census of India: Incidence of Polygynous Marriage in India, 1971.

Due to lack of authentic statistical data at the national level, it is rather difficult to state the exact incidence of polygyny among Muslims of contemporary time. However, individual survey conducted by the scholars of different places in this country show that Muslims were found to be least polygynous in comparison to other castes and communities. Their studies concluded with the facts that polygyny is steadily decreasing among Muslims specially among the educated section of the population. Ali (1976) noted 2.15 per cent of polygynous marriages among the Muslims of Ranchi district in south Bihar. Rokiya Begum (1992) recorded 1.84 per cent polygynous marriage among Muslims of rural Bengal. Jain (1986) reported that there was not even a single case of polygynous marriage while studying the Muslims of Jaipur city in Rajasthan. Menon (1981) observed 3.33 per cent of polygynous marriages among the Muslims of Kerala. Roy (1979) stated a vary low incidence (0.33 per cent) of polygyny among the Muslims of Lucknow city. Siddiqui (1976) recorded that the practice of polygyny among Muslims in India is very negligible. Similar view has also been held by Mistry (1991).

All the above facts cleanly reveal that incidence of polygyny is rather marginal among the Muslims. Polygyny is specially related with the material prosperity. Religious reform movements, legislative action, spread of education and declining of material prosperity among the classes which had earlier practised polygyny, gradually reducing the incidence of such practice among the Muslims. Further, the sex ratio of the Muslims is not very balanced. According to 1981 Census, the sex ratio of Indian Muslim population was 937 per 1000 males. Thus it is not possible to practice polygyny by the Muslims as there ought to be a competition for getting even one wife. Similarly, the growth rate of Muslim population is not accelerated due to polygyny as it is rare in practice among them (Bhatia, 1990).

It is usually believed that the rate of divorce is very high among the Muslims, but it has no empirical validity. It is true that divorce is permitted in Muslim society on appropriate cases, even then it is not liked by the people all over the country. So far that empirical data are available, it is seen that the divorce is rare in Muslim community. Due to paucity of data it is rather difficult to get the actual national picture on incidence of divorce among Muslims in India. However, out of case studies conducted by the scholars a picture can be drawn on this issue. Irshad Ali (1976) observed a lower frequency of divorce among the Assamese Muslims. Rokiya Begum (1992) noted 0.92% of divorcee among Muslim women of rural Bengal. Jain (1986) noted 0.8% of divorcee among the Muslim women of Jaipur. Menon (1981) observed, the incidence of divorce is not very high among the Muslim women of Kerala. Lateef (1990) stated the incidence of triple *talaq* was rare among the Muslims in India, specially in urban areas. Roy (1973) recorded 0.99% of divorced ladies among the Muslims of Lucknow city. These facts show that in empirical context divorce or *talaq* is very limited among the Muslim community mainly for three reasons. Firstly, marriages having been initially well considered and settled, thus the possibilities of divorce are rare considering the prevalent social circumstances. Secondly, the tradition of faithfulness in marriage which prevail among the families are such that both the parties, specially the women, are ready to put up with problems, however difficult and somehow make things agreeable. Thirdly, as divorce defames both, so social norms are abided by the people.

Case Studies in West Bengal

A study was conducted on incidence of polygyny and divorce among the Muslims of ten villages in ten different districts of West Bengal. The results of the study are presented in Table 2.

TABLE-2

Incidence of Polygyny and Divorce in Some Muslim Villages of West Bengal

Name of Villages	*District*	*Percentage of Polygyny*	*Percentage of Divorce*
Digol-hati	Cooch Behar	4.90	1.85
Tari-jote	Darjeeling	6.89	1.28
Sihole	Uttar Dinajpur	2.42	0.94
Kastore	Malda	1.63	1.23
Nagar	Murshidabad	0.69	0.51
Agardanga	Burdwan	Nil	2.14
Bansjore	Birbhum	2.10	1.43
Boersingh	South 24 Parganas	3.68	0.98
Gopalpur	Midnapore	1.00	0.97
Chakbomekha	Howrah	1.18	1.90
Total	—	2.45	1.32

The study shows that the practice of polygyny and divorce among Muslims of rural West Bengal is rather minimal. A detailed enquiry on these issues in the villages under study reveals that polygyny and divorce, in the experience of the respondents, are very rare. Actually very few women are concerned with these problems and there is lack of knowledge and awareness on the part of affected women about their rights on these issues. There is a feeling that polygyny was an earlier practice among some affluent Muslims of higher social status (*Asraf* or *Khas*), while oral *talaq* was often invoked by the persons of lower socio-economic group (*Ajlaf* or *Aam*) to get rid of unwanted wives.

The polygynous marriages, whatever recorded in the villages, are mainly the cases of double wives, where the concerned husbands are maintaining two wives (with their children) separately in different households. Owing to the practice of polygyny these persons are not even liked by their own family and kin members. In the context of divorce it has been noted that such incidences are not the cases of *talaq* in true sense of the term, but actually those are the instances of informal separation or desertion mostly on dowry question. Such males favouring break of marriage caused problems to the Muslim women. Thus the women who suffer due to polygyny and divorce are very much critical about the prevalence of such practices in their society. Though there are safeguards to protect and maintain the divorced women out of Mehr money, yet there is total lack of monetary support to them from their respective husbands. Thus the oath of *mehr* undertaking is merely a ritual and not the practice. Further, there are instances where women after marriage freeing their husbands from *mehr* obligation for love and faith on them and thereby they lose right in their favour resulting to total lack of support during crisis.

Conclusion

The analysis of Islamic norms and values in the context of ploygyny and divorce clearly shows that these are permitted only in certain circumstances and at the same time there are safeguards to defame from such practices. Provisions to protect the rights and interests of the affected women are also made in Islam. But in spite of all such rules and restrictions there is a wide impression that the Muslim women are treated unfairly by their religion. Thus, this impression has nonvalidity in the context of ideal Islamic principles.

The empirical data indicate that the incidence of polygyny and divorce among Muslims are very low. Thus they are not as high as it is believed to be. The facts presented in the foregoing pages seem to be of considerable importance, as they are contrary to the prevailing notion that incidence of polygyny and divorce are high among the Muslims than among other communities. The prevalence of social and legal sanction behind them might have caused the development of such a myth and resentment.

REFERENCES

Engineer Asghar Ali *Rights of Women in Islam* (Delhi, 1996).

Roy, Shibani, 1979. *Status of Muslim Women in North India.* New Delhi: B.R. Publishing Corporation.

Siddiqui, N. A., 1976. *Population Geography of Muslims of India.* New Delhi: S. Chand & Co. (Pvt.) Ltd.

Wolf, R. Eric, 1951. The Social Organization of Mecca and the Rise of Islam, in: *South West Journal of Anthropology,* Vol. VIII, No. 4 (Winter).

Yasmeen, F. & S. Ahmed 1989. A Sociological Study of Marriage and Divorce in Islamic Law, in: *Islam and Modern Age,* Vol. 20, No. 4, pp. 341-67.

7

Mobilisation of Muslim Women for Gender Justice

Sabiha Hussein

The main thrust of the study is to highlight the emerging trend of mobilisation and growing awareness of Muslim women about the misuse of Islamic rights and to some extent deviated interpretation and practices of Islamic principles with regard to marriage and family. Also, an effort is made to capture the emergence of new efforts amongst Muslim women both at individual and organisational levels about their assertiveness for their rights and status over the last few years. Women's demand for change in the existing practices related to marriage and family have also been discussed on the basis of interviews with 250 educated, semi-educated Muslim women of North Bihar (Darbhanga) where the Muslim are in good number and running a few Muslim general and technical institutions. The women under study felt that the institutions and laws meant to safeguard the interests of women must be made more gender just and sensitive to problems of women specially in matters of marriage and family. The opinion of a few Muslim men had also been sought to know their approach towards Islamic principles and reality with regard to marriage, divorce, maintenance, remarriage, custody of children etc. Thus, the first part of the paper deals with empirical data followed by a discussion on Islamic principles in reality and women's struggle for gender just laws.

The Sample

The women in the sample were selected through purposive sampling. The sample included college students, educated housewives and women in teaching and government jobs. About 37.2 per cent (98) of the girls were unmarried, (above the age of 18); 57.2 per cent (143) were married, 1.6 per cent (4) were widows, and 4.4 per cent (10) were divorced. Similarly 39.2 per cent women were from Non-Ashraf families and 56.8 per cent (142) belonged to Ashraf families and 8.0 per cent (20) did not respond queries regarding this. As far as the duration of stay of the respondents in the town was concerned 23.0 per cent (59) women in the sample were natives of that town while 17.0 per cent (43) had been living there for two generations and 59.2 per cent (198) were the new settlers of the town. A large bulk of the women were either graduates or doing their final year of graduation (50.0), followed by 35.2 per cent (88) doing first year of graduation or had passed 12th, and 14.8 per cent (37) were postgraduates and above. An interview schedule was administered on them to seek their opinion on various issues related to marriage, fixation of *Mehr*, consent taken by the girl, divorce, remarriage, inheritance, Muslim Personal Law, role of religious elite (ulemas and Qazis) and Muslim social institutions etc. Apart from this, intensive case studies of divorced women were also done to highlight how Islamic provisions were being personalised and the act is justifie in the name of Islam.

Problems faced by Muslim Women in Fighting for their Rights

The Muslim women in their ongoing struggle to achieve their rights have to face some specific and distinct difficulties:

- (i) lack of information concerning the rights which Islamic law confers upon them',
- (ii) corruption of the original message, both by accretions derived from less authentic sources and by (Mis) interpretation of the Qur'an and law which tend to emphasize male privilege at the cost of female rights;
- (iii) lack of a common plattorm or organisation and even

movement where women can raise their voice against the un-Islamic practices;

(iv) Non-existence of reformists or ulema or community leaders to fight for the cause of women like Sir Syed Ahmed Khan, Ameer Ali, Nawab Muhsinul Mulk, Maulvi Khudabaksh, Maulvi Mumtaz Ali (*Huququn Niswan*), Maulana Ashraf Thanvi.

While on the one hand these difficulties along with low socio-economic status of community as a whole and above all increasing communalisation of our society has made life of women more pathetic. On the other, the conservative elements from within the community are trying to maintain community identity by exerting greater control over women's lives which has added to women's misery in their struggle for gender justice.

Therefore, the struggle and mobilisation of Muslim women for the assertion of their rights and gender just laws has to be carried out at two broad levels: against the orthodox elements of their own community and secondly, rise and spread of right wing majoritarian communalism.

Empirical Findings

It is well known that Muslim marriage is a civil contract. This written marriage contract (*nikahnama, kabin-namas* and *sanad-e-nikah*) have been in practice among certain sections of upper class Muslims in India since Mughal times. It became more general in some parts of the country since the movement launched by the late Sharifa Hamid Ali four decades ago.[1] (Fyzee : 95-98 : 1973). The conventional marriage in practice mainly includes names of parties, witnesses and amount of *mehr* etc. (other essentials as initiated by a few Muslim women's organisations and individuals will be discussed later).

Since it is a contract, any kind of condition/s can be stipulated from either side which are deemed to be binding on both as long as the marriage exists. Secondly, either party can break the marriage if it does not work. Therefore, consent becomes vital to marriage because the persons entering into this contract should be fully aware of all that it implies. This principle of marriage is based on gender justice which disapproves any coercion on any party wishing to marry and procreate.

Consent at Marriage

When we look at our data regarding consent of girl in marriage, we find a great contrast as in 90 per cent cases the women were neither consulted before nor was their consent taken at the time of marriage. The direct consent of the girl was not also taken by the Qazi for Nikah. Although, in principle the Qazi with two other witnesses had to hear the acceptance by girls but in practice this hardly happens.

It was seen that the Qazi with one of the girl's relatives, either brother or uncle (Chacha or Mama) comes to the girl for taking her consent. The girl normally sits behind a *purdah (chadar)* from where she is not seen by the Qazi and the witnesses; they can only hear her voice. When asked by the Qazi, he said that in the majority of cases, the acceptance was given on behalf of the girl by an elderly women sitting with her.

TABLE 1

Consent to the Marriage

	No. of Women	Percentage
Yes	47	18.8
No	18	7.2
Not directly	80.	32.0
Not applicable	105	42.0
Total	250	100.0

Table 1 shown above reveals that more than fifty per cent of the women did not give direct acceptance for their Nikah; either they kept quiet (considered as consent) or an elderly lady on her behalf had given the consent. While 18.8 per cent had said "yes" and 7.2. per cent had not indicated acceptance either directly or indirectly; rather they started crying and the ladies conveyed to the Qazi that she had accepted. It may be possible that on account of their rather young age, they may not have been able to understand. A few women expressed that there is no use of seeking girl's consent at the time of Nikah because at that time due to social pressure and for the sake of family's honour, a girl had to accept it. However, a girl who knows that she will have to in any case be married to a boy of her parent's choice usually agrees. She has probably been socialized into accepting a marriage of this kind. At the same time the incidence of boys and girls marrying persons of their own choice was also found in this present study (3.4 per cent).

Thus, "girls must be consulted by parents or relatives before the settlement of marriage and girl's consent should be sought directly by the Qazi three times (acceptance must be heard) along with two witnesses", this was stated by 22.4 per cent (56) unmarried girls (out of 42.0 per cent). Not only that, a few of them (9.8) per cent further added that since marriage is a crucial phase of a woman's life so it would be better if she could get a chance to decide it rather than imposing upon her the wish and liking of parents or guardian. Therefore, the girl's consent should not be just a token or mere ritual but must be taken as her independent right given by Islam.

Age at Marriage

The data reveal that out of 58.0 per cent (145) married women, 46.4 per cent (67) were married between the age of 21-24 years, 27.5 per cent (40) between the age of 16-20 years, 13.7 per cent (20) between the age of 25-29 and 12.4 per cent (18) below the age of 15 years. The average age at marriage was found to be between the age of 20-24 years. This trend further reflected the respondents' attitude towards the age at marriage for girls, when about 70 per cent of them said that it should be between the age of 18-25 irrespective of caste, class and occupation. The argument was that by that time they would be able to finish their graduation. Not only the educated but uneducated or semi-literate women of daily wage earners (another study done by the author) had also advocated the age at marriage for their daughters as between the age of 17-21 years.

Therefore, we conclude that the average age at marriage has definitely increased for various reasons and they also gave reasons for their daughter's age at marriage. As far as the consent of the girl at the time of marriage is concerned, it was never really operationalised in the manner in which the Shariat suggested. Most of the women really do not have a choice. The variations in the conditions of women depends on the socio-economic class to which they belong. However, the hold of patriarchy can be seen overruling the Shariat which had been to a great extent liberal and empowering, especially with regard to women.

Nikahnama

In Bihar the Nikahnama is not in vogue. In our sample of 145 (58.0 per cent) married women only 14 (9.6 per cent) had their Nikahnama. These 14 women had to have the Nikahnama, 12 (8.2 per cent) had it because they had to join their husbands who were working outside India. Otherwise in the majority of cases there is no *nikahnama*, even though the Shariat Court in Bihar (Imarat-e-Shariah Phulwarisharif) had this provision that all Nikahs have to be registered. When the respondents were asked about the provision of Nikahnama, majority of them (48.5 per cent) felt no need of this, while 32.8 per cent were strongly in its favour and 18.7 per cent did not know about this. These women who felt that *nikahnama* must be made, pointed out that even the Qazis who perform the Nikah, hardly bothered about this document. The worst is that 95 per cent of the women did not even know about the provision of registration of marriage at the Imarte-shariah. That is the reason that since 1993 to 1997 only 717 marriages were registered and marriage certificates were issued from Shariat court which seems to be a drop in the ocean if we look at the Muslim population of this state. In spite of the fact that branches of shariat courts (Darul Qaza) do exist in each commissionary of the state (see appendix) and the proforma of Nikahnama is available at each Darul Kaza, the making of Nikahnama has not been taken into account.

While talking to Nayab Qazi of Darululum, Muzzaffarpur, and Imam of Jama Masjid, Darbhanga about the Nikahnama, the consent given by the bride in the form of *Qabul Hai,* at marriage, fixation and payment of *Mehr*, they did accept that in most of the Nikahs solemnized by them, they had hardly heard the voice of the girl, in spite of his request to speak loudly. Most of the time one lady conveyed the acceptance of the bride. He is unable to see the nodding of the bride or any other indication because the girl sits behind a *purdah* with other married ladies. He further adds that from Shariat point of view the girl has to accept the Nikah by saying *"Qubul Hai"* but the social practice is different. About Nikahnama, he explained that most of the parents specially from the boys' side hesitate to sign any document on account of fear of blackmailing from the bride's side regarding the returning of Mehr and Dahez (cash and kind) in case of break of marriage. The Nayab Qazi shariat court (Phulwari Sharif, Patna) did advocate the making of the Nikahnama because it helps in the proceedings of divorce (i.e. claiming Mehr and Maintenance) and for other documentary proof.

Mehr

Islam has not decided lowest or highest amount as *Mehr.* It may range from a Rs.100 to thousands or it could be in kind from a little ring to a heap of gold. If *mehr* is not paid, the wife can claim it through court of law. It is not that it is to be paid only if a divorce takes place. But what is the practice? Do women really get their Mehr before the consummation of marriage? Do they ever ask for *Mehr*?

Discussing this with the women under study it was found that the amount of mehr remains between Rs.500 to 51,000 (plus five gold coin) (depending on the class to which the women belong). Some women are not even aware of their Mehr (mostly illiterate women from both Ashraf and Non-Ashraf families). But the majority of the women were aware of the amount of their *mehr.* When asked if they had received it, or if they had ever asked their husband for *mehr*, 65 per cent said they had not, because they visualise it as a kind of pressure of binding on the husbands or as future security in case of divorce.

About 27 per cent had received it either in the form of land, jewellery or cash and 8 per cent had waived it in favour of the husband. Most of the women who received the *mehr* were in their forties.

> When talking about *mehr* to the Imam of Jama Masjid (Darbhanga) he said that nowadays young educated men fixed the amount of *mehr* in the form of kind (gold) and paid it on the same day. The guardians specially from the educated class also insist upon heavy amount of *mehr*. He was citing one incident of Nikah performed by him where the mother of the girl had great reluctance regarding the mehr fixed by the groom's side. She insisted on Rs. 75,000 as *mehr* and that too had to be fixed in the name of her daughter. After lots of argument the amount was fixed at Rs. 60,000 (plus five gold coins called 'Surkh Dinar") and the Nikah was performed. When I met this lady (by profession headmistress of high school) she said that the women must come forward in favour of more socio-economic and psychological security of their daughters. After all we spend so much of money willingly or unwillingly on our daughter's marriage. We must educate our daughters on these issues. It is very unfortunate that majority of the women are ignorant of their rights Islamic as well as legal. She further said that fixation of *mehr* should be in correspondence with the amount to be spent on the marriage.

Thus, the majority of the women never ask for the *mehr*. This amount is generally seen to be given if a divorce takes place. To a great extent, women also see it as a kind of mental security and a weapon to ensure continuation of marriage.

Divorce

Muslim marriage is a contract, both the parties are given the right of separation under certain circumstances. Through *khula'* shariat gives the woman the power to dissolve marriage for which no reasons have to be assigned (Khan, S. 1997:26). The Prophet said, "if a woman is prejudiced by a marriage, let it be broken", Islam has also put no restriction on remarriage.

But what is the reality? Did women really know about the different forms of divorce? Did they know the procedure of divorce or the authorities to be approached for maintenance of themselves and of their children or other related issues? Were they aware of the grounds on which they could obtain divorce? These were some of the questions put before the respondents. The finding reveals that more than 62 per cent respondents were unaware of the most laudable pattern of divorce, *(Talaq-e-sunnah)* only 30 per cent had the knowledge while 8 per cent did not respond. As far as Khula' is concerned 57.2 per cent (143) of the women were aware of *khula'* but not the procedure. It is surprising to notice that 96 per cent of the women did not know anything about the Dissolution of Muslim Marriage Act, 1939 which has given women number of valid reasons to obtain divorce.

Similarly 98 per cent of women are ignorant of Section 125 of Cr. P.C. under which any Indian woman could claim maintenance on divorce till she is remarried. A vast majority of women were ignorant of Muslim Women's (Protection of) Right on Divorce Act, 1986 including those who were educated.

When asked about the change or modification required in Unilateral system of divorce or the way in which it is practised, it is surprising to note that 70 per cent of the respondents did want "change in this system and a few of them even went beyond saying that this kind of Talaq has to be banned because women are under constant threat of being divorced by their husbands even for no fault of hers. Secondly, it hurts the self respect and dignity of women. The All India Muslim Women's Convention held in Delhi also demanded that the practice of triple *talaq* be made illegal (Pioneer, 25.3.96). However, the provision of *Faskh* and its procedure is known to only a thin stratum of women.

The responsibility of the Waqf Board and Baitulmal towards the destitute widows and orphans is hardly known by women under study. Thus, knowing of Shariat law, its procedure and how to approach it, has further worsened the condition of women. Majority of the women,

83 per cent, did not know about what kind of cases are being dealt in Shariat Court, how to approach the court for obtaining *faskh* and other disputes related to marriage and family. In few states the Waqf Board does not even exist. Most of the Waqf property is under litigation and encroached upon. Besides the Waqf Board is plagued by shortage of funds and is unable to pay the salary of its staff, let alone maintaining destitute or divorced women. Among other things, a divorcee has to seek a court order that she needs Waqf maintenance as a proof that her family cannot support her.

> While talking about the responsibility of providing financial help to destitutes, widows and orphans from Baitulmal, the Mufti of Imarat-e-shariah said that they do provide financial help to such persons, provided they approach the Imarat, (the amount varying from Rs. 150-300 p.m.).

Although, divorce is not very common in this part specially in the educated middle class families but the incidence is on rise for the last few years. The reasons are: incompatibility between spouses, inadequate dowry, adjustment problem with other relatives in the family etc. and in some cases a second marriage.

As said earlier, among 250 women surveyed, ten were divorced. Among these ten cases of divorce, six divorces were in the form of triple Talaq, three in the form of *khula'* (where women initiated the process) and two were in the form of Faskh (through Shariat court). In six cases of divorce, three were due to the husband's involvement with someone else, two were due to incompatible match (because of girl's low education) and in one case, there was no specific reason as such. The triple pronouncement of Talaq occurred in anger without any witness or valid reasons. All these women were either in their early twenties or mid-twenties and all of them had one or two children who were minor at that time. Five of them neither got their *mehr* nor maintenance either for themselves or for their children even for the period of Iddat. The dowry *(jahez)* in the form of cash or kind was not returned. Two of them got their *mehr* in instalments. Maintenance was provided for three months that too after lots of pressure through the local panchayat. None of them were remarried as late as 1998.

The reasons for *khula'* were licentious nature of husband and husband's continuous demand to bring cash 50,000, (this may be because the amount of *mehr* was 51,000 and he could not manage to pay) from parents which she refused and this resulted in physical torture. In both the cases the wives had to sign an agreement that there would be no claim of *mehr* or maintenance either for themselves and their children, or claims on any moveable or immoveable property would ever be made.

The reasons for Faskh was humbugery on the part of husband and impotency. Both the reasons were difficult to prove. Although in Faskh a wife is entitled to have her *mehr* and other claims but in both the cases they did not receive any of their claims in spite of the order issued by Shariat court to the husband. The two women had tried several times to approach the Shariat court either by visiting personally or through correspondence but in vain.

> When this question was put before the Nayab Quazi of Shariat court (Phulwari Sharif, Patna), he said that we give the judgment, but we do not have the law enforcing machinery. At most we can persuade the person to obey the judgment. More or less the same opinion was expressed by some of the members of Muslim Personal Law Board that Islamic laws are often misused in the absence of any effective redress mechanism.

All of these divorced women were either living in a rented house (three of them are in teaching profession) or with their parents along with their grown-up children. The rest of them were getting economic support from their fathers who are now old and they wish that their daughters could get remarried. A few of them resumed their education and have become independent. A few of them were still living on the economic and social support of their parents but were unsure of how long they would be supported.

Maintenance and Custody of Children

When these issues were addressed to women, we found that (31.3 per cent) of the women said although a woman is entitled to get three months maintenance from her husband after divorce but the reality is different (as is going to be discussed below). Her responsibility also falls on father and brother or uncle and if they are not there then the responsibility falls on the Wakf Board. At the same time, they did point out as to how many divorced women ever remarry, and get respect and support either from the family or other religious institutions. They also argued if a woman is divorced in her mid and late thirties her future prospects of remarriage is distant dream.

If we look at our data of divorced women we did find the same trend. Out of six cases of divorce in the form of triple *talaq,* five of the women never got any maintenance for themselves even for the period of three months. In two cases they did get the maintenance for the minor child, that too only for a few months. The husband never came to claim the custody and guardianship of the children even after few months or one and two years of divorce, they remarried either of their own choice or arranged by parents. The children remained the mother's responsibility. They themselves said that as per the Islamic principles, responsibility of children lies with the father, but the father never bothered to give maintenance or other facilities to the child. In almost all the cases of *talaq*, the grown up children till the time of study were living with their mother, either in their Nana's (maternal grandfather's) house or in independently rented or own house.

Inheritance and Polygamy

While most of the women (75 per cent) were well informed about the share of daughters in inheritance, none could actually give us an example of how property is divided amongst all the daughters and sons. (See annexure) When asked about whether (married) they had claimed their share (in case not given) most of them had relinquished their share of property to their brothers in the name of emotional attachment. Secondly, they felt the *Jahez* given to them as well as expenses incurred on their marriage is another form of giving the daughter's share.

Regarding polygamy, the majority of the women irrespective of their educational, occupational and economic background strongly felt that at times men use this povision at their convenience without having any reasonable grounds so it should be banned (as in the case of other Muslim countries). If at all be permitted, there must be certain rules and grounds which the men have to prove in order to get married a second time (as in the case of Faskh in which women have to prove the ground on which she wants to dissolve the marriage). However, in the sample of 250 women only two cases of polygamous marriage were found. Both the women are living with their parents (after their husband's second marriage) along with their children (one has two daughters studying in class IX, XII; other has one son in B.A. and two daughters in schools). The husband is not giving any maintenance for their children because both the women are in teaching profession (one at the time of writing the paper had applied for Faskh).

Islamic Principles Vs. Reality: A Question of Gender Justice

If we look at the Islamic principles with regard to women and its present applicability in practice from gender perspective, we are bound to ask: Are rights given to women in Islam really applied in practice?; Does personal law and its application in Indian context reflect gender justice?; Are not women doubly disadvantaged? Are women not living under the double disadvantage of the Shariat Law and customary practices of Indian society?

As we found in our study that among all those interviewed, there were hardly any instances of brothers or fathers offering their sisters/ daughters rightful share in family property nor did the women go to the court for their share, one of the reasons being ignorance of the procedure. For most interviewees, consent at marriage was more a kind of ritual than exercising a choice. In spite of the provision of *nikahnama*, in majority of the cases there was no *nikahnama*. In most of the cases *mehr* was not given to women not even after divorce had taken place, neither in *khula* nor in Faskh. No divorced women were given maintenance either for themselves or for their children in spite of their persistent approach to Shariat courts. A few of them got back their *jahez* (dowry) that too after lots of pressure from the local Panchayat. No man even took the responsibility of his children after divorce although as per Islamic law the children become the responsibility of father. No divorced woman ever got remarried in spite of the Islamic provision of remarriage. She does not even have the right to reject the partner of her parent's choice. Mehr has become a status symbol for most families and not a protective shield as envisaged originally in Islam. Can these all be considered as Islamic? Obviously not. The practice of Islamic principles and laws are far behind the gender justice for which Islam stood and advocated 1400 years ago.

Her tragedy becomes ever greater because she neither has a platform (if there is no knowledge, no support, no access to reach that) of social or political representation like her counterparts nor do social norms (superseded over Islamic principles) give her freedom to change and grow. No doubt Islam has given her undesirable rights, exalted status and a constructive role in society. But that is what Islam has given her. The most important and pertinent point is, what does the community give her as a member of society? Most of her rights are confined within the pages of the rule book. The rights granted to women by Islam are rarely in practice.

Mobilisation of Women for Gender Justice

It is said that pain does not wait to visit any particular caste or religion, so why should Muslim women not assert and claim for her rights first from within the community and then State at large to which they are entitled. The first and foremost step to restore her to her former glory is to recognise, acknowledge and solve her problems firstly by mobilising the women and then the community and lastly the larger society in which they are equal sharers. This can be done at two levels: from within the community i.e. effort of individuals and the organisation in which first of all women have to come forward and assert for their rights then support from different organisations working for the cause of Muslim women. For achieving this aim, a mass education drive (religious, as well as modern) for women and men is badly needed particularly in matters related to Islamic tenets, Shariat law, women's rights and the anti-custom, anti-conventional spirit of Islam.

There is also an urgent need for the circulation of information provided to women specially at grass roots level for making them aware about their legal and Islamic rights with regard to education, marriage, divorce, maintenance, etc. This can be done through writing in regional languages, street plays and by IJTIMA (religious gathering) of women etc. The responsibility lies both on individual and on the organisation working for the cause of Muslim women. The support of men cannot be ignored as it has been pointed out that during pre-independence period, the Muslim women who fought and wrote about the rights of women, left observing *purdah* or got themselves involved in various socio-political activities, got full support either from their husband or father (Minault : 271 : 1998). So men and women equally have to sensitized for their rights and duties towards each other. Equally important is to conduct surveys to ascertain the conditions of women before advocating any reform in laws and to launch a crash programme for making men and women aware about their rights and duties.

The role of Ulama or religious elite is of great importance in providing women their due rights in which they can exercise in practice and in removing misconceptions of Islamic principles from the masses, specially in matter of marriage and family. For example, in the pre-independence era, Ulama like Maulana Mumtaz Ali Khan wrote a book called *Huquq-e-Niswan* (rights of women), where he wrote in defence of women's rights and superiority of men against women in different matters. Similarly Ulama like Maulana Mohmmad Ali, Sir Syed Ahmad Khan, Allama Iqbal and Maulana Azad insisted that pronouncement of triple *talaq* in one sitting is not in accordance with Qur'anic verses so they argued for reform in that system. The work of Maulana Ashraf Thanvi and Syed Suleman Nadvi cannot be overlooked. They took initiative to usher in some necessary reforms. Thanvi wrote a book in Urdu to help women and also helped in passing Muslim Marriage Dissolution Act of 1939 which gave great relief to women (Engineer, 1997 : 47). So it is time that Ulama deliberated on the cultural and social perspectives and on the recent changes in personal law in most west Asian countries and Pakistan. They should evaluate the scope of reform in the Muslim personal law in the country, (Jung, 1996).

However, a few women have started their struggle for their rights particularly related to divorce and maintenance (as shown in the study) through the civil courts under the provisions of the Muslim Women's Act 1986 as well as Section 125 Cr. P. C. [The case of Saru (Kerala, 1987) Nargis Bano (Chennai, 1999)]. While in the former case the Kerala High Court granted a life long maintenance to a divorced Muslim woman (1993) in the latter case the civil court gave Nargis her benefit of maintenance (Laxmi, C.S. *Hindu* 3rd Sept., 1999). The Supreme Court's judgement in the case of Bai Tahera (1979) for maintenance went in favour of divorced women. The case of Fazlunbi was filed a year later in which the Supreme Court's judgment went in favour of divorced women. (Carroll, 1996). The case of Anwar Begam who filed a case for maintenance and Justice Bahrul Islam of Guwahati High Court had fixed the maintenance under Section 125 of Cr. PC (Ahmad, 1994). [The case filed by Hamida Hanif in the Bombay High Court claiming maintenance from her husband]. The judge upholds the right to maintenance even after the period of iddat and stated that she can move any civil court of law if her husband refuses a "reasonable and fair provision" (Justice S.N. Variawa). He ruled that Muslim Women Act of 1986 does not restrict the maintenance right of divorced women to the period of iddat. "Such an interpretation will be contrary to and against the object of the Act" (1997). Similarly, Ms Raheena had in a case filed [in the chief judicial magistrate's court] for maintenance, received Rs. 2.5 lakhs as maintenance for five years, from her ex-husband and paid money under the Muslim Women Act of 1986 (Sundern, 1996).

Women's organizations had welcomed this ruling by saying that it gives hope to the Muslim women majority of whom are uneducated, unemployed at the time of divorce. Agnes (1999) a senior lawyer says that it provides for a lump sum settlement amount to the divorced wife, much more than that given under Section 125 of Cr. P.C.

Women are not only struggling for their maintenance after divorce but also for their minor children who in practice become the sole responsibility of mother or mother's parents. In a recent case, Noor Saba Khatoon, a divorced woman filed a case of maintenance against her husband for her three minor children. The Supreme Court under Section 125 made maintenance of minor children for two years as void by pronouncing that the father has to maintain minor sons until they acquire independent sources of living and daughters until marriage. This legal provision reinforces and extends the limit under the Muslim Women Act, 1986 (Khan, 1997). It is amazing that this judgment of Supreme Court did not create any controversy or debate among hardcore Muslims on the ground that it violates the Shariat. This judgment definitely had given boost to divorced Muslim mothers.

Thus, on the basis of the above observation one could say that the struggle or mobilisation of women for gender justice at individual level is getting momentum. The basic hurdle in their demand for a gender just law and rights is lack of religious and legal knowledge of their rights, non-accessibility of information about the procedures to claim for their rights, non-existence of family courts all over India specially at the district level where they can approach for their cases, indifferent attitude of ulama in reformulating the Shariat law, etc.

In this regard Sumbul, a Delhi High Court lawyer says, "The basic requirement to improve the status of women is to bring about greater awareness of the existing provision of the Shariat law and the actual implementation of those provisions. For example, (the Nikah contract) has all those provisions which could go in women's favour like the husband can delegate the power to divorce to the wife as well. Other provisions like her upkeep and that of the children there but most of us do not know of these clauses and those who know about it do not implement it. (Qureshi, 1996).

Mobilisation of Women at Organizational Level

The mobilization and struggle of women for the assertion of their rights is not confined to the individual level but has extended to the organizational level too, with the organisations working for the cause of Muslim women from within the community. Steps have been taken by these organizations through different ways to make women aware of their status and rights which were or still not been utilised by them due to ignorance of women and the community.

It is true that majority of the ordinary Muslims are not in favour of Uniform Civil Code, not that they do not want any reform or change in personal laws but they would like to be initiated by the Muslims (ulama and scholars who possess religious as well as legal knowledge and others) within the framework of Islamic prescription. At the same time they do not want any interference from the majority community in the reformulation of their laws. Thus both the attitude hardly add up to being against any social reforms.

As said earlier that there is an urgent need to make an evaluation of certain customs and practices which are being upheld in the name of Islam specially those affecting the women and efforts have to be made to eliminate them. In this direction progressive Muslim (men and women) from all walks of life are joining hands and efforts are on to make laws more gender just. In Bombay a group of progressive Muslims comprised of five women activists and four men who have deep understanding of the problems of women, have worked on drafting a model Nikahnama (marriage contract which has in-built safeguards to protect women's interests). They are trying to get this model Nikahnama approved and propagated by Muslim Personal Law Board. Others who helped in drafting this Nikahnama are four Muslim men, one is advocate, fighting the cases of Muslim women; one of them happens to be a Qazi and the second a lawyer, a member of Muslim Personal Law Board. This group before drafting this model Nikahnama had organised a meeting with Muslim women and identified the problem areas and tried to incorporate appropriate safeguards into this model code. The group's interactions with ulama regarding this model Nikahnama were favourable and they were asked to finalise it and send it for discussion. The Muslim Personal Law Board is also preparing a model Nikahnama based on the same mentioned above which has to be circulated to the Muftis and Qazis all over India. The main objective, is to check gross misuse of Islamic laws regarding divorce, non-payment of Mehr and maintenance. The board is in the process of setting up Shariat courts in all districts and Taluqas to solve various disputes.

Nisha a Muslim women's forum at Kozhikode in Kerala represented by P. Suhara as convenor and S. Beebi as joint convenor, is working for the cause of Muslim women specifically as regards triple *talaq* in one sitting, misuse of polygamy etc. They had launched a signature campaign among divorced women to represent before the union government against the "divorce at will" being commonly and freely practised by Muslim men. They are strongly in favour of allowing divorce only through Court of law. (Surendran, 1997).

The Islamic Fiqh Academy, Aligarh, in its annual conference, Maulana Saud Alam Qasmi, director religious affairs in the department of Sunni Theology AMU talked about the proposal to introduce basic reforms related to marriage and divorce, would be an important step in ensuring justice to women in the light of our own religious scriptures.

One of the major reforms envisaged is a draft of Nikahnama which will include a special clause that will make it "very difficult" for a Muslim to take a second wife. The penalty for breaking this contract will also be there.

The (conditions laid down in Nikahnama) according to him, will, for the first time, give Muslim women in India the right to divorce. Although this provision has always existed in theory but somehow never been enshrined in the Indian Muslim Personal Law. Under this provision a Muslim woman will need the support of just three withnesses to obtain divorce. (Hasan, 1996).

The Bihar Muslim Intellectual Forum has formulated a draft bill named as "Muslim Family Council Act" proposing several changes in the most glaring areas of Muslim Family Law within the Islamic ethos especially marriage, divorce and succession. This Council should consist of one Hight Court judge and six other members who could be nominated by State Government from the Panel made by chairman.

The Council should be constituted at district level and chaired by the District Judge nominated by the chairperson of the state level.

Forum convenor and former vice chancellor of Patna University M. Mohiddin said that the clause 5(2)(a) of the draff bill proposes that only Talaq-e-Ahsan shall be permissible to Muslim husband married under the Muslim law. It is stated in the bill that any man who wishes to divorce his wife shall, immediately after the pronouncement of the first *talaq,* give the chairman of the District Council notice in writing and shall supply a copy of the same to his wife and to Naib of the block. First efforts of reconciliation between the two would be made by Naib failing which the district council will examine the justification of divorce and shall be effective only if they approve the divorce.

The District Council shall also have the power to pass the necessary order for payment of all dues to the wife which will be recoverable under the Public Demand Recovery Act or Code of Criminal Procedure. The bill also seeks to confer equal rights on women to divorce their husband by talaq-e-tafweed.

According to 5(1) of the draft bill, no person during the subsistence of marriage shall contract another marriage without the written consent of his existing wife and without obtaining the approval of the district council which will examine if the proposed marriage is necessary. The permission will be granted only when the Council is satisfied.

The bill states that the Qazi who performs Nikah shall issue a marriage certificate that has to be recorded by the block level officer who will be appointed by the Council for this purpose. It shall be the duty of Naib to send a copy of all Nikahs registered with him to the State Council.

The bill also proposes to establish a Muslim family court also in the state with retired judge of High Court or District Court and will function as the appellate authority which will take into account the problems of divorce maintenance and polygamy faced by Muslim women (Engineer Asghar Ali, 1996).

Another organisation named **Anjuman Action Committee,** a

group of progressive Muslim intellectuals in Dhanbad (South Bihar) working for religious reform specially in matter of marriage, divorce and maintenance of Muslim women.

Another organisation **Awaze-e-Niswan** (Women's Voice) of Bombay for the last twelve years is working mainly among the Muslim women to generate awareness about the importance of education, women's rights in personal law, counselling and helping those women who became the victims of domestic violence, divorce, deprived of maintenance, custody of children etc.. They also organised workshops, networking with other groups in the city working for the cause of women. Last year they organised a three day national workshop in which women from all over India had participated. The subject was Muslim Personal Law and women in which some of the important issues like Registration of Marriage, banning of triple *talaq,* matrimonial rights, custody and guardianship of children and adoption were discussed.

WRAG (Women Research Action Group) is another organisation mainly working on the condition and problems of Muslim women in India. Although it is basically a research organisation but its members go to women and listen to their problems and educate them about various issues. Majlis which is basically a legal and cultural centre working to provide legal aid to women and work towards familiarising women with courts and litigation procedure and also doing campaigning about the registration of marriages.

These efforts on the part of different organisations to mobilise the Muslim women for their rights and their demand to make personal laws more gender just is very bold and outstanding step for the whole community. These efforts to improve the status of women in general and community in particular is now realised by the religious elites (Ulama) who previously had strong opposition to listen to any word of change and modification in Shariat law. "Many of the ulama care deeply about Muslim women, about which they have been kept in the dark, by our social workers. With the women experienced in and committed to constructive practical work on the board, so much can be done" (Jyoti, P. 1996). It is high time that the progressive Muslim women and their organisations, the progressive Muslim intellectuals and the Ulama should come on a common platform to think about the problems and plight of Muslim women resulting from illiteracy, ignorance of their Islamic and legal knowledge of their rights, putting a check on misuse of Islamic provision by men, to reformulate the Shariat law in more gender just manner. The responsibility equally lies on the secular force of the majority community to create an atmosphere of pluralistic democratic culture in which Muslims can evaluate their own laws and modify it according to Islamic prescription.

Thus, the question of women's legal rights and the best means to implement gender justice through law has entered a new phase in India today. The best indicator of this situation can be seen in the controversies over bringing in a uniform civil code for all Indian women. Different groups and women's organisations have taken very different positions on this issue. Problems have arisen as a result of the highly communalised situation that we are currently living in, and which are showing no signs of abating. Muslim women in particular are the worst victims of this situations, both within their own communities and in the face of the growing power of the Hindu right.

Most of all, the situation and problems faced by Muslim women is not well understood, and many routes to their advancement appear to be blocked. Nevertheless, in this paper, I have argued that there are forces at work that can improve the situation. For instance, mobilisation is possible and is taking place around questions concerning the relationships between Islamic principles concerning women, the Shariat law as it currently exists in the statute books on Muslim personal law, and the actual practices prevailing in specific regions.

However, instead of making a concluding remark on the Islamic principles on questions of marriage, divorce and so on which are, on the whole, more gender just and favourable to women than current practices, the issues which have to be incapsulated are: In a communally vitiated atmosphere can Muslim women be successfully mobilised through:

1. A better understanding of these Islamic principles?
2. Initiating changes in current practices as the result of such knowledge?
3. Pressurizing leaders of the community to adhere more closely to these principles?
4. Working for reform of existing personal laws themselves?

These issues are open for further discussion from all concerned.

APPENDIX

LIST OF DARUL QAZA IN BIHAR AND ORISSA

1. Darul Qaza, Imarate Shariah, Purnea

2.	-do-	

3. Darul Qaza, Imarate Shariah, Supaul, Darbhanga

4.	-do-	Kishanganj
5.	-do-	Khankah Rahmani, Mungyr
6.	-do-	Begusarai
7.	-do-	Samastipur
8.	-do-	Saharsa
9.	-do-	Gir dih
10.	-do-	Chatra
11.	-do-	Rohtas
12.	-do-	Muzzaffarpur
13.	-do-	Bettiah
14.	-do-	Jogbani, Arania
15.	-do-	Jamshedpur
16.	-do-	Siwan
17.	-do-	Dumka
18.	-do-	Khagariah
19.	-do-	Arania
20.	-do-	Katihar
21.	-do-	Madhubani
22.	-do-	Madhubani
23.	-do-	Godda

24.	-do-	Sitamarhi
25.	-do-	Basoria
26.	-do-	Ranchi
27.	-do-	Raurkela (Orissa)
28.	-do-	Cuttack (Orissa)
29.	-do-	Dinajpur (West Bengal)
30.	-do-	Purulia (West Bengal)
31.	-do-	Asansol (West Bengal)

Notes

1. Sharifa Hamid Ali was a prominent worker in the cause of women's rights, a leading firm of solicitors in Bombay who drafted an agreement to ensure to a Muslim wife in India the fullest possible rights of obtaining for freedom by the rules of law as applied to Talaq-e-tawfid which is to be signed Before the Nikah ceremony.

2. Until the enactment of Muslim Marriage Dissolution Act 1939, the Muslim women in India (Hanafi) had virtually no right to secure a divorce in the absence of her husband's agreement to divorce her extra-judicialy by Talaq or Khula'/Mubarat. The only grounds on which she could apply for judicial dissolution were impotency of husband and husband's false accusation of adultery against her in the ritual known as LIAN (Carroll, 1986, Journal of Indian Law Institute; 364-376). But this Act improved the situation of Muslim wife (Hanafi) by adding other grounds such as desertion, cruelty, failure to maintain, leprosy and veneral diseases which she has to prove.

3. Divorce

It is to be noted that triple *talaq* which is actually not in accordance with Quranic verses, also absent in Fatawa-e-Alamgiri (religious decree of Aurangzeb on which the Shariat Laws of India, Pakistan and Bangladesh are based).

4. Inheritance

Although there are wide differences in the law of various sects and subsects, the inheritance rights of women under Islamic law be broadly classified as:

* The daughter inherits half the share inherited by son.
* The wife inherits one eighth of the husband's property.
* The mother inherits one sixth of the property.

5. Faskh

Divorce sought through Shariat Court on different grounds prescribed in Muslim Marriage Dissolution Act, 1939.

REFERENCES

1. Agnes, F., *Law and Gender Inequality,* Oxford University Press, New Delhi, 1993.
2. Ahmed Furqan, *Triple Talaq : An Analytical Study,* Regency Publication, 1994, New Delhi.
3. Balasubramaniyam, Vimal," a Model Nikahnama "*Mainstream,* 33(41), Sept. 3, 1995.
4. Bihar Muslim Forum's draft bill on Family Law, *Hindu,* March 23, 1996.
5. Carroll Lucy, "Divorced Muslim Women in India" in Lucy Carroll and Harsh Kapoor (ed.) *Talaq-e-Tafweed: The Muslim Women's Contractual Access to Divorce,* Leader's Compilation series, Women living under Muslim Law Publication, 1996, France.
6. Engineer, Asghar Ali, Indian Islam and Reform Movements in Post-Independent India, *Dossier* 20 (December) 1997 Women living under Muslim Law Publication, 1997, France.

   --------------- Muslim Women An Attempt at a New Legislation, *Mainstream* 34 (24) May 18, 1996.
7. Fyzee, A.A., *An Outline of Mohammdan Law,* The Oxford University Press, 1974.

8. Hasan Tariq, "Muslim Law Reforms are on anvil", *Times of India,* Sept. 9, 1996.

9. Jung Zafar, "Indian Muslim Needs in-house reform" *Indian Express,* August 8, 1996.

10. Khan, Mumtaz Ali, "True Islamic Spirit" *Decan Herald,* August 5, 1997.

11. Minault Gail, *Secluded Scholar: Women's Education and Muslim Social Reform in Colonial India,* Oxford University Press, Delhi, 1998.

12. Punwani, Jyoti, "A change from Within", *Telegraph,* January 28, 1996.

13. Quraishi, Humera, "Need for Reform", *Pioneer,* Nov. 11, 1996.

14. Raikar Mhatre Samedtia, "Judge upholds right to maintenance even after iddat", *Indian Express,* Oct. 10, 1997.

15. Surendran, P.K., Muslim Women wins Maintenance Claim, *Times of India,* Jan. 1, 1996.

"Kerala Talaq" Victims will fight Polygamy, *Times of India,* June 6, 1997.

8

Divorce and Remarriage Among Muslims of Mumbai

Neelofar Saeed Akhtar

There is growing domestic violence all over the world and it is said that in 21st century the common problem all over the world will be matrimonial offences. Women represent half the world population and play a vital role in human development in all spheres. In Islam, women have rights, obligations and opportunities as men have. For human development men and women have mutual dependence where one cannot exist without the other. The Creator has assigned to each some specified rights and responsibilities. Islam is the only religion which has given a number of rights to women like the right to inherit property, right to refuse or consent to a marriage proposal, have *mehr* maintenance, custody, education, freedom of expression, individuality, to retain husband's property for unpaid Mehr and li'an.

The Holy Quran, the perfect Divine Book and man's eternal guide, reveals to us that social laws must be framed in accordance with human nature. Al Quran 30.30.

One must not analyse the doctrines of Islam on the basis of the action of some Muslim at a certain time and place. It is observed that Islamic tenets are being negated in some Muslim lands which imitate the Western culture. It should not be concluded that governing laws agree with those of Islam even if millions of Muslims do follow the westernized ways of life. Careful examination will reveal that if an

Islamic dictate apparently seems ineffective, that is so due to neglect of other Islamic injunctions, inadequate religious education, moral and spiritual decadence in the present society, and not because Islamic laws are defective for any period of time and place.

The Islamic law, which is wrongly called as Mohammadan Law, is understood, practised and applied, based on Holy Quran. In India, Islamic Law is not codified, except in the matters of divorce where two acts are the Dissolution of Muslim Marriage Act 1939 and the Muslim Women (Protection of Rights on Divorce) Act, 1986 have been passed. Under Act 1939, there are about 16 to 18 grounds for dissolution of marriage and they are impotency, imprisonment, whereabout not known, insanity, veneral disease, non performance of matrimonial obligation, physical or mental cruelty, force to lead immoral life, obstruction in performing religious profession, unequal treatment to wives, leading immoral life, failure to provide maintenance, Prepudiation, disposal of her property without her consent. It is in this background one must analyse the topic. The most progressive modern concept of Jurisprudence on matrimonial dispute in civilized and advanced countries is conceptualised as a private family affair. The dispute, if any, in matrimony is to resolve itself by dissolution without indulging into long drawn legal battle and thereby saving the prime time of both the spouses. Needless to say, the most sufferers are the children.

This modern concept was known to Islam as far back as 1400 years ago. The majority wish to dissolve their marriage by mutual consent without assigning any reason valid or otherwise. The modalities apart, the fact is that marriage is considered as a dissoluable tie which Islam taught and practised for centuries. This very principles is, if looked into with pros and cons in it's proper context of the time, well founded, most practical and logical.

It is a misconception that Muslim men only are given right to dissolve the marriage. A woman has equal right to dissolve her marriage through *khula*. She need not give any reason for it, but she need to pay Iwaj or compensation to her husband. Foregoing *Mehr* is always Iwaj or compensation from her. She can also obtain divorce under delegated authority of the husband to divorce herself known as *Talaq-e-Tafweed* form. She can even apply to the court for divorce on several grounds. In *Talaq-e-Tafweed*, a wife can incorporate many stipulations at the time of *Nikah* and violation of any of these stipulations, the woman can divorce herself or dissolve her marriage. This practice has been recognised and enforced in many Muslim countries. In modern times this practice is being preached, propagated and developed all over the world. This has also come to be recognised and practised in India in educated and affluent families.

A wife can also dissolve her marriage by mutual consent, this is known as Mubarat or bilateral divorce. If the stipulation indicates such assurance on mutual divorce, then also such right of woman can be exercised for obtaining divorce.

Experience does indicate that educated Muslims are realising that instead of having any interference of the Court or any authority, the matrimonial dispute can be sorted out without washing dirty linen in public. We may also incorporate a clause of arbitration which has divine injunction. Quran Sura 4 Ayat 35 provides provision for arbiters in case of family dispute. This will obviate the cumbersome and tortuous procedure of going through litigation which sometimes take precious time of the spouses. The experience at Bar has shown that if proper counselling is done people part their ways in a civilised, dignified and amicable atmosphere; if there is any litigation initiated by either party, it is revengeful and passion packed. In modern times well recognised principle of dissolution of marriage by women should be well understood in the context of social conditions and status of the concerned spouses.

In Islam marriage is a simple ceremony in which free consent, consideration of *mehr,* consummation of marriage and capacity are very important. The marriage in Islam is solemn pact Quran 4.21 which does not require any formal proof. Even long duration of stay, admission of relationship of husband and wife are enough for Muslim marriage. No sooner the matrimonial bond is established, it creates rights and obligations for the spouses. Islam casts obligation upon the husband to maintain and look after and keep his wife happy. He is bound to be a provider and the wife is entitled to inherit the properties from the husband as her absolute right. Keeping this view in mind, Islam has made dissolution of marriage simple.

At the time of *nikah*, women have been given right to receive *mehr* which may be instant or deferred being an essential element of Muslim marriage. Quran warns against depriving woman of her dowry or *mehr* of marriage which belongs wholly and exclusively to her only and should never be taken by husband unless offered. Mehr is not a bride price and is connected with the modesty and chastity of a women. It is necessary for her honour and respect that she should not give herself up freely to the authority of man but should give herself a worth. *Mehr* is a gift from man as token of his sincerity. Ayat 4.4 says "Give the Women their Dower as a Gift Spontaneous". It is token to truthfulness and earnestness of the affection of a man. *Mehr* is also a symbol of new relationship of husband and wife. It can be anything, may be gold, land, money, rent, jewellery or property. Quantum and mode of payment or delivery is fixed at the time of *nikah*. If *mehr* is not given, she can claim it through court. A wife may decrease or forego her *mehr*. *Mehr* is never invalid due to its excess. She can retain the property of husband for her unpaid *mehr*. This right to receive *mehr* survives even after the death of her husband. The wife's or widow's claim for unpaid portion of *mehr* is an unsecured debt due to her. It is an actionable claim. The wife has an option of refusing the husband his conjugal rights until the prompt *mehr* is paid.

Triple Talaq is a practice that has caused maximum damage to institution of marriage. Families should be safeguarded, and marriage should be strengthened. Quran Ayat 22 of Sura 2 allowed a man to pronounce *talaq* only twice during whole of his life. Codified laws of many Islamic countries require prior permission or intervention of an appropriate authority. It is, therefore, necessary that the Muslim Personal Law in India be codified by religious experts, scholars and Ulama, and these laws, must be interpreted only by recognised authorities of Islamic law, Islamic scholars and Ulamas and not by any court and parliament.

A Muslim husband in India can divorce his wife by his unilateral action and without intervention of any authority or court. There are different modes of *talaq*. *Talaq-e-Ahsan* is the most approved and *Talaq-e-Hasan* is approved mode. Talaq may be single, triple and irrevocable pronouncement. This is known as *Talaq-e-Bidat* or triple *talaq* which is very common in India. In majority cases husbands pronounce irrevocable triple *talaq* which denies chances of reconciliation. However, a husband who divorces his wife by triple *talaq* cannot remarry her unless she marries another man through valid *nikah* and then the man consummates the marriage as ordained in verse 230 of Sura Bagarah of Holy Quran.

In India, Islamic law is practised on the basis of text. There is no codification of Islamic law in India except two legislative enactments namely Dissolution of Muslim Marriage Act 1939 and Muslim Women (Protection of Rights on Divorce) Act, 1986. Under this, the wife has to go to court to get the relief.

The basic reason for divorce may be financial problem, and lack of basic concept of marriage. In places like Mumbai, the shortage of accommodation, poor economic conditions, lack of consistent income to create insecurity in women. As a result, the divorces are taking place within 6 months to five years. Generally, the majority of divorce cases are in lower middle class families, on account of financial constraints. Amongst the financially well off couples, the reason for divorce may be lack of interest in the spouse, incompatibility, differences in educational standards and differences in age. Divorce is taking place irrespective of community and occupation. There are about 50 per cent cases where there are no disputes or differences of opinion between husband and wife, but there are conflicts of personality amongst the respective elders of the spouses either on the grounds of nearness of relation or social status of the relatives. Normally after the birth of first child the dispute surfaces. In 70 per cent cases, the husband shows his willingness to maintain the child without any *bonafide* intention but to deprive the mother of the custody of the child. The husbands normally marry the second wife within a year of divorce (about 65 per cent). In 65 per cent cases, the husbands marries a younger virgin and financially more sound woman, and divorcing wife remarries on account of several varying factors like rich, well settled, aged man. She may marry a man involved with her. In 50 per cent of cases she may not marry, as she does not get proper match, or she has to look after children, or aged parents who have provided her shelter. In 75 per cent of cases the man if willing to marry her does not want the responsibility of the children of her previous husband. The parents of the divorcee girls undertake to look after her children. In all such cases, the mental state or upbringing of children is disturbed, due to single parenting. In 60 per cent of cases if proper counselling is administered by correctly diagnosing the reason of discord, the marriage can be saved. In majority of cases if the parents of the respective spouses interfere or put their prestige at stake (which is false) the divorce is inevitable. However, it is found that where there is reasonable approach and scope for willingness to compromise and adjust, the marriage can be saved. The joint or extended family system has its own advantages and disadvantages. In such families there is elderly person whose word is last, all the other spouses in the family follows the norms, but if the head of the family is unreasonable, discriminatory and lacks depth and foresightedness, the family leads into discontentment; eventually either the marriage breaks down or if the couple is financially independent, they branch out and the entire family is disintegrated. In all such cases, one factor is very dominant and that is if the head of the family controls the entire financial aspects and is sufficiently well off only then it works. The joint family business is also a factor which keeps the family together. If there is cohesion in the family it works to its advantage. In all such cases the central factor is money power which keeps them intact. The nature of complex society, demanding time and money are also factors which preserve the joint family. However, in such joint families there is craving for independence of the couples. If there is curb, it again leads to disputes and differences which may in the longer run, as said before, either result in branching out or divorce.

In majority of cases, if the couples are given proper counselling at the teething stage of matrimonial life, the marriage may be saved. In joint family system elder members do such counselling; but where the couples are living on their own without any guidance or elderly family members, they result into disputes and dissolutions of marriages. In 90 per cent of cases, the custody of the children always goes to mother but mothers find it difficult to maintain them. In the event of her demand, the husbands normally offer to maintain the children with no intention to look after the children. In 80 per cent of cases where husbands get married second time, irrespective of their status and education, they do not look after their children and they avoid to pay maintenance. There is no fixed number of children when the divorces take place; it may be from none to 3 or 4 children. In 90 per cent of cases divorces are not finalised through intervention of court. People approach Jamat of their community like Ghachi Bohras, Agakhans or the Moulvies of respective mosque of their locality. The educated come to legal advisers, either referred to by some friends or relatives. These parties come alongwith the parents. In all cases women are always accompanied by parents, brothers or sisters and the men by their either friends or parents. There are many social organisation in Mumbai which refer matrimonial disputes to panelled legal advisers of their organisations, where counselling is done in 3 or 4 meetings and in 85 per cent of cases matters are settled.

There is growing tendency to get the Nikah Faskh (termination) and the reason for such tendency is that the husband is employed outside India and he neglects and fails to look after the wife and the child, if any. The wife is left high and dry. In that eventuality people approach Moulvies/Kazis. In 80 per cent of cases there is no difficulty in payment of *mehr,* the reason being that the amount being meagre. In affluent class where *mehr* is on the higher side the husbands can normally afford to pay. In cases where woman is involved with another man, she forgoes her *mehr* and is ready to dissolve her marriage by *khula*. In 80 per cent of cases the women avoid to resort to legal remedies. Nowadays in view of several NGO's espousing the women's cause, women are coming out to resort to legal remedies. In Mumbai such legal remedies lie on the Magistrate's Court. In almost 99 per cent of cases, after the death of husband widow foregoes *mehr*.

The *jahez* articles are not returned to the wife in the event of her leaving the house and is used as lever for bargain. The jurisdiction for enforcing the *jahez* is with the Magistrate's court and the same factors as said before deter the wife from going to courts. The *jahez* is given as per the financial capacity of father or brother. Nowadays, in accordance with the policy of the state, women cell attached to the police stations call upon husbands for a meeting and in 90 per cent of cases the husbands return the *jahez* articles. In 10 per cent of cases out of vengeance the husbands damage or destroy them. In 95 per cent of cases *jahez* list is prepared and signed by both parties.

In 99 per cent of cases there is no remarriage after divorce with the same spouse, but in only one per cent case the husband is ready and willing to remarry the same woman for financial reason.

Amongst Muslims the remarriage is not a taboo. On the contrary, women marry within a span of one year to five years. In places like Mumbai, there is no question of compromise, on the contrary the spouse may get a better spouse. There is no negative attitude to remarriage. It is true that elderly women with children find it more difficult to get a proper match than the younger women without children. Another factor which plays a vital role in remarriage is employment or financial status of the woman. She gets many proposals for remarriage. Thus, the employed women have better chances for remarriage. In Mumbai, the other factor for remarriage is owning of a residence. Among Muslims in 80 per cent of cases there is no demand of dowry, but such allegations are used as a lever.

There is no real bonafide intention of resumption of co-habitation. If any husband has any bonafide intention for making a family he needs no proceeding. In 95 per cent cases, proceedings for restitution of conjugal rights are instituted without any intention and to take advantage of his own wrong.

Dissolution of Marriage of Apostacy

In Mumbai, there have been many instances of interreligious marriage. Many non-Muslim women have married Muslim men. The women have high expectations of living with Muslim husbands. They embrace Islam, learn Islamic *tehzeeb* but Muslim men do not live upto their expectations. They treat their wives very badly. The wives never expect that the Muslim husband will come drunk, and treat them with physical cruelty. Such wives cannot accept the fact that the Muslim husband consumes the prohibited liquor and beats his wife. The other family members of the husband instigate him to desert her. Being fed up with everyday behaviour towards her, she returns to her natal family and the divorce follows. In such cases, the blame squarely falls on Muslim community which failed to appreciate her sacrifice. Even the legal professionals are ignorant about the procedure of dissolution of marriage of "apostacy."

Such women face hardships as she has no perspective husband at hand as no Muslim or non-Muslim is ready to accept her and the presence of her children further add to her misery. Children born from such wedlock, also suffer socially, psychologically and emotionally. One can imagine what they will be in their lives.

The general perception of people by and large has been that the divorce Muslim woman being the victim become prostitutes. But the fact which is based on research carried out by one of the leading social organisations is that such cases are less than one per cent .

The element of vengence of taking revenge by the wives among Muslim is rarely found. Their aim and goal is to get them relieved from matrimony. They do not mind foregoing Mehr, Jahez articles expenses incurred for the marriage and claim of maintenance.

In 90 per cent of cases the Muslim women's cause is true. However they take inspiration from maintenance demanded by their counterparts in other religion and such numbers are growing, and thus they too demand maintenance and provision for their life.

In Muslim marriage one of the important ingredient of complete marriage is its consummation. In 99 per cent of cases the marriage is consumated. We hardly come across of divorce cases on ground of impotency of the husband. There is no case of annulment of marriage on account of non-consummation.

In 99 per cent of cases there is no allegation of illicit relationship with father-in-law or brother-in-law. A salient feature of Muslim marriage is that each and every Muslim marriage has a proof of *nikahnama*. There is an entry in the register maintained by kazi for all marriages. The consent of bride is always obtained and thereafter the *nikah* is performed.

By and large Muslims in Mumbai are not happy with the practice of triple *talaq* and the women feel aggrieved with *talaq* without assigning any reason. The women desire some check on unilateral divorce by husbands. Such unrest in the Muslim society can be conveniently, consistent with Shariah can be sorted out by arbitration proceedings.

The most advantageous factor in Muslim society in Mumbai is that there is no dowry deaths. The spouses do not waste their time, money, energy, human resources and suffer humiliation in long drawn proceedings of divorce. The exceptional cases do not lay down the rule. Factors like false projection in media, wrong guidance given by certain social organisations, misguidance by professionals and lack of knowledge of Islamic law create confusion, and people resort to wrong remedies and thereby complicate the issues. In the ultimate analysis, it is the next generation who suffers the most.

If Islamic law is not understood in its proper perspective, the community will lose its culture and value. Somewhere on the way, our identity will be lost.

9

Muslim Women and the Law

Khurram Shah Durrany

Introduction

The Muslim woman in India has become a subject of interest in academic and social circles for her human rights. Though the Muslim women's movement is very weak, their voices are heard in other women's outfits where they openly criticize and expose inconsistencies of Muslim Personal Law. They have some real grievances against Muslim males in matters of divorce and maintenance of their wives. Certain provisions of Muslim Personal Law, they feel, are discriminatory against women and they favour men. They question legality of triple *talaq* and polygamous marriages, recognized by the Muslim Law, in the context of Indian Constitution and other laws. However, the general principles of Muslim Law cannot be challenged.

Progressive Principles

The Muslim Law is a pioneering family law in our country. It recognizes the distinct personality of a woman independent of her father, husband and other male members of her family. The dictum that "husband and wife constituted one person and the husband was that person," never applied in case of Muslim woman. The progressive principles taken here are drawn from an article of Mr Danial Latifi, an eminent advocate of Muslim Law, entitled "Muslim Personal Law Reform" published in the Journal of Constitutional and Parliamentary Studies, 1970. According to this article, Muslim marriage is a civil contract where woman retains her full legal personality to acquire, hold and dispose of her property without any intervention of her husband; she continues her identity with her father's family; she has a right to demand from her husband protection of marriage ties and *mehr*. The husband has no right to claim any dowry from his bride. The woman has right to remarry after divorce or widowhood. Moreover, the wife has option to put appropriate terms and conditions to secure her matrimonial rights. She may also impose a condition that husband shall not marry a second wife during her life time and that she shall have right to divorce herself at will or subject to conditions specified in the marriage contract *(nikahnama)*. And further it may include a condition in every marriage contract that wife shall not be required to observe *purdah*, nor shall she be hindered in the pursuit of her studies or any other activity or association reasonably connected with, or required in the interest of, her business, profession or vocation. This is the ideal situation for the law of marriage and divorce. The article of Mr Danial Latifi was followed by an Annexure—The Muslim Personal Law (Shariat) Application (Amendment) Bill, 1969 which intended to reform the Muslim Personal Law as contained in Section 2 of Shariat Act, 1937 as:

> "2. Notwithstanding any custom or usage to the contrary, in all questions (save questions relating to agricultural land) regarding intestate succession, special property of females, including personal property inherited or obtained under contract or gift or any other provision of Personal Law, marriage, dissolution of marriage, including *talaq*, ila, *zihar*, *lian*, *khula* and mubarat' at, maintenance, dower, guardianship, gifts, trust and trust properties, and wakfs (other than charities and charitable institutions and charitable and religious endowments) the rule of decision in cases where the parties are Muslims shall be the Muslim Personal Law (Shariat)."

Need for Reform and Codification

Most of the provisions of Muslim Personal Law are uncodified. They are scattered in religious and legal texts of jurisprudence which are beyond common scholars' reach for they do not understand language. The Holy Qur'an and Hadith are fundamental religious texts and have the status of divine commands The rest of the literature has no such sanctity.

It is believed in the orthodox religious circles that entire Muslim Personal Law is God-given and hence immutable. It cannot be reformed or codified. This position is not correct. The Muslim Personal Law has not only been reformed or codified in other countries but it has been codified in our own country. Some of the provisions of Shariat has been totally replaced during the British Rule. The laws relating to Muslim Wakfs have been codified and amended several times since 1913.The present Muslim Wakf Act, 1995 (Act No. 43 of 1995), is the reformed law. The Dissolution of Muslim Marriage Act (Act No. 8 of 1939) is the reformed and codified law. But the law of *talaq* is not codified. It must need immediate attention of the Muslim leadership to reform and codify the Muslim Law of Marriage and divorce, as the Parliament has codified. The Muslim Women (Protection of Rights on Divorce) Act, 1986 (Act No. 25 of 1986). This Act has very limited scope but it serves good purpose.

The Muslim society is conscious of the plights of divorced Muslim women. The intellectuals, activists and even religious leaders realize that the practice of irrevocable triple divorce is wrong and polygamous marriages are exploitative. The intellectuals like Danial Latifi and Asghar Ali Engineer should work for a better law of Muslim Marriage and divorce. Maulana Mahfoozur Rahman speaking for Islamic Fiqh Academy (India) said that the husband who has wrongly divorced his innocent wife should be made to agree to pay more money and face rigorous imprisonment for 6 months (Ishtarat-e-fin nikah by Mujahidul Islam Qasmi). But the suggestion of the Maulana will not serve any purpose without a properly codified law. The Muslim Law of Marriage and Divorce is inconsistent with the constitution, secular laws and the codes of other communities. This inconsistency can be removed only by agreeing to the State securing a uniform civil code for all of its citizens as provided in Article 44 of the Constitution or by making such efforts as to have gender just laws in matters of marriage, maintenance, divorce, etc.

Indian Constitution and the Law

The Constitution secures for all its citizens (including Muslim women), Justice, social, economic and political; Liberty, of thought, expression, belief, faith and worship; Equality of status and opportunity, and to promote among them all Fraternity assuring the dignity of the individual. The Constitution guarantees Fundamental Rights of equality before law (Art. 14): prohibition of discrimination on grounds of religion, race, caste, sex or place of birth (Art. 15) and equality of opportunity in matters of public employment (Art. 16). The State has imposed a duty upon itself that it will protect the fundamental rights of citizens by declaring the inconsistent laws as void (Art. 13). The inconsistency of Muslim Law of Marriage and Divorce become void in the light of this article. The discriminatory and inconsistent provisions of Muslim Law are in force because the State has not taken any step to reform the Muslim Personal Law under Article 372 which reads as follows:

> "....all the laws in force in the territory of India immediately before the commencement of this Constitution shall continue in force wherein until altered or amended or replaced by a competent Legislature or other competent authority."

The State has reformed and codified the entire Hindu Law which was inconsistent to the principle of equality and equal justice. In this regard the State policy is itself discriminatory and inconsistent with the constitutional policy of secularism and equality before law. The community can resist amendments of inconsistent law for all times. How people can tolerate if two persons under same Constitution treated differently even under criminal law. For example, the Christians, Hindus and Muslims are treated differently under Section 494 of IPC and Sections 125, 127 (3) (b) of CRPC.

The Role of Judiciary

The duty of Indian judges is to defend Constitution and laws thereunder. The judges can not defend the customary laws which are inconsistent to the provisions of the Constitution for they take oath under Article 219 and Article 124 (6) which provide under the Third Schedule the oath to the Judges of High Court and the Supreme Court takes as:

> "that I will bear true faith and allegiance to the Constitution of India as by law established, (that I will uphold the sovereignty and integrity of India), that I will duly and fully and to the best of my ability, knowledge and judgment perform the duties of my office without fear or favour, affection or ill-will and that I will uphold the Constitution and the laws."

In view of this oath, therefore, what should be the duty of a judge who sits to decide a petition of a Muslim woman who pleads that she is a very devout wife for about 16 years and lived with her husband and three children in her matrimonial home. One day her husband informed that she should live with her parents and he will provide her residence and maintenance but also should not come back to this home, if she disobeys this command, she is divorced irrevocably. The reason for this command was that the husband has securely married a second wife who wanted to live with him. He failed to provide her residence and maintenance. The aggrieved wife filed a case of cruelty with the State under Section 498-A of IPC. He formally divorced her and sought a *fatwah* from the Deoband Mufti who allowed the dissolution of their marriage under Muslim Law. The Sessions Court asked the husband to make an amicable settlement with the wife or face trial under said IPC provision..The husband preferred Appeal in High Court which upheld the proceedings of the Sessions Court. The husband made the terms of settlement at wife's behest who demanded permanent maintenance for life, residential accommodation, besides Rs.80,000 fixed deposit with an increment @8% over Rs. 1500 per month maintenance for life. This case may be seen in Crl. M(M) 2100/95 and Crl. M. (M) 1080 of 1996 at Delhi High Court dated: 15-11-96. This relief to the victimised women was not possible under Muslim Personal Law.

In a judgment of Bombay High Court dated 22nd, 23rd April and 4th May 1999 by A. Savant and T.K. Chandrasekhar Dass J.J. in between Jaitunbi Mubarak Shaikh vs Mubarak Fakhruddin Shaikh the Court has interpreted Section 3 (I) (a) of Muslim Women (Protection of Rights on Divorce) Act, 1986, where there was provision for *mataun bil maroof* that is a reasonable and fair provision and maintenance to be paid to the divorced wife within *iddat* period by her former husband and the reasonable and the fair provision should be such that the divorced woman can maintain herself for food, clothes, shelter, healthcare etc. This provision should be made for entire future of the divorced woman and be paid during the period of *iddat*. The judgment has noted the fact that husband has married a second wife while the wife has not married. The judgment has also suggested that the parties in dispute may exercise the option available to them under Section 5 of the 1986 Act according to which both parties can file an affidavit to the effect that their dispute for maintenance may be settled under Section 125 of CRPC.

Another judgment of Punjab and Haryana High Court was published in *Qaumi Awaz*, an Urdu Daily dated 27-10-97 wherein the Muslim husband was instructed to maintain his wife even after *iddat* period. Justices Harpal Singh Barar, Shivmant Kumar and K.S. Kumaran directed the husband to pay maintenance to his divorced wife w.e.f. May 19, 1985 @ Rs. 200 per month and Rs. 75 per month to their child within 3 months.

Uniform Civil Code

The role of judiciary, while interpreting the provisions of customary personal laws opens up a controversy on Uniform Civil Code which adversely affects the Muslim Women. The personal laws based on religion are no laws within the meaning of Article 13 of the Constitution, but they have force of law under Article 372. But this provision is in the process of amendment as seen in the judicial verdicts. The Parliament is a competent authority to replace the discriminatory provisions of personal laws by enacting a Uniform Civil Law based on the principal of gender justice. Though Shah Bano Judgement was replaced by the

Muslim Women (Protection of Rights on Divorce) Act, 1986, it is still the basis of many High Court judgements some of which we have mentioned above while interpreting the Islamic principle of *mataun bil maroof* a provision of maintenance for divorced Muslim Women to be paid during *iddat* period as an equivalent of the provision of Section 125 of CRPC for divorced women of all communities. So far as the justice is concerned there should be no difference before the judges between the personal laws and secular laws.

However, Muslim Women are in more disadvantageous position in Muslim Personal Law as practised in India in matters of marriage, divorce and maintenance. But the Uniform Civil Code seems to be a remote dream for equal justice to all women irrespective of caste and religion.

The Uniform Civil Code is a constitutional provision for securing common law to all citizens of India to be enacted by the Parliament. It means a secular law to replace the religious laws or laws based on tradition, customs or usage practised by the people for centuries. It has become a contentious issue among the people since the time of making of the Constitution. Some people especially the 'draftsmen' of the Constitution, favoured its enactment, and others opposed it on the ground that it is in contravention to their personal laws. Here is a humble attempt to resolve the perennial controversy by reforming the personal laws of different religious communities by themselves.

Various factors contribute to keep uniform civil code (U.C.C.) into cold storage. Aggressive communalism, political opportunism, mass illiteracy and backward notions of culture and religion, do not help people to come together and think together about the common beneficiaries of the U.C.C., i.e., the women and children. The Constitution only empowers the state to endeavour to secure a uniform civil code for all citizens throughout the territory of India in Article 44 of Directive Principles of State Policy which are beyond the reach of the courts. The Indian National Congress won for us independence to protect the religious and cultural interests of different people. It looked at India as a country of composite culture and numerous traditions of centuries old practices. The Congress never made any attempt to secure uniform civil code for all citizens. The Muslim amendment to the Draft Constitution in the constituent assembly:

> "That any group, section or community or people shall not be obliged to give up its own personal law in case it has such a law", and "that the personal law of any community which is guaranteed by the statute shall not be changed except with the previous approval of the community ascertained in such manner as the Union Legislature may determine by law"

-- was rejected and yet the Article 44 was not made a time bound provision. It remained as a dead letter till reminded by the Supreme Court judgements in 1985 and 1995. The political interests took advantage of these judgements and started their movement for capturing power. From June 1985 to the destruction of Babri Masjid on 6.12.1992 and later the Bombay blasts of 1993 the Uniform Civil Code was in the background of communal flareup.

The National Executive of Bharatiya Janta Party (BJP) which has been pursuing an ideology of exclusive Hinduatva in the name of cultural nationalism has adopted a resolution on uniform civil code welcoming the recent Supreme Court judgement. It reads:-

> "We have today a paradoxical situation in the country where almost all laws are applicable uniformally to all citizens. We have a common criminal law. We have common laws in relation to property, rent, commercial transactions and taxation. It is only in the matter of marriage, divorce, succession and gift that we are permitting personal laws to be applicable to members of various religious denominations....when we look at the different personal laws in India, they present a pathetic spectacle. A Muslim woman can be turned out of her matrimonial house on the three oral utterances of 'talaq' without an adequate provision for her maintenance. She can be driven to destitution without remedy. She can be compelled to live with three other wives under the same roof. Polygamy has no place in any

> modern society. A Christian woman is not entitled to the same rights and grounds of divorce as her male spouse is. A Hindu woman may be a co-sharer of residential house but has no right to claim its partition. A flagrant violation of gender equality and right to live with dignity visible in different personal laws...The Bharatiya Janta Party feels that 'rituals' in relation to marriage and death can be guided by religious practices; but 'rights' emanating from them must be regulated by law. This law should be reasonable, non-discriminatory, based on gender equality and respect—dignity to all citizens—man and woman".

The BJP's good gestures for women of India through the promise for uniform civil code should not be read in isolation to the opening remarks by Sh. L.K. Advani, President of BJP while inaugurating the National Executive on July 15, 1995. He says

"BJP's ascendency, we must appreciate, heralds the rise both of idelogy as well as of ideoalism. The party's phenomenal growth in the past few years owes much to our nationalistic stand on Kashmir, Ayodhya and Uniform Civil Code."

Thus, for the BJP the implementation of the Uniform Civil Code is identical with the destruction of Babri Masjid on 6.12.1992 which put the entire nation to shame in the eyes of the world. The BJP's love for the U.C.C. is bound to be opposed by various sections of people—political as well as non-political.

The most important opposition to BJP's love for the U.C.C. has come from the Prime Minister in power to declare that:

> "We are not going to interfere in the personal laws of any community; it is not the agenda of the Government to do anything against the existing traditions of the various communities. These are strictly personal laws of the communities and I cannot bring any uniformity" said the then Prime Minister Mr. P.V. Narasimha Rao. "It is not at all practical to force them to change those traditions overnight. It was not a matter of concern for the Hindus and the Muslims as it was purely a personal affair, not a legal one. Can I dare to change

such things without the will of the people", he asked (i.e. 28/7/95).

The failure of the political parties to convince all sections of religious communities for having a Uniform Civil Code for all citizens envisages a duty and responsibility on the leaders of religious groups to reform their personal laws in conformity to the egalitarian provisions of the constitution.

The Christian minority community has already initiated an open debate on the uniform civil code. The church leaders gave positive response atleast to continue the debate within the church and the society. The laity has been made aware on the subject of the uniform civil code. In spite of some differences of opinion among the church leaders there seems to be no visible resistance or annoyance against the U-C-C. There is discussion on demand for changes in the Christian Personal Laws within the community forums. The case of Muslim community is different. The representatives of the community in the Constituent Assembly appreciated the ideal of uniform civil code but opposed it on religious grounds. Even today our religious leaders instigate the Muslim masses, against the provision on political plane with the same zeal of Hinduatva force who are now resolved to implement the Article 44 of the Indian Constitution. The orthodox Hindus and Muslims are aggressively opposed to each other in this regard. There is no voice of reform in personal laws for Muslim community.

The Parsees form a very small minority community in the country and they have their personal laws. They had codified their Marriage and Divorce Act as early as 1865 (Act No. XV of 1865) and amended it in 1936 (Act No. III of 1936). The Scheduled Tribes of the country have their own Tribal Laws which are excluded from the purview of Hindu Personal Laws within the meaning of clause (25) of Article 366 of the Constitution. The other religious communities namely the Buddhists, the Jains and the Sikhs are covered under the Hindu Personal Laws, which have been reformed through Hindu Code Bill. The reforms in Hindu Personal Laws were made by Hindus themselves, "No other community from outside tried to influence the course of reform within the Hindu Community," says KG Kannabiran.

As pointed out ealier the essential character of all Indian personal laws is religious and they are based on scriptures, customary rites, usages and ceremonies. The Hindu Marriage Act, 1955 (Act No. XXV of 1955) as amended by Act 2 of 1978 is not a secular piece of legislation and therefore fails to inspire any reforms in the personal laws of other communities. The personal laws are very important cultural ethos of Indian secular state. They deserve to be retained in the statute books but in the modified form.

Let us see again the community movement for reforms in personal laws of Christian community. A woman leader of that community declared:

> "As Christian woman we need to highlight changes required in the Christian personal laws, Marriage, Divorce, Succession and Adoption. This is necessary in the light of our Christian understanding of justice"

before the most enlightened gathering of National consultation of Christian women leaders jointly organised by Catholic Bishop's Conference of India (CBCI), Women's Desk and All India Association for Christian Higher Education (AIACHE) held at Bangalore in May 1993. It was said in the presence of Archbishop Alan De Lastic, Bishop Bosco Penha, Archbishop Alphonsus Mathias. The lady leader also said:

> "If we are to begin to act—to influence the social process at various levels—the only instrument is raising collective voice leading to collective action, even if it means combating leadership in our own country and church."

However, by this we do not mean that the church leadership accepts the changes in Christian Personal Laws as pointed out by the lady leader, "but at the same time"; said Archbishop Alan De Lastic, "I fully support the freedom, the spontaneity with which their views were expressed." The reasonable understanding of voice of dissent by religious leadership of the community opens the door for reformation.

And this has been happening in Christian minorities. Let us wait for the outcome.

In Muslim society there are large number of victims of certain inadequate and outdated provisions of personal laws. The Dissolution of Muslim Marriages Act, 1939 (Act No. 8 of 1939) consolidates and clarifies the provisions of Muslim Law relating to suits for dissolution of marriage by women married under Muslim Law. A Muslim married woman shall be entitled to obtain a decree for the dissolution of her marriage on several grounds to be proved before the judge. Even for a cruel husband she has to wait for seven years or more if the ground is sentence to imprisonment U/s 2 (iii) and if the ground is for disappearance of husband for four years she has to wait for him $4^1/_2$ years. Hundreds of Muslim women want divorce from their husbands but they do not divorce them for fear of loosing maintenance for minor children and wife for *iddat* period and giving back dowry and gifts to wife received by the husband from wife at the time of marriage. The provisions of Muslim Woman (Rights on Divorce) Act 1986 Section 125 of CrPC, Section 498-A of IPC check Muslim husbands from divorcing their wives, but for habitual assaults and cruelties.

On the other hand the Muslim husband can divorce his wife at his will without the intervention of a court.....The wife cannot divorce herself from her husband without his consent. The Muslim law of divorce is very peculiar as held by the courts: "If the words of divorce used by the husband are "express", the divorce is valid even if it was pronounced under compulsion, or in a state of voluntary intoxication, or to satisfy his father or some one else." However the Shia Law considers this divorce invalid. The Muslim law of divorce is so powerful that it can defeat an order made against husband U/s 125 CrPC for maintenance of his wife. It does not provide any punishment for violators of laws. It ultimately encourages male dominance of worst kind.

Therefore, this law needs to be reformed, codified and made uptodate by the religious-leaders of Muslim Personal Law Board and it be enacted by the Parliament.

The process of reforms should start right now, and such subjects be specified as marriage (polygamy be made permissible subject to strict conditions), the right of divorce should not be a unilateral affair, the maintenance of Muslim wife and children should be reasonable. And any other matter of public interest which the religious leaders consider necessary to be reformed. This will create a goodwill among all sections of society and pave the way for Muslim progress.

10

Women's Presence in the Mosque : A Viewpoints

Diane D'Souza

Over the last three years the question of Muslim women's participation in congregational prayers and their entry into the mosque has become, if not a "sensational debate,"[1] at least an issue receiving some national attention.[2] In this paper I review and analyze the arguments of both those who support women's presence in the mosque and those who oppose it. I will also look briefly at how ordinary Indian Muslim women regard the issue. One assumption I question is the equation of women's participation in Friday prayers with gender parity: is women's entry into the mosque really a victory? And if so, for whom? I suggest that the larger issue in the debate is not whether women join men for worship in a place many of them see as male-centred, but the control of women's religious expression generally.

Reaching the Headlines

It was women's participation in congregational prayers at the Palayam Jama' Masjid in Kerala's capital city of Trivandrum that gave national attention to the issue of women's entry into the mosque. Although women have been praying for some time at various mosques in different regions of the country,[3] their participation generally has not been widespread.[4] The popular notion among many Indians that women never go to the mosque also lent the reporting of the incident a revolutionary feel.[5]

The man seen as behind the move was the chief *imam* of the mosque, P.K.K. Ahmed Kutty Mawlvi, a fifty-six year old "active supporter" of the Jama'at-i-Islami,[6] a religious reform movement started by Abul a'la Mawdudi in 1941. P.K.K. Ahmed Kutty was no stranger to controversy. Nearly twenty years before he had caused consternation by suggesting that the community take the assistance of a local astronomical observatory in sighting the new moon rather than using the naked eye for this critical task.[7] He was also reportedly one of the first *imams* to encourage the use of the local language, Malayalam, rather than Arabic as the medium for giving the weekly sermon at the mosque.[8]

The opposition to his latest move, encouraging women's participation in congregational prayers, was strong. The religious leaders of the two hundred and eighty three *jama* 'at (congregation; sing. *jama'* at) in the district met and formed an Imams' Council. A *fatwah* (opinion or judgement by a religious authority) was then delivered, calling the move "un-Islamic" and "unauthorized by the Holy Scriptures."[9] The body also argued that none of the four major law schools allowed for women's participation in mosque prayers. Protests continued, including a *dharna* in front of the mosque staged by the Sunni Yuvajana Sangham, another public protest by "conservatives" on the eve of the Bakrid festival, a denunciation of those who supported the move by the Samastha Kerala Sunni Student's Federation,[10] and a "door to door" campaign to warn people about the "negative consequences" of permitting women to pray inside mosque organized by a section of Sunni 'ulama' in Mallapuram and Kozhikode districts. Still, women continued to attend in considerable numbers, especially for Friday congregational prayers.[11]

To better understand this controversy and its implications, we need to look at the arguments used on various sides of the debate, as well as the assumptions which underlie them. One set of assumptions concerns the place of the mosque in the Muslim community and the requirements for congregational prayers. We will start, then, with a brief overview of this aspect of Muslim life.

A Place for Assembly and Prayer

Most Muslims are well aware that no special hallowed ground is needed for worship. The Prophet reportedly said, "The earth is a mosque for you, so pray wherever you happen to be when prayer time comes."[12] Still, the Muslim community has traditionally given value to a place of assembly where mundane affairs as well as prayer can be conducted, whether it be the majestic Masjid al-haram at Makkah or Prophet Muhammad's simple mosque-cum-home in Madinah.[13] The word "mosque" comes from the Arabic work *masjid* the noun form of *sajdah*—meaning a "place where one prostrates oneself in worship".[14] The Qur'an calls mosqueas:

> .... houses of worship which God has allowed to be raised, and His name remembered in them. His praises are sung there morning and evening, by men (*rijalun*) who are not distracted from the remembrance of God by trade and commerce or buying and selling, who stand by their devotional obligations and pay the *zakat*, who fear the day when hearts and eyes would flutter with trepidation that God may reward them for the best of their deeds and bestow more on them of His bounty.[15]

In addition to being a place for offering the daily prayers (*namaz* or *salat*), the mosque serves a number of other functions: providing a place for children to learn the rudiments of their faith, most importantly how to read and recite the Qur'an; offering a stopping place for travellers; and providing a meeting place for formal or informal discussion of local events or matters of importance to the community. Besides the daily *namaz*, spiritual activities at the mosque may also include non-obligatory prayers, the recitation of the Qur'an, *dhikr* (the repetitive praising of God), and the recitation of melodious pious poetry such as *qasidah* or *na'at.* During the fasting month of Ramazan, men may spend a number of days in retreat there, many others join for the special *tarawih* prayers.[16]

Once a mosque is built it becomes obligatory, according to Sunni Muslim legal opinion, for the five daily prayers to be offered there by congregation. Although most 'ulama' agree that any given individual need not offer all their prayers in a mosque, most see the community members as having a responsibility to seeing that a congregation offers prayers there daily at the five appointed times.[17] There is general consensus that attendance is required at the Friday *zuhr* (mid-afternoon) prayers, which most commonly include a sermon along with the regular ritual prayer.

According to expressed legal opinion, among those exempted from fulfilling the duty for congregational prayer are women.[18] We will look in detail at reasons for this exemption, and one opinion on how it came into being, in a later section. Here it is sufficient to note that there is general agreement on most sides of the current debate in the Indian context that women, unlike men, are not *required* to join the congregation for Friday prayers. The issue then, is that of women's optional participation.

Before concluding this part of the discussion, it is important to note that attitudes and practices vary considerably among Muslims. For example, among Ithna 'Ashari Shi'ahs, the mosque has a relatively less important place than among Sunnis, particularly given the existence of the central Shi'i meeting place-cum-shrine known as an *'ashurkhanah* or *imambarah*. For Khoja Muslims, the *jama 'at khanah* is an essential gathering place where both men and women participate in the prayers, recitations and sermons, as well as in social events.

Whatever the variation among different communities, however, we find that, with few exceptions the mosque is commonly described as having a "central" place within Muslim society.[19] Is this an accurate description? If one visits mosques across the Muslim world, one is often struck by the relative scarcity of women.[20] In India, even in mosques where there is no restriction on their participation, women's absence is particularly visible. Is it true, to say that the mosque is the special centre of Muslim religious life? If so, one must ask, for whom is it the centre? Or, more to the point, who defines the centre? We will return to this important point in the conclusion of this paper. For now, let us turn to look at different positions on the debate regarding women's participation in congregational prayers, starting with a feminist viewpoint.

The Feminist Viewpoint

In her book *The Forgotten Queens of Islam*, Morrocan feminist and sociologist Fatima Mernissi argues that gradually, over time, women were declared "strangers to the place of worship." She calls this a "betrayal of the Prophet," whose mosque in Madinah was "open to all, welcoming all those interested in Islam, including women."[21], Mernissi traces the writings of various authoritative *imams* down through the centuries to demonstrate how this happened.

In the *Kitab al-Jum'ah* (Book of Friday) of Imam Bukhari—written two centuries after the death of the Prophet—we find what Mernissi calls a "famous" *hadith:* "do not forbid the mosques of Allah to the women of Allah."[22] A century later, Imam Nisa'i, wrote his book of traditions in which, Mernissi notes, he never forgot to give directions for arrangements between men and women during prayers. In his chapter on *"al-masjid",* for example, he gives specifications for the rows of men and women: how crowded they may be and how far from each other. The problem, according to him, is to regulate the coexistence of the sexes in the mosque and not to forbid it, as happened later.[23]

Imam Nisa'i, Mernissi records, first reminds his readers that "the Prophet said that saying one's prayers in the mosque is worth a thousand prayers said elsewhere, with the exception of the Ka'ba." He also adds that the best way to wash away sin is to go to the mosque. Therefore, concludes Imam Nisa'i, quoting the words of the Prophet a man has no right to forbid his wife's participation in community prayers. He goes on to note that the Prophet only ever forbade access to the mosque to people who came smelling of garlic or onions.

Moving her investigation forward three more centuries, Mernissi look at the writings of the Hanbali *imam* Ibn al-Jawzi (d. 597 A.H.) who wrote a chapter on "Women's Services" in his book on the laws governing women in Islam (*Kitab ahkam al-Nisa*). Here, Mernissi notes, we find the seeds of misogyny being sown. Although he could not deny women's right to attend congregational prayers—the *hadith* being, in Mernissi's words, "incontrovertible"-Ibn al-Jawazi took four critical steps which created doubt:

* He said the prayers of men who are seated behind women are worthless. This, speculates Mernissi, arose in the context of men coming to the mosque late and being blocked by women who had arrived on time. She notes, "It is very easy to imagine the fatal next step: ban women from the mosque, since the mere presence of women risked creating a problem."
* He asked, "Is it permitted for women to go to the mosque?" (even to pose this question is, according to Mernissi, a "betrayal of the ancient texts."). Al-Jawzi's answer: "If she fears disturbing men's minds, it is better for her to pray at home" (giving women, quips Mernissi, a "distressing responsibility").
* He concludes from the *hadith* which says not to forbid women the mosques of God, that "the Friday service is not a duty for them."
* He dwells at length on the need for women to avoid going out, implying that it is a dangerous and impious act for women.[24]

The practice of denying women access to the mosque soon became widespread, and then institutionalized. Mernissi cites the twentieth century Indian scholar Muhammad Sadiq al-Qannuji (d. 1308 A.H.) who quoted in his chapter on "What has been said on the Friday service not being a duty for women," the "dubious hadith" (Mernissi's words): "The Friday service is a duty for all Muslims, with four exceptions: slaves, women, children and the ill." According to Mernissi :

This is betrayal of Muhammad's ideal community: women are declared strangers to the place of worship. Women, who had the privilege of access to the mosque as *sahabiyyat*, companions of the

Prophet, very quickly became the polluting, evil beings they had been in the *jahiliyyah*, the pre-Islamic era. From the ashes of that era was reborn a misogyny whose roots reached deep down into archaic fears of femaleness and ignored the Prophet's endeavours to exorcize them by insisting on the necessity for the Muslim man to share everything with his wife. The biography of the Prophet, the *Sira,* always shows him carrying out with his wives the two most important acts of Islam from its very beginning: praying and making war. Not only will there be the fabrication of false *hadith* that exclude women from worship. Memory will be custom-tailored to show that the appearance of women in the mosque brings disorder and turpitude.[25]

Mernissi concludes her foray into history with an impassioned plea to uncover the marginalized voices of not only women, but also peasants and the poor. It is, she suggests, the currents of resistance and counter-resistance from these quarters which are never reflected in Islam's official discourse.[26]

In Fatima Mernissi, then, we find a woman's re-reading of history: a tracing of the path of women's marginalization through a critical selection and re-assessment of *hadith*. In her analysis, the ground has shifted from what Islam does or does not say, to who has said what on behalf of Islam and for what purpose.[27] The importance of recovering women's history is part of feminist agenda; a necessary move to counteract attempts to legitimize women's subordination.[28] We hear a similar echo in the words of a December 1995 resolution from the All India Democratic Women's Association: "The Holy Koran is considered as the divine revelation by Muslims and is therefore sacrosanct. But the interpretation of the Koran and the Hadith is not."[29]

Women Have a Right

Not all those who argue for women's participation in prayers at the mosque see themselves as feminists. However, a common element which unites those who seek women's equality on this issue is the use of examples taken from the time of the Prophet to buttress an argument.[30] These stories, recorded through the *hadith* or "traditions," are particularly important given that the primary source of guidance—the Qur'an—provides no clear direction on this particular question.[31] Muslim scripture endorses men's and women's equal responsibility in carrying out prescribed religious duties, as well as their equal treatment by God in receiving reward or punishment for their action.[32] But it does not shed direct light on whether it is better for women to pray in their homes or at a gathering place for the whole community.[33]

As already noted, those who argue for women's right to pray in the mosque inevitably use as their point of reference the earliest days of Muslim history. Thus, for example, Ernakulam-based Justice P.K. Shamsuddeen, in explaining why he supports women's entry to the mosque, notes that, "Women had the freedom to go to mosques even at the Prophet'stime."[34] South Asian scholar C. M. Naim goes into greater detail, quoting the following *hadith:*

Abd Ali b. Umar reported the Prophet (may peace be upon him) as saying: Allow women to visit the mosques at night. A son of his (Bilal) said: "I swear by Allah, we shall certainly not allow them because they will defraud." He (ibn Umar) abused him and became angry at him and said: "I tell you that the Apostle of God (may peace be upon him) said: Allow them; yet you say: we shall not allow them."[35]

Naim notes that the Pakistani university professor who translated the volume containing this *hadith* included the comment: "...[the son's] interpretation might be correct but his tone and response were audacious." Naim challenges the implication that women do not belong in the mosque, attributing it to the obsessive fear that some inherent evil lurks within all women. This fear, he points out, persisted across fourteen centuries of Islamic history. Naim then goes on to briefly address the question of woman's right to be an *imam*, again using the *hadith* as a primary source to strengthen his argument.[36]

A number of supporters of women's right to enter the mosque argue similarly, including Basheer Hussain, Professor at Bangalore's Government Law College, and Mawlana Ryazur Rehman, *imam* of that city's Jama' Masjid.[37] The *hadith* they cite as proof of their interpretation are numerous and differ in context. Some, for example, refer to: women leaving before men from the mosques, or women leaving the mosque clothed in outer garments which kept them from being recognized, or women praying behind the men of her household, or women keeping their heads lowered in prayer until men raised theirs in order to preserve modesty, or occasions on which the Prophet advised women to refrain from using scent or to keep their dress and ornaments simple when coming to the mosque.[38] In all these different *hadith* it is clear that women were praying in the mosque during the time of the Prophet.

"Let Women Come, But...."

Although some Muslims argue unreservedly for women's place in the mosque, others adopt a more provisional view. In fact, some of those who acknowledge women's right, encourage, women not to make use of it. In a letter to the editor of the popular *Radiance Viewsweekly,* Waheed H. Hashmi of Hyderabad writes that women have a right to offer their prayers at a mosque, including during the congregational prayer time, as long as they occupy a place from where they cannot be seen by men. The writer adds, however, that women should not go because "mixed congregations of both sexes tend to breed evil thoughts in human minds.[39]

This is also the opinion of Abdussattar Yusuf Shaikh, the Secretary of the conservative All India Muslim Personal Law Board. Abdussatar Yusuf admits that the practice of women praying at the mosque is not "un-Islamic" but it is better if women stay in *pardah* and pray at home.[40] He expands on his argument by saying that a women who prays at home is worthy of greater spiritual reward than one who prays in a mosque. This, Abdussattar Yusuf states uncategorically, is the opinion of the Prophet. The only time the value of the prayer's blessing changes, he adds, is at the Muslim world's two major mosques. One prayer at the *masjid al-haram* in Makkah is equivalent to one lakh prayers elsewhere, and performing the *namaz* at Prophet Muhamad's mosque in Madinah is just like performing fifty thousand prayers in an ordinary mosque. These special blessings, Abdussattar

Yusuf says, are the reason for the "relaxation" of the general policy of exclusion in these locations.

One influential person from whose writings men like Abdussattar Yusuf perhaps draw is the Indian founder of the Jam a 'at-Islami, Mawlana Abu a' la Mawdudi (d.1979 C.E.). In Mawdudi's popular book *Purdah and the Status of Woman in Islam,* he devotes a full chapter to "Divine laws for the movements of women."[41] The segregation of women is a main feature in Mawdudi's strategy for avoiding the "tragic" social consequences of modernity and secularization. Moreover, it is a strategy which he defines as quintessentially Islamic.[42]

In the section titled "Permission to visit the mosque", Mawdudi explains that God's commands for "the foremost obligatory duty in Islam" differ between men and women. Prayers offered in congregation are the best prayers for men, while to pray at home in seclusion is the best for women. He quotes a *hadith* from the collections of Imam Ahmed and Tabarani to buttress his point:

> [Umm Humaid Sa'idiyyah] said, "O Prophet of Allah. I desire to offer prayers under your leadership." The Holy Prophet said, "I know that; but your offering a prayer in a corner is better than offering it in your closet; and your offering the prayer in your closet is better than offering it in the courtyard of your house; and your offering the prayers in the courtyard is better than your offering it in the neighbouring mosque; and your offering it in the neighbouring mosque is better than your offering it in the biggest mosque of the town."[43]

Mawdudi argues that since God gives greater favour to women when they pray at home and to men when they pray in the mosque, God's "real intention" is to prevent the mixing of the sexes. He concedes, however, that women have been permitted to come to the mosques. In expanding on this he cites not only Bukhari's famous *hadith* quoted earlier, but also another version of that *hadith,* this one recorded by Abu Daud. The difference between the two lies in the significant concluding line: "Do not prevent your women from coming to the mosque, though their houses are better for them".

This small but vital difference—the inclusion of little more than half a dozen words—completely changes the tenor of the Prophet's statement. Women may go to the mosque, but "their houses are better for them." In her study of the issues surrounding women and the mosque in India, Vijaya Kumari notes that most of those who argue against women's participation in public prayer, cite the latter half of this particular *hadith* as the reason for their position.

Conditions of Participation of Women

Those like Mawdudi who provisionally acknowledge women's right to be included among the worshippers at a mosque note that there are certain conditions for their participation. These include:

* Women joining the congregational prayers only under the cover of darkness, when the lack of light serves as an aid to their *hijab* (this is exempted for the Friday prayers).
* Women refraining from coming to the mosque with either perfume or decorations—including fancy clothes.
* Women avoiding mixing with men. They are not to stand in the front rows, but must always stand separately behind the rows of men.
* Women avoid raising their voices during the prayer. Unlike men, who may correct any errors of the *imam* with a word, women in such an event should only tap their hands.[44]

Mawdudi supports each of the above conditions with references from the *hadith*.

Uzma Naheed, Mumbai-based member of the All India Muslim Personal Law Board, echoes Mawdudi's interpretation. She expresses reservation about women going to the mosque for prayers, although she grants that it may in some ways be a "very good step, an Islamic step." Her concern is that women who exercise the right to pray in the mosque without the true spirit of worship *(ibadat)*, will destroy the very purpose of praying.

This happened in some *Jama'ats* in India where this right already exists. Women come to pray decked up with jewellery and full make-up. Often boys and girls decide their future [on whom to marry or not to marry] here. Surely this is not the purpose of this step.[45]

Naheed recommends that to offset this danger, certain precautions must be taken. She recommends separate arrangement be made for women; for example, a separate mosque entrance, space for women to pray in the back rows or in a separate room, or at least have a cloth curtain to separate men from women.[46] A recommendation that such special arrangements be made in all mosques was put forward by the newly formed Muslim Women's Council, Delhi. In its December 1998 seminar on "The problems of Muslim women in a changing modern society", the body also resolved to ask the All India Muslim Personal Law Board to take initiatives to reach an Indian-wide consensus on the contentious issue of women praying at the mosque.

So far we have encountered Muslims who argue for either full or provisional participation of women in community prayers. Given the clear evidence of women's presence in the mosque during Prophet Muhammad's lifetime, it is difficult to imagine the basis on which some Muslims argue that the practice is un-Islamic or should be stopped. In the next section we will analyze the writings and arguments of two *imams* who have clearly opposed women joining men for the congregational prayers.

In her Master's thesis on women and the mosque, Vijaya Kumari draws our attention to arguments advanced by two Hyderabadi *imams* whose unpublished papers on this issue were written and circulated as an elaboration of their earlier *fatwa*.[47] I will focus on only two of the points which Mufti Shakeel Ahmad Rahmani and Mawlana Khaleel Saifullah Rahmani raise to explain why it is better for women to pray at home.[48]

The first is a fairly common argument; namely, that during the lifetime of the Prophet, society was "more righteous." Mawlana Khaleel Saifullah Rahmani notes that during those early days, men responded and took care of "unlawful acts" in society. This is no longer the case. Who now, he laments, will be responsible for safeguarding the modesty of women? He expresses his doubts that the management committee of a mosque can prevent "any kind of mischief" from taking place within their precincts. Look at the incidents already taking place in the markets and bazaars when women go shopping, or at *dargahs* (shrines) or other places of religious gatherings. Who can guarantee women's lives if they come to attend congregational prayers at the mosque? It is far better, he urges, if women do not go out in the first place.[49]

A similar argument is used by Haroon Rashid, the editor of *Inquilab Daily,* who favours women s presence at congregational prayers provided "the right social atmosphere" exists, Rashid notes that it is the responsibility of men to create a conducive atmosphere where, for example, women would not be teased or harassed by men. If such social problems cannot be contained, he warns, it is advisable for women to stay away from the mosque.[50]

This argument is not new. Valerie Hoffman-Ladd points out that the medieval Muslim theologian al-Ghazzali (d. 1111 C.E.) saw the "popular ban" on women's participation as justified given the "widespread moral degeneration" which rendered public spaces unsafe for all but elderly women.[51] Hoffman-Ladd goes further. Drawing on ethnographic studies from different countries, she identifies a widespread belief within Muslim communities that somehow women's presence in public is a source of temptation and social discord.[52] "The exclusion of women," she observes, "is thus considered necessary to preserve the holiness and dignity of religious ceremonies."[53]

Both Khaleed Saifullah Rahmani and Shakeel Ahmed Rahmani justify their ban on women praying in the mosque by quoting a *hadith,* reportedly narrated by Aisha, which cements their argument about the historical deterioration of moral values since the time of the Prophet. They note that the youngest wife of the Prophet herself commented:

> If the Prophet had seen the innovations *(bid'ah)* that women had included in their lives, he would have stopped them from going to mosques. The women of Bani Israel were prevented from visiting places of worship by the early prophets for a similar reason.[54]

This, then is a more subtle argument against women being allowed inside the mosque. It is the hard-hitting accusation of innovation *(bid 'ah)* which is the main focus here. For many Muslims, *bid 'ah* is equivalent to unbelief, for departing from the way *(sunnah)* of the Prophet it is worthy of complete approbation. This *hadith* suggests that the reason for women's ban from the mosque rests squarely on women's shoulders. What was it that Aisha was hinting at in her reference to "innovations"? Was it women's behaviour or dress or maybe even a glance that evoked such a severe accusation? Was it real or imagined? In the absence of any elaboration, one is limited only by one's imagination.

Of course, one of the crucial aspects in the current debate centres on the acceptability of the *hadith* literature. Not all Muslims accept the hundreds of traditions recorded and collected by earlier scholars. Some will regard only certain collections as valid, while others speak of strong and weak *hadith,* referring to the likeliness of their being true and accurate reporting of the Prophet and his times. The debate is large and complex and well beyond the scope of our discussion here. I would simply note, however, that as wholeheartedly as Shakeel Ahmed Rahmani argues for the importance of Aisha's remarks about women and *bid'ah,* Fatima Mernissi argues just as wholeheartedly that it, and many other *hadith,* are fabrications devised to support men's misogynist views.

Muslim religious practice is most commonly described in terms of five major "pillars": the confession of faith *(shahada),* ritual prayer, fasting *(saum),* alms-giving *(zakat)* and pilgrimage *(hajj)*. Yet, among these prescibed activities, women's unrestricted personal participation is possible in only two: the recitation of the *shahadah,* and the paying of alms (assuming, in the case of the latter, that the woman is earning or is responsible for her family's finances).[55] Women learn that they cannot touch the Qur'an or recite its words during their menses and immediately after giving birth since blood from the womb is considered ritually unclean. For this reason, women are excused on those occasions from performinng their prayers or observing the fast. Women are also not permitted to perform the *hajj* unless accompanied by a husband, male relative or guardian. When they do make the journey, although men and women mix together, during the congregational prayers women, as always are confined to the periphery. Even women's exemption from the mandatory symbolic dress of pilgrimage *ihram* is, in the opinion of anthropologist Carol Delaney, a symbol of the clear gender biased "brotherhood" of Islam.[56]

In other words, when we lock from the perspective of women, we find Islam's defining practices somewhat less than normative. I would like to suggest that, in the same way, the mosque does not have the same meaninng for many Mus im women as it does for men. When Vijaya Kumari interviewed a diverse sampling of women in Hyderabad, she heard it commonly said that, whether at mosque or home, the rewards for performing one's prayers were the same. Most of the women seemed uninterested in attending congregational prayers, explaining that domestic responsibilities kept them too busy. Although many felt that their religion either did not require them to attend, or actively forbade their presence, there seemed to be little inclination to claim what they clearly saw as a male space. As Vijaya Kumari recalls, "When I raised the question about their desire to attend Friday prayers in the mosque, most of the interviewers [sic.] did not show their desire to go... ."

I once asked a woman who had been active in the building and running of an all-women's *'ashurkhana* whether she thought Shi'ah woman would ever unite in a similar way to establish a mosque. Her reply and its accompanying chuckle were dismissive: "Mosques are for men." My friend could not imagine women having any interest in such a project.[57]

Perhaps the reason many Muslim women feel disinclined to attend the mosque is that, with few exceptions, it remains a male-dominated space. For example,

* Women are situated behind the men or in partially or wholly secluded areas literally on the margins of the mosque;
* Men command the mosque's leadership role (the common

understanding being that women cannot hold the position of *imam*);

- Men deliver the *khutbah* at the Friday congregational prayer,[58] on at least some occasions using the opportunity to espouse misogynist interpretations of Islam;[59]
- Religious authorities *('ulama)* teach that women are to be silent during prayer,[60] effectively curtailing their voices in discussions of matters concerning the community as a whole.

Moreover, women's presence in the mosque becomes an occasion for men to try to "correct" women's religious knowledge. In an editorial entitled "Needless Paranoia," the editors of the Indian monthly *Islamic Voice* argue,

> Women's participation in collective prayers in mosques is expected to enhance their role in community affairs. Congregational sermons could equally benefit them and throw light on their special responsibilities. It is also likely to expediate universal acceptance of *Hijab* [modest dress, veiling] and may even bring uniformity in its form. It was women's participation in daily prayers that made headscarves the common denominator of the Muslim sartorial scene in the United States. Five-time prayers in the mosques could also obviate the need for seeking alternatives for satisfaction of instincts for social intermingling among the womenfolk.[61]

For some men, then, encouraging women to come to the mosque opens up opportunities to spread ideas of segregation and veiling, to draw attention to women's primary role as wife and mother, and to provide an alternative to women's visits to *dargahs* and other places of meeting. In other words, it gives a chance for men to have more say in the space women inhabit, as well as to influence their religious understandings and expressions.[62]

Given these factors, it is little wonder the women with whom Vijaya Kumari spoke gave excuses why they could not attend the mosque prayers. Perhaps for women, sensing a sphere of greater marginalization and increased control by men, the more empowering course is to choose non-participation. Remaining at home—or even working outside the home—women have the power to direct and shape their own religious and social expression.[63] Although in many cases this power may not be comprehensive or complete it nevertheless offers, in at least one aspect of women's lives, comparatively greater control.

Some Conclusions

This study focuses on women's participation in prayers at the mosque, starting with a recap of the event which brought the question to national attention, and a summary discussion of the place of the mosque in the Muslim community. It then explores various perspectives on this issue including those offered by people who see the practice as inherent to Islam and others who argue for a restriction or complete curtailment of women's attendance at the mosque. The larger questions are particularly significant here, for example, that the view of the mosque as central to Muslim religious life is a male perspective which does not find its echo in many women's perceptions. I also point out that women's participation in the rituals at the mosque as a marginalized group within the larger community can also have costs, since at least some of the men see the occasion as an opportunity to "correct" women's ideas and behaviour, bringing them more in line with conservative interpretations of the faith. In other words, just ensuring that women have "equal rights" to enter the mosque does not necessarily guarantee women's equal partnership with men. In fact, it may signal an opportunity for encouraging even greater restrictions on how women see their lives and their own religious expression.

Finally, should we conclude from their relative absence from the mosque that religion is unimportant for most Muslim women? My own research suggests that the problem lies not so much in women failing to see spirituality as important. It was women's spiritual practices being seen by others as somehow less than "pure religion". That women's religious practices are crucial to their lives—at least in South Asia—is clear from a 1988 Pakistani study on "Women,

Religion and Social Change". Commenting on what she calls "one of the significant" findings of that study, activist Farida Shaheed notes that for the more than four hundred Pakistani women interviewed for her study, prayer, ritual and other religious practices emerged as some of women's most powerful strategies for survival. This finding, she notes, cut across region, class, economic circumstance, and community group. Shaheed explains that religion operates on different levels: personal faith, social customs, as well as a mobilizing force in the political arena, where it can be used either to legitimize existing structures and relations or to challenge them. Religion also operates as a means of self-identity and provides a source of identification with one's environment. She writes:

> In sharp contrast to that strain of feminist analysis—both within and outside Pakistan—that sees religion as a major source of women's oppression, women themselves do not view everyday experiences of religion as either oppressive or a factor of constraint... The extent to which religion is internalized can be gauged from the failure of women in the study to mention any religious activities when describing their daily routines. The integration of religion into women's routine appeared far more dramatically in response to direct questions on religious practices, indicating that rituals and practices—as much as household responsibilities, childcare, agriculture or care for livestock, studies or a job—shape and structure a woman's day in Pakistan, irrespective of whether she is a Christian, Hindu, Parsee, or Muslim, or whether she lives in a rural or urban setting, is poor or rich.[64]

Shaheed observes that religion allows women a level of social interaction which, for most women, is "unsanctioned and unattainable" in other forms. Yet, Shaheed argues, it is more than the social aspect which makes women welcome religious events:

> Many women expressed a sense of communion and peace in praying which, even forgetting for the moment the spiritual/ psychological aspects, provides adherents a break from their

> daily routines and chores, allowing women space which is theirs absolutely. It is in its capacity to provide self-affirmation at the personal psychological level as well as that of the social collectivity that religion is unique. Through its rituals, practices, and structures, religion provides a feeling of participation and belonging in the most immediate sense, unavailable to vast numbers of women in other aspects of their lives.[65]

It is not likely, then, that women, at least in South Asia, will choose to abandon spiritual practices which both give their lives meaning and provide occasions for empowering interactions. Whether they can find such sustenance in congregational prayers is still questionable.

REFERENCES

1. N.V. Vijaya Kumari's assessment. See her "Religious Participation of Women in the Mosque," unpublished M.Th. dissertation. Senate of Serampore College, March 1999, p. 75.

2. Interestingly, Barbara Freyer Stowasser seems to imply in her brief reference to the broader Muslim debate on this issue that it was an "ongoing debate" only during medieval times. See her *Women in the Qur'an, Traditions and Interpretations* (Oxford: Oxford University Press, 1994) p. 163, note. 103.

3. For example, in a letter to the editor titled "What's New?" A. Iqbal Ahmed of Tiruchy notes that "separate praying places for women are common in several mosques, especially in Tamil Nadu. For Ramazan prayers, in almost all mosques...." *Communalism Combat*, Mar. 1977, p. 22. C.M. Naim recalls at least "one or two" women always being present at various congregational prayers in Uttar Pradesh in the 1940s and '50s; see his article "Don't leave it to the men," *Communalism Combat*, Mar. 1998, p. 39. Uzma Naheed reports that women "regularly" pray at mosques in Kashmir; see her interview in *Communalism Combat*, Feb. 1997, p. 3. I myself have observed women praying at a number of mosques in a very small minority.

4. Most notable among the exceptions to this are Khoja and Bohra communities.

5. For example, the front page of the February issue of *Communalism Combat* highlighted the issue with the headline, "In Allah's home at last".

6. Information about his connection to the Jama'at was gleaned through Jose Abraham's 1998 interview with the present *imam* P.K. Hamza Farooki. See Kumari, *op. cit.*, p. 66 By September 1998, P.K.K. Ahmed Kutty had been "transferred" from the Palayam Jama Masjid to another mosque.

7. The Muslim calendar is a lunar one, the appearance of the new moon signaling

the start of a new month. This sighting assumes particular importance when Ramazan, Safar and Muharram begin, for each of these new months is linked with certain religious festivals, observances or attitudes.

8. P.K. Surendran, "Gender parity is a cardinal principle of Islam" *Communalism Combat,* Feb. 1997, p. 3.

9. "Claims for women's entry into mosques," *Communalism Combat,* May 1997, p. 6.

10. "Muslim women and congregational prayers", *Muslim India,* 117 (Mar. 1997), p. 118.

11. When Vijaya Kumari visited during the Friday prayers in September 1998, there were nearly two hundred women present. See Kumari, *op. cit.*, p. 62. That the women continued to gather despite opposition is noteworthy since an earlier attempt to make space for women at the mosque had led to violence and a halting of the practice; see *ibid*, p. 4, 61. The issue eventually went to the Kerala High Court, which in January 1999 ruled in favour of women's entry. For an analysis of the factors contributing to the movement for women's participation at the Palayam mosque, see *ibid.*

12. "Masijd", *The Encyclopaedia of Islam,* new edition, eds. C.E. Bosworth, E. Van Donzel, B. Lewis and Ch. Pellat (Leiden: Brill, 1991), Vol. 6, p. 644. This tradition finds its root in the Qur'anic verse, "To God belong the East and West. Wherever you turn the countenance of God is everywhere: all pervading is He and all knowing" (2:115).

13. For a more complete discussion see "Mosque," *The Oxford Encyclopedia of the Modern Islamic World,* ed. John L. Esposito (Oxford: Oxford University Press, 1995, henceforth Oxford Encyclopedia) Vol. 3, pp.133-151.

14. Muslim, *Sahih Masajid,* quoted in Juan Eduardo Compo's section on "Historical Development", q.v. "Mosque", *Oxford Encyclopaedia.*

15. 24: 36-37. All translations from the Qur'an used in this paper are taken from Ahmed Ali, *Al-Quran: A Contemporary Translation* (Delhi: Oxford University Press, 1987).

16. For an example of guidance about their recommended form, see Altaf A. Kheri, *A Comprehensive Guidebooks of Islam,* rev. ed. (Delhi: Adam Publishers, 1994), pp. 251-53. J. Pedersen (*Encyclopedia of Islam,* q.v. *Masajid*) makes a brief reference to Ibn Battuta's record of "women singers" taking part in the *tarawih* prayers in Delhi during his visit there in the mid-fourteenth century. Unfortunately, I have not been able to pursue this tantalizing reference which may shed some light on gender equations and Indian Muslim practices of the time.

17. See Qazi Thanaa Ullah, *The Essential Hanafi Handbook of Fiqh,* trans. Mawlana Yusuf Talal Ali al-Amriki (New Delhi: Kitab Bhavan, 1963), pp. 60-61. See also Kheri, *op. cit,* pp. 253-254. Legal opinion on the minimum number of people which constitute a congregation differs, ranging from two to forty; Thanaa Ullah, *op. cit.*, p. 85.

18. *Ibid.* Also exempted are children, travellers, slaves, those who are sick and, according to some interpreters, those who are blind.

19. See, for example, articles like "Building a mosque—A divine intention", *Mahjubah,* 17:8 (1988), p. 11. Certainly the premier orientalist reference, *The Encyclopedia of Islam,* makes this assumption in its lengthy article on "Masadjid." N.V.Vijaya Kumari expresses a typical view: "(The mosque) is the center of worship, learning and social activity." From this starting assumption flows the logical extension: "Listening to the Qur'an and to public speeches [in the mosque] influences the social, religious and political life of the community, strengthening its unity. In a sense, then, prohibiting women from entering the mosque is the equivalent of preventing them from participation in the religious and social affairs of the community." Kumari, *op. cit.,* p. 6.

20. There are, of course, exceptions.

21. Fatima Mernissi, *The Forgotten Queens of Islam,* trans. Mary Jo Lakeland (Minneapolis: University of Minnesota Press, 1993), p. 82.

22. See, al-Bukhari, *Sahih al-Bukhari,* trans. Muhammad Muhsin Khan (New Delhi: Kitab Bhavan, 1980), 12:824.

23. Mernissi, *op. cit.,* pp. 80-81.

24. *Ibid.,* pp. 81-82.

25. *Ibid.,* pp. 82-83.

26. *Ibid.,* p. 82. Just as there is a whole range of differing interpretations of Muslim history and scripture, so also there is diversity in attempts to recover women's history. In contrast to Mernissi's picture of a gradual curtailing of women's access to the mosque, Valerie Hoffman-Ladd cites the eleventh century scholar al-Ghazzali, who opined that women were banned altogether from the mosque in the generation after Muhammad. Hoffman-Ladd argues that during Umar's caliphate itself (634-644 C.E.) women began to pray in the mosque in a separate room from men, with their own *imam.*

27. The paraphrased words of an unnamed Iranian feminist quoted in Seema Kazi, "Women Beyond the Veil," *Communalism Combat,* May 1997, p. 23.

28. *Ibid.* For a brief assessment of Mernissi's unique feminist approach to trends in Islamic modernism, see Stowasser, *op. cit.*

29. "Resolution of AIDWA national convention on equal rights, equal laws," *Muslim India,* 14: 161 (May 1996), p. 212.

30. The other common argument, which I do not go into here, is the fact of women's attendance at mosque prayers elsewhere in the Muslim world. P.K.K. Ahmed Kutty Maulvi uses this argument in explaining his decision to allow to join the prayers at the Palayam mosque. He, like a number of others, including Zeenat Shaukatali, Professor of Islamic Studies in Mumbai, notes that even the major mosques at Makkah and Madinah permit women.

31. Not all Muslims see the Qur'an as a complete and single source of guidance.

For example, many Shi'ahs understand the Qur'an's guidance to be perfected through the guidance of the *imams,* while the Ahmadiyya (whom some Muslims regard as non-Muslims), do not see the Qur'an as God's last revelatory act.

32. See for example, 33:35, 9:71-72, 3:19.

33. Vijaya Kumari argues that two indirect references in the Qur'an do suggest that women participate in prayers with men. The first reads (according to her translation by Mohammed Marmaduke Pickthall): "O children of Adam *[ibn-i Adam].* Look to your adornment at every place of worship *[kulli masjidin],* and eat and drink but be not prodigal" (7.31). "Children of Adam", Kumari argues, implies both men and women. Interestingly, a different translator (Ahmed Ali) translates *ibn-i Adam* as "sons of Adam," which is also grammatically correct. The second reference Kumari cites is 62:9, which reads, according to Ahmed Ali's translation: "O you who believe, when the call to prayer is made on the day of congregation, hasten to remember God, putting aside your business..." The "day of congregation" or assembly is Friday. Here, Kumari argues, the general reference to "you who believe" can encompass both men and women, especially given that the Qur'an was revealed "for all times for the entire human race." The problem with this argument is that there are also references to worship in the mosque which unequivocally speak of men (*rijalun*) as those who are present to glorify God's name. See, for example, the earlier cited 24:37. Another difficulty I have with Kumari's argument is that is does not seem to emerge from within a Muslim community or context, thus making it difficult to know whether or not there are Muslims who would agree with her interpretation.

34. "Muslim women and congregational prayers", *Muslim India,* 14:171 (Mar. 1997), p. 118.

35. Naim, *art. cit.,* p. 39.

36. Naim, art. cit., Dr. Tahir Mahmood, Chairman of the National Commission for Minorities, also linked women praying at the mosque to the issue of women's religious leadership generally. In a speech to participants at a women's conference on education, he derided as "alien to Islam" the concept of confining women to their homes. When asked about the legitimacy of women praying at the mosque, he opined that women do not need permission from their menfolk to attend congregational prayers. He went on to encourage women further by citing "Islamic precedents" for women becoming *qazis* and *muthawallis.* See "Call for Muslim Women's University at Chennai" *Islamic Voice,* Jan. 1997, p. 3.

37. See Kumari, *op. cit.,* pp. 42-43.

38. Most of these are reported in *ibid.,* pp. 15-19.

39. "Women in the Mosque", *Radiance Viewsweekly,* 30 Mar.-5 Apr. 1997, p. 25.

40. Interview in *Communalism Combat,* Feb. 1997, p. 2.

41. Stowasser records that the book was translated into Arabic and published in the early sixties under the title *al-Hijab.* It is, she notes, widely available

in the Arab world from a variety of publishing houses and, along with the rest of Mawdudi's writings, has inspired conservatives and fundamentalists all over the Islamic world (*op.cit.*, pp. 127 and 187, note 72).

42. *Ibid., pp.* 127-128.

43. Mawdudi, *op. cit.*, pp. 202-203. He also cites a very similar *hadith* from the collection of Abu Daud. It is worth noting that feminists like Fatima Mernissi would reject this *hadith* as a later accretion. For a fascinating book which offers illuminating examples of modern feminist exegesis see, *For Ourselves: Women Reading the Qur'an* (n.p.: Women Living Under Muslim Laws, 1997).

44. Mawdudi, *op. cit.*, pp. 205-207.

45. Interview in *Communalism Combat*, Feb. 1997, p. 3.

46. This view is also supported by others including the Member of Parliament and Editor of *Muslim India* Syed Shahabuddin. See "Shahabuddin's statement on access of Muslim women to Mosque, 25 Feb. 1997", *Muslim India*, 14:171 (Mar. 1997, p. 118). The well known Nagpur-based theologian Mawlana Abdul Kareem Parekh also stresses that every mosque make such arrangement for the admittance and segregation of women. (Kumari, *op. cit.*, p. 44).

47. Mufti Shakeel Ahmad Rahmani, "Khawatin ka masjidon men namaz ka masla Islami ta' limat ki roshni men," and Mawlana Khaleel Saifullah Rahmani, "The issue of women coming to the mosque , trans. A.R. Khaleel. Both articles were written in Hyderabad in 1998.

48. We have already drawn attention to many of the other issues which these two authors raise, particularly in our discussion of Mawdudi's position. Arguments which they use which we have not yet considered include the observation that women could only gain religious knowledge at the mosque during Muhammad's time, whereas now women have many other options; the fact of women having a God-given responsibility for the domestic household which makes it difficult to take time off to go to the mosque; and the fact that women's "biological problems" earned them a respite from the religious obligation to attend congregational prayers, thus helping to safeguard their modesty. On this latter point, see Mawdudi, *op. cit.* p. 203, note 1.

49. Rahmani, quoted by Kumari, *op. cit*, p. 53.

50. Interview in *Communalism Combat*, Feb. 1997, p. 3. It is interesting that this same argument—society changes, therefore what was true at one point in Muslim history is not necessarily always true is the same argument used by Muslim feminists and others to argue for changes in women's roles and their greater rights in society.

51. Hoffman-Ladd, *art.cit.* p. 327.

52. Stowasser elaborates further on this, recalling the classical argument of women's lower nature, and her power to wreak social anarchy *(fitna); op. cit.*, p. 184, note 45. An interesting rebuttal to such arguments is given by Anees Syed, an Indian Professor of History, who lays the responsibility for

restrictions on women squarely with "dominant male opinon". In her own strong words: "Anyone who says that if women come to pray in mosques it will jeopardise the moral environment should be ashamed of saying so. Women come to the mosque to pray just like men and they have every right to do so. Besides, where in the Qur'an does it say that Muslim women should not be well-dressed, or look presentable? The real problem is not women but the thinking process of men. Segregation is no guarantee against the social ills and problems that so exercise the minds of our men. In so far as any problem is anticipated it is not women so much as men who need to be taught to behave. Islam was the first religion to talk about *masawat* (equality) between the sexes. Anyone who opposes this violates a very basic principle of Islam." See her interview in *Communalism Combat,* Feb. 1997, p. 3.

53. Hoffman-Ladd, *art. cit.,* p. 327. Hoffman-Ladd notes that this is starting to change. Many recently constructed mosques in the Middle East are providing considerably more space for women than earlier ones, a change which she attributes to a widespread Islamic resurgences since the 1970s. She notes however, that women's spaces are still on the peripheries, reinforcing women's marginality to life in the mosque.

54. Quoted by Shakeel Ahmed Rahmani, reproduced in Kumari, *op. cit.,* p. 50.

55. For a brief but well reasoned arguments supporting this point see Valerie J. Hoffman-Ladd's article "Women and Islam: Women's religious observances" in the *Oxford Encyclopedia.*

56. Carol Delaney, "They hajj: Sacred and Secular" *American Ethnologist,* 17 (1990), p. 528, note 19.

57. This is not meant to be universal assessment. Women in different regions have, from time to time, contributed economically to the building or maintaining of mosques. To the best of my knowledge, however, this largely has been an effort confined to the elites.

58. The *Khoja* community is, of course, one exception on this point.

59. As has been related to men on more than one occasion.

60. See, for example, S. Abul A'la Mawdudi, *Purdah and the Status of Women,* trans. and ed. Al-Ash'ari, 3rd ed. (Lahore: Islamic Publications Ltd., 1976), p. 206.

61. March 1997, p. 4.

62. An article in the monthly magazine *Communalism Combat* points out the irony of self-proclaimed "progressive and secular" voices assuming conservative agendas on other fronts. It cites as an example the weekly Urdu tabloid *Jadid Markaz* which projects itself as being on the forefront of the modern sccular movement for pluralism and human rights, yet, on another occasion espouses the "maximum possible *purdah*" for Muslim women. See "Muslim Press and Purdah". May 1996, p. 11. N.P. Chekkuty and Geetesh Sharma make a similar point regarding the *Jama at-i Islami,* which is actively promoting women's presence at congregational prayers (as long as they

observe modesty and the proper dress code), while simultaneously being involved in a "systematic and aggressive" campaign against sufism, one of the areas where Indian women have traditionally found nurturance in expressing their piety. See "The Enemy Within", *Communalism Combat,* March, 1999, pp. 8ff.

63. For examples of the diversity of Muslim women's religious and other rituals, see among many others, Anne Betteridge, "Domestic observances: Muslim practices", *Oxford Encyclopedia,* vol. 1, pp. 404-407; *idem,* "Gift exchange in Iran: The locus of self-identity in social interaction", *Anthropological Quarterly,* 58:4 (1978), pp. 190-202; Lila Abu-Lughod, "Islam and the gendered discourses of death, *International Journal of Middle East Studies,* 25 (1993), pp. 187-205; Mary Hegland, "Shi'a women of northwest Pakistan and agency through practice: Ritual, resistance, resilience," *Political and Legal Anthropology Review,* 18:2 (1995), pp. 65-79; Fatima Mernissi. "Women, saints and sanctuaries," *Signs,* 3 (1977), pp. 101-112; Robert A. Fernea and Elizabeth W. Fernea, "Variations in religious observances among Islamic women," in *Scholars, Saints and Sufis,* ed. Nikki R. Keddi (Berkeley: University of California Press, 1972), pp. 385-401; Pnina Werbner, "Sealing the Koran: Offering and sacrifice among Pakistani labour migrants," *Cultural Dynamics* (1988), pp.77-97.

64. Farida Shaheed, "Networking for change: The role of women's groups in initiating dialogue on women's issues," in *Faith and Freedom: Women's Human Rights in the Muslim World,* ed.Mahnaz Afkhami (Syracuse: Syracuse University Press, 1995), pp. 90-91.

65. Farida Shaheed, "The Other side of the Discourse: Women's Experiences of Identity, Religion and Activism in Pakistan," in *Shaping Women's Lives: Laws, Practices and Strategies in Pakistan,* eds. Farida Shaheed, Sohail A. Warraich, Cassandra Balchin, Aisha Gazdar (Lahore: Shirkat Gah, 1998), p. 431. Shaheed's work in this project is at least partly motivated by the fact that urban based, vocal, middle class activist women tend to "level out" the "very real differences in women's experiences and locations" and impose their own analysis of reality as universal and primary for all women. In the context of women and their relationship with religion, activists have generally dismissed religious commitment and expression as unimportant or actively hurtful to women. See Farida Shaheed's article, "Women, Religion and Social Change in Pakistan: A Proposed Framework for Research-draft," *Women Living Under Muslim Laws: Dossier,* 5/6 (1988/89), pp. 41-44.

Women and the Tablighi Jama'at

Yoginder S. Sikand

From its origins in early twentieth-century north India, the *Tablighi Jama*'at (TJ) has now grown into what is probably the single largest Islamic movement of contemporary times. Writing in 1992, one scholar observed that the movement had a presence in around 165 countries (Faruqi, 1992: 43). It would not be wrong, then, to say that the TJ is today active in almost every country in the world where Muslims live. Despite the obviously great influence that the TJ has on the lives of millions of Muslims throughout the world, scholars have hitherto devoted little attention to it.[1] Even within the existing limited corpus of writings on the TJ, almost no mention has been made of the participation of women in the movement. This paper is an attempt to address this serious lacuna in our understanding of the role of women in the TJ. It does not claim to be a complete account, though, for given the nature of the movement, the subject of women in the TJ can only be properly studied by a female researcher, preferably a Muslim, with access to female *tablighi* respondents who rarely appear before 'strange' *(ghayr)* men.

In exploring the question of the role of women in the TJ, this paper begins by tracing the historical context within which the movement emerged. It then moves to a discussion of the portrayal of the ideal Islamic woman in *tablighi* tracts. The *tablighi* agenda for women follows from this. In the concluding section we turn our attention to what implications *tablighi* work might actually have for

Muslim women, both activists in the movement as well as others.

The Historical Context

Emergence of' Ulama

The decline of Muslim political power in South Asia towards the end of the eighteenth century witnessed the emergence of several reformist *ulama,* crusading against the widespread observance of local customs, often seen as 'Hinduistic', and calling for Muslims to abide strictly by the Shari' a instead. For these reformists, the decline of the fortunes of the Mughals was a result of Muslims' straying from the path of the Shari' a. Hence, they stressed, Muslim power could only be salvaged if Muslims were to begin to govern their own lives according to the dictates of Islamic law (Ikram, 1963, 14). In pursuit of this aim, they began increasingly devoting their attention to ordinary Muslims who were seen as the bastion of 'un-Islamic' customs and practices. This represented a noticeable shift from past precedent, for at the height of Muslim power in the subcontinent the *'ulama'* seem to have been primarily concerned with the ruling elite, remaining distinctly aloof from common Muslims.

The growing power of the British, culminating in the overthrow of the Mughal dynasty after the aborted revolt of 1857, saw the Indian *'ulama* making new efforts to cultivate links with the Muslim masses who, with the Mughals now gone, increasingly began to be viewed as the new repositories of Islam. With the eclipse of Muslim political authority, from now on it was to be ordinary Muslim who came increasingly to be seen as the protectors of Islam. Purged of local customs, beliefs and practices, the reformed Muslim man, and, later, woman as well, was to be the new defender of the faith. This concern was best exemplified by the movement spawned by the Dar-ul 'Ulum, a seminary established at the town of Deoband, near Delhi, in 1867.

By training *'ulama,* by issuing opinions in matters of religious law (*fatwa*) and, most of all, by taking advantage of new printing technology by publishing popular books and tracts in the vernaculars, the Deobandi *ulama'* as they came to be called, sought to disseminate the message and teachings of reformist Islam among ordinary

Muslims. Of particular concern to them was the religious instruction of ordinary believers in the fundamentals of the faith, including basic ritual practices and beliefs (*'aqa'id*). Marking a distinct departure from the past, they began paying increasing attention to Muslim women, whom they saw as bastions of 'Hinduistic' customs and traditions. The reformed Muslim woman was now seen as playing a central role in the project of reforming the Muslim family and, in the process, the Muslim community as a whole. This concern for women on the part of the Deobandi reformists was most strikingly illustrated with the writing of a voluminous text specially for women, the *Bahishti Zewar,* by the leading Deobandi *'alim*, Maulana Ashraf 'Ali Thanawi (d.1943) in the early years of the twentieth century.[2] This book, more than any other, grew into the most popular reformist tract for the proper religious instruction of Muslim women in India, a distinction that it enjoys till this very day.

As a product of the Deoband *madrasa* and a student of Maulana Thanawi, Maulana Muhammad Ilyas (d. 1944), the founder of the TJ, was particularly concerned to popularize the teachings of the new Islamic reformists among ordinary Muslims, including both men and women. The first target of Ilyas' early *tablighi* (missionary) efforts, starting in the mid-1920s, were the tribe of nominal Muslim converts known as the Meos who lived in the region of Mewat, to the immediate south of Delhi. In the course of his work in Mewat, he strove to encourage the Meos to cultivate faith (*iman*), to improve their knowledge of the basic beliefs of their religion, and to abide strictly by the rituals of Islam. From its humble origin in Mewat, the TJ gradually grew into the vast international movement that it is today.

In the early years of the TJ, the movement was directed almost entirely at men. Once his movement had established a significant presence in Mewat, Ilyas seems to have realized that his mission would remain incomplete if he did not bring women into active involvement in it. Accordingly, he approached some leading Deobandi *'ulama* with a proposal to start *tablighi* work among women. The *'ulama,* however, initially recoiled at the prospect, arguing that this was 'an age of great disorder' (*fitna ka zamana*), with women going out of their homes without covering themselves 'properly', and that *tabligh* tours might actually be used by women as an 'excuse' for 'turning towards freedom'.

Despite the *'ulama's* initial hostility to his proposal, Ilyas kept up his pleas for women to be allowed to participate in *tabligh* work, until the noted Deobandi *'alim*, Mufti Kifayatullah, finally relented and gave him his consent. Thereafter, Ilyas approached a close disciple of his, one Maulana Abdus Subhan, who was persuaded to let his wife begin missionary work among Muslim women in Delhi, where Ilyas lived and where the TJ currently has its global headquarters. This women is said to have, under Ilyas instructions, formed a small group of women who went off for a few days to Mewat in the company of their husbands and, under the supervision of one Maulana Daud, started preaching among the Meo women of that region. After that, we are told, women's participation in the form of the TJ gradually picked up in many other parts of the world as the movement began to expand outside the confines of South Asia (Ferozepuri n.d., 105-7).

This is one of the only references we have in the available literature to the actual work of women in the TJ, and even here they remain faceless, nameless people about whom we are told but little. We do know, however, what they and other TJ women activists were, and still are, taught and learnt as participants in the movement, and to that we may now turn.

As in the case of Muslim men, the TJ sees every Muslim woman as playing a central and active part in the effort for the revival of Islam. The method in which this is to be done—the-*tariqa-i-tabligh*—is, for the most part, common to both men and women. Ordinary Muslim women are encouraged to take off and form a group or *jama 'at* that travels to various places to do *tablighi* work, preaching the message of reformist Islam among the Muslim womenfolk in the areas they visit. To begin with, ideally, they should spend three days at a stretch every two months in this way. After they have gained enough experience they should start to go on fifteen-day *jama' ats*.

Thereafter, this should be increased to a *chillah*, or forty days at a stretch, or even longer, during the course of which they should be encouraged to visit other countries to carry on *tabligh* work there.[3]

The Jama'at Tour

Only married women may go out on a *jama'at,* and they must always be accompanied by a male relative. This should preferably be the husband. If, for some reason, the husband is unable to accompany a woman, she must have her son, brother, father, grandfather or some such *mihram*[4] relative with her. The male *mihram* should, if possible, be one who has already spent a *chillah* doing *tabligh*. In addition, he must have a beard, testifying to his commitment to Islam (Waliul Islam, 1996: 17).

Ideally, the *jama'at* should consist of ten women and ten male *mihram* relatives (*Ibid.*, 16). While on a *tablighi* tour, all decisions regarding the working of the *jama'at* are to be taken by the menfolk accopanying the women. The head (*amir*) of the *jama'at* must in all cases be a man. In consultation (*mashwara*) with the other men he is to oversee the working of the group. Decisions taken by him are relayed to the women through the medium of a woman whom the women choose from among themselves. This woman is told of the *amir's* decisions by her own husband or *mihram* relative who is accompanying her, and she, in turn, conveys this information to the other women in her group (Ferozepuri n.d., 108).

When the group reaches its destination the women are taken to the house of a local *tablighi* activist, where arrangements have been made to keep them in strict *pardah* (seclusion). Such a house must have toilet facilities for women inside; women are not to step out of the house to relieve themselves in the fields, as is the practice in much of rural South Asia. If the house does not have a toilet, one must be built, says a *tablighi* elder, before the women arrive (*Ibid*, 107, 109). The menfolk accompanying them are put up in separate quarters nearby or may stay in the local mosque. For a few days the women live together like a small community.

Daily Schedule and the Principles of Tabligh Chhebaten

The daily schedule for the women is formulated by their husbands or *mihram* menfolk in consultation with each other. After they have chalked out the women's programme for the day, it is written down on a sheet of paper and slipped under the *pardah* to the women's quarter (Waliul Islam 1996, 15). Much of the day is to be devoted to improving the women's own knowledge and practice of basic Islamic ritual observances. In the course of their stay the women activists are expected to learn, among other things, the principles of *tabligh*, which they are to popularize among the women of their own families once they return to their homes. Of central importance is the learning of what is called in *tablighi* parlance the *chhe baten* or the 'six points'. The first of these is the *kalima* or the Islamic creed. The second is *namaz*, Islamic prayer. *'Ilm*, or knowledge about the basic Islamic ritual practices, and *zikr*, litanies in remembrance of God, come next. Here, women are expected to memorize a number of Arabic supplications that are to be used for various different occasions. This is followed by *ikhlas-i-niyyat*, 'the purification of intention'. Here, the women are expected to learn that every thought and action of theirs must be motivated solely by the desire to gain the pleasure of God and to acquire *sawab* or religious merit. Sixthly, and last, is *ikram-i-muslimin*, in which women are expected to learn about the importance of respect for other Muslim, particularly the *'ulama*.

Besides the *chhe baten*, while on *jama'at* the women must busy themselves in reading in a group from the books of *faza'il* (heavenly rewards). This genre of *tablighi* literature consist largely of books containing short episodes from the lives of the early Muslims recounting their piety, and highlighting, in particular, the great rewards that are to be expected in Hereafter if one follows in their footsteps.

The daily recitation from the books of *faza'il* is to be accompanied by *bayāns*, or lectures, that are delivered to the women by a learned and experienced male *tablighi* activist, who may either be one of the husbands or *mihram* relatives of the women or a local Muslim. The *bayan* is to be delivered from behind a curtain so that although the women may hear the speaker, they may not see him and nor can he see them. The lecture should focus on the need for all Muslims to engage in *tabligh*, to strengthen their faith, improve their practice of the Islamic ritual observances, and to bring Islam into their own personal lives.

Women activists who are experienced in *tabligh* and well-versed in its principles may also address the other womenfolk. However, here extreme care should be taken that a woman does not speak in an authoritative tone as if she is delivering a lecture. The reason for this, says a *tablighi* elder, that this is the age of *fitna* (disorder), of great corruption and degeneration, and 'much evil', he warns, can come out of this (Ferozepuri n.d., 109). Just as women should 'always keep their bodies completely concealed', he says, so too 'must their voices be kept in complete *pardah*' (*Ibid*., 111). 'Unlike a man, who can give a lecture from the pulpit (*minhar*) or while sitting on a chair, if a woman is to address her sisters she must, like them sit on the floor and speak to them. In no case should she stand up to speak to the others, as that goes against what are seen as notions of feminine modesty (Waliul Islam, 1996: 16). She must speak as she would in an ordinary conversation and not try to imitate the forceful, emotive style of male *tablighi* speakers.

As well as serving as a learning forum for the women *muballighin* or *tablighi* volunteers, the *jama'at* also functions as a means for communicating the *tablighi* message to other Muslim women in the places that the *jama'at* visits. Local women are to be invited to join the *muballighin* in the house in which they are put up. This is done by the husbands or male *mihram* relatives accompanying the women *muballighin*. They first approach local male *tablighi* activists, and along with them go from house to house exhorting the men to send their wives to join their women in *ta'lim* or learning sessions. When going to the venue of the *ta'lim*, local women should be accompanied by their husbands or a male *mihram* relative and must be covered in full *pardah*. Like the female *muballighin*, they must be very simply dressed. There must be no ostentatious display of jewellery or fine clothes, and every effort should be made to conform to a standard or radical equality.

Besides occasions when women's *jama'ats* visit a place, local *tablighi* activists are expected to arrange for weekly meetings (*ijtima's*) for women, where local women get together to learn about the *chhe baten*, listen to narrations from the books of faza'il and imbibe the teaching of the TJ. Such *ijtima's* must, however, be started only after getting permission from the local *tablighi* headquarters (*markaz*).

Women's *jama'ats*, as well as the periodic local-level *ijtima's*, also serve as occasions where women can gather, an opportunity rarely afforded to them in families where strict *pardah* is observed. Although they are expected to spend all their time in meditation, prayer and learning, as well as teaching other women about Islam, women can find in these occasions spaces where they can share their own stories, their own joys and sorrows, with each other. Thus, Rukaiyya Begum, a woman who works in a non-governmental development agency in Barisal, Bangladesh, speaks of how some male *tablighi* activists in her town are critical of the women's *jama'ats* and *ijtima's*, because, according to them, 'women who attend them spend much of their time simply gossipping with each other rather than taking and thinking only about the *din* (religion)'. 'They might talk about their children's problems with their mothers-in-law or even about the rising price of rice and fish,' she says, and this irks the men because they see these as worldly (*duniyavi*) matters that completely distract one from the single-minded pursuit of the *din*.[5]

Women's *jama'ats* can also prove to be occasions for women to get away from domestic chores and family responsibilities for a while. They are not allowed to take their children with them on *jama'at*, as otherwise their attention might be diverted from the mission of *tabligh*. Thus, for a few days, women can leave their household tasks and their children in the care of other women and gain a respite from the drudgery of domestic work. Gulshan Siddiqui, a housewife from Dhaka, who once travelled on *jama'at*, but is now no longer involved in the TJ, describes her experience thus:

> I had been married for seven years and every day, day in and day out, it was the same old routine—cooking, washing, cleaning, making endless cups of tea for my father-in-law, scrubbing the floors... I badly needed a break. My husband was deeply involved in *tabligh* in those days. One day, he came home from the *markaz* and told me that we both should go for a few days on a *jama'at*. At first, I was apprehensive. I did not know what I would have to do. But, later I found that I had really enjoyed myself. I learnt so much, and besides that, visited some places that I had never been to before. And those few days provided me some respite from the monotony of housework.[6]

Tablighi Notions of Femininity and the Ideal Muslim Woman

The pedagogical function of the women's *jama'ats* and local *ijtima's* is not simply limited to imbibing the teachings of the *chhe baten* and the stories from the books of *faza'il*. Women's groups in the TJ serve as crucial arenas where women's identities are sought to be crucially re-defined in line with *tablighi* understandings of the ideal Muslim woman. Indeed, this can be seen, in some sense, as the central function of all *tablighi* work among women. Through the lectures of the *muballighin* and *tablighi* elders and through numerous *tablighi*-type texts, an attempt is made constantly to communicate and reinforce the image of model Islamic womanhood.

Tablighi notions of ideal Islamic femininity echo, for the most part, traditional Islamic understandings of the role of women as wives and mothers. As a wife, the Muslim woman must constantly remember that God has appointed her husband as her master (*sardar*). To obey him (*uski itaa'at karna*) is a duty (*farz*) that is binding on her (Ferozepuri n.d., 104). Participation in *jihad* not being a *farz* (religious duty) for a woman, she can again the same divine reward simply by being obedient to her husband (Azmi 1993, 1-2). If her husband should, for any reason, get angry with her, a woman should bear his wrath cheerfully and not complain ('Alam 1995, 11-12). One *tablighi* writer approvingly quotes a Hadith, according to which the Prophet is said to have declard: 'O Woman! Your heaven and hell is your husband' (Azmi 1993, 2). This, he says, implies that a woman 'will enter heaven if the husband is pleased with her and hell if he is displeased with her. He goes on to adduce a long list of forty more such Hadiths to prove his point that in order to gain bliss in this world and the hereafter, a woman must follow every command of her husband, should bear his anger cheerfully, and should not protest when he does wrong.[7]

This view is repeated in several other tracts written by other writers associated with the TJ. Some of these texts are specifically targeted at a female readership. A good illustration of this is a book entitled *Muslim khawatin ke liye bees sabaq* ('Twenty Lessons for Muslim Women'), written by a leading Indian *tablighi 'alim*, Maulana Ashiq Elahi Bulandshahri. This book, says the author, 'should reach every single house' in order to 'put an end to the increasing deviance (*ghaflat*) on the part of women'. In addition, he strongly recommends that it be included in the school curriculum for Muslim girls (Bulandshahri n.d., 4).

A central concern of this book is the portrayal of the ideal Muslim wife. Quoting numerous Hadiths, the author argues that only that wife who willingly obeys the commands (*hukm*) of her husband and does not answer him back shall gain entry into heaven. According to a Hadith he cites, the prayers of three people shall not be accepted by God: the runaway slave until he returns to his master; a person in an intoxicated state; and a wife whose husband is angry with her. The Prophet, he says, had declared that the majority of the inhabitants of hell would be women who were ungrateful of their husbands and used foul language (*Ibid.*, 56-57).

The ideal Muslim woman is seen in *tablighi* discourse as bound within the four walls of her home. The moment she steps out of the house, says Bulandshahri, the devil (*shaytan*) himself begins to accompany her (*Ibid.*, 78). 'God has told men that he has made women for them' and 'she is the ornamentation (*zinat*) of your home', another *tablighi* activist tells his (presumably all-male) readers. She must be hidden 'even more carefully than silver, gold and precious stones'. Allowing her to go out of the home will result in all manner of *fitna,* he warns. Just as if costly things are left outside the home, robbers and dacoits and even otherwise honest people will be tempted to steal them, so also if a woman 'is paraded outside without *pardah'*, the 'lascivious eyes' of men will fall on her. This will 'open the doors of adultery (*zina*)' and the woman will lose her shame and modesty (*haya*) (Ferozepuri n.d., 103). Furthermore, care should be taken that women do not adorn (*banao-singhar*) themselves, for they might otherwise become 'a great source of temptation' for men and, consequently, a perennial source of *fitna*. Such women are assured that they shall 'neither gain admittance into heaven and nor even get to smell its fragrance' (Khan n.d., 5). Likewise, and for the same reason, women should wear only very simple clothes and should not use any make-up, for the Prophet has declared that God had cursed the Children of Israel (*banu isra'il*) for having let their women dress in such a manner (*Ibid.*, 10).

Since woman is a thing that must be hidden (*chhippana*) from *ghayr* males, if, under dire necessity, she has to step out of the house, she should do so only in the company of a male *mihram* relative, and that too in strict *pardah*. On such occasions she must cover herself, says a *tablighi 'alim*, with a *burqa* (veil) that stretches from head to foot, covering the entire face as well. So as not to attract any male attention, the *burqa* must be as simple as possible. It should not be decorated or embroidered.[8] Even in the house, she must not appear before any non-*mihram* male. She should never even see any such man, even though the man may be blind. This is because just as it is forbidden (*haram*) for a man to see a non-*mihram* woman, so, too, a woman never see a non-*mihram* man (Khan n.d., 3). She must not be present at any place where she can see a non-*mihram* man.[9] She must not even open a window to look out if her face is not covered. If she goes to the market she must not, under any circumstances, lift the veil from off her face, not even to see what she is buying

(Bulandshahri n.d., 75). Indeed, says this *'alim, pardah* is so important in Islam that it must be observed with the same degree of strictness as with non-*mihram* males with certain classes of non-Muslim (*kafir*) women. Interestingly, under this category he mentions only women from the 'low' Hindu *Dhobi* (washermen), *Bhangi* (sweeper) and *Chamar* (cobbler) castes, though he does not specify why he singles these out among all others (*Ibid.*, 76-77).

Since, the ideal Muslim woman must be confined to the house, her sphere of work is the myriad household tasks that she must perform. These tasks must not be seen as drudgery, however, for great heavenly rewards await the woman who performs them cheerfully as religious duties. Thus, a leading *tablighi* elder writes that the woman who massages the tired body of her husband without having been asked acquires the merit equivalent to giving seven *tolas* of gold in charity (*sadaqa*). However, if she were to do this only on being requested by her husband, she still gets a reward, but this time only that for giving away seven *tolas* of silver (Khan n.d.,5). Elsewhere, this source puts the reward for the former as equal to half of that of a martyr (*shahid*) (*Hadiser Aloke*). Great divine blessings also await that woman who does all her domestic chores properly and tends to her children (Khan n.d., 2-5). Thus, the woman who feeds her child with her own milk gets the reward of one good deed (*neki*) for each drop that is drunk. The woman who sweeps her house while engrossed in *zikr* will receive with the reward for sweeping the holy Ka'aba itself (*Hadiser Aloke*).

Domestic works alone is the proper sphere for women. While performing all these tasks, she should constantly be engrossed in *zikr*, the remembrance and praise of God. Her spare time she should spend in *zikr* and *namaz* and in counting her rosary (*tasbih*). She must say her prayers five times a day in a space kept apart in the house itself, for that is her mosque. She should recite (*tilawat*) portions of the Qur'an every day as well as a number of Arabic supplications. She should also make adequate arrangements for the religious training (*tarbiyat*) of her children. In this regard, she should strive to follow the example of Hazrat Khamsa, a Muslim woman, who, during the rule of the second caliph 'Umar, cheerfully sent her four sons on *jihad* against the unbelievers where they all lost their lives on the battlefield (Akhtar-ul 'Alam 1995, 3-14).

Besides properly carrying out the various domestic tasks that have been assigned to her, a woman is promised great heavenly rewards if she takes care of her own appearance to please her husband and to conform to the demands of proper Islamic hygiene. Thus, according to one leading *tablighi* elder, if a woman lowers her head in humility, properly combs her hair with a central parting (*chir*), uses a tooth-stick (*miswak*) to clean her teeth, cuts her nails regularly, shaves her pubic hair and arm-pits, uses a cloth during her menses and properly cleans herself after excretion (*paykhana*), she will receive the enormous reward equal to that of a hundred martyrs (*shuhada*), and shall be blessed with the intercession (*shafa'at*) of Muhammad on the Day of Judgement (*hashr*), because that is the blessing that God has announced for every Sunna of the Prophet, both great and small, that has gone into disuse and is revived in this age (*Hadiser Aloke*).

No Longer on the Margins?: Muslim Women and the TJ Islamization Project

The active involvement of women in public *tabligh* activity, an arena hitherto completely closed to them, coupled with the traditional images of Muslim womanhood that the TJ seeks to project and constantly reinforce, provides what seems, at best, an ambiguous and confused portrayal of the role and status of the ideal woman *tablighi* volunteer. Is the *tablighi* agenda for Muslim women to be seen simply as bringing them to participate actively in their own subordination and confinement within what some might see as the iron cage of tradition? Much evidence suggests that the concern of the TJ with the question of women can, in fact, be seen as a reaction on the part of male defenders of tradition to the threat of increasing female independence. Thus, in his introduction to a pamphlet directed specifically, at women written by a leading *tablighi* elder, a *tablighi* activist writes that the need for *tabligh* work among women is today 'particularly urgent', as increasing numbers of females are 'going in for co-education, have started reading novels and stories (*afsane*), are watching television and going to the cinema, are strolling freely in parks, and are increasingly going out of the house without a *mihram* male to accompany them'. This, he says, is making women lose 'all sense of shame'. He castigates Western feminism as having only 'further bound' women in heavy chains. As a way out of what he sees as this growing 'irreligiousness'on the part of women, he suggests that girls and women must 'always remain in strict *pardah*, mix only with pious Muslim women and should read only those books that strengthen their faith', particularly those that contain stories about the wives of the Companions of Muhammad and brave Muslim women.[10] In a similar vein, another *tablighi* activist puts the entire burden of women's low status on the fact that they are 'abandoning the *pardah'*, all in the name of 'female liberation' (Palanpuri 1995, 35-36).

However, to see Muslim women in the TJ as simply passive collaborators in a project designed to curb all assertion and agency on their part would, perhaps, not be doing justice to the great complexity of the situation. For, although the movement aims at reinforcing the traditional gender division of labour, it affords, in the process, new role models for women to emulate which can be seen as providing, at one level, significant departures from traditional gender norms. What is particularly interesting here is the central role that women come to be seen as playing in the spread of normative Islam, a role that traditional Islam in South Asia at least, had hardly envisaged for them before.

In some *tablighi* accounts women are portrayed as, in some sense, capable of making greater sacrifices for Islam than men. God, says the late Enamul Hassan (d.1995), the third *amir* of the TJ, has made women weak (*kamzor*) and emotional, as opposed to men, whom he has made strong, brave (*bahadur*) and comparatively hard-hearted (*sakht*) (Nizami 1993, 21). Because of their 'tenderness', many Muslim women have displayed a greater receptivity to Islam than have many men. Thus, Abū Lahab an uncle of the Prophet, stiffly opposed Muhammad, and another uncle of his, Abū Talib, refused to recite the Islamic creed of confession even on his death-bed despite being convinced of Muhammad's (PBUH) divine mission, while all of Muhammad's (PBUH) aunts had accepted Islam in his lifetime (*Ibid*, 23). Likewise, the first martyr in the cause of Islam was a woman, Samiya, and it was a woman, 'Umar's sister, who was instrumental in bringing 'Umar, later the second Sunni Caliph, into the Muslim fold. In the same manner, Akramah, who later went on to sacrifice his life in a battle for Islam, was brought to Islam by his wife (*Ibid.*, 25-27). Muslim women are exhorted to take these women as role models to emulate, as also the Prophet's wives—Khadija, the first convert to Islam, who helped Muhammad (PBUH) by consoling him when he was the target of oppression by his enemies in Mecca and assisted in his mission with her wealth, and 'A' isha, a renowned narrator of Hadiths herself, who taught the Qur'an and the Prophetic traditions to the Muslim women of Medina (*Ibid.*, 33-35, cf. Qasmi, 1995: 25-26).

As active agents in the project of Islamization, Muslim women need first to enhance their own knowledge and strengthen their own practice of Islam through participation in the work of the TJ. They are then to share this knowledge with others, although keeping strictly within the confines of *pardah*. Most importantly, they must now see themselves as playing a crucial role in transmitting Islam to their children, bringing them up to be pious, committed Muslim. They are, a *tablighi* elder writes, to consider themselves as the first *madrasa* of their children (Khan n.d., 12). Women must also make every effort to encourage their husbands to spend as much time as they can on *tablighi* work. A woman who sends her husband 'on the path of Allah' for *tabligh* and maintains her modesty while he is away will, or so promises a *tablighi* elder, 'enter heaven 500 years before her husband, where she will be crowned as the sardar of 70 thousand angels and heavenly houris'. She will, he says, 'be bathed in the waters of heaven and, seated on a horse made of *yaqut*, she will await the arrival of her family' (ıbid., 2-3). The rewards for encouraging their menfolk to go regularly on *tabligh* may actually be received by women in this world itself for, according to a Bangladeshi *tablighi* activists, 'It is possible that husbands doing Tableegh would be comparatively more religious and be loyal to their wives' because, by being fully engrossed in *tablighi* work, 'they might have less time to run after other women' (Shamsul 'Alam, 1993: 727).

Within the familysetting, *tabligh* may open up new spaces for women, who now may appear to exercise greater say in religious affairs than has hitherto been allowed for. At least half a hour must be set apart every day when the family should get together for what is called the *ghar ki ta' alim* session (Qasmi n.d.). Here, the *Faza il-i-Amal* (Zakariyya, 1990), the main book of *faza'il* used in the TJ, and the *Chhe baten* should be read out by the husband, wife or children. According to one *tablighi* source, women, in fact, should actually take the responsibility of organizing the *ghar ki ta' alim* because their menfolk have usually to go out of their houses to work (Akhtar-ul-'Alam, 1995: 5). Another part of the day should be fixed for the husband and wife to discuss how best they can improve the Islamic milieu of their home. From here they can progress to planning *tabligh* work for their locality, city, country and, eventually, the whole world. Women must also make every effort to spread the message of *tabligh* to all their female relatives, guests, and neighbours who come to their homes, as well as even to female beggars who knock on their doors, soliciting alms (Nadwi 1983, 40). Women, thus, are provided with a new instrumentality that they hitherto have lacked.

One can also observe in tablighi discourse on women a hidden critique of certain traditional notions of femininity and domesticity. Exhorting women to follow the example of the wives of the Prophet, Enamul Hassan writes that whereas today women find themselves in the kitchen almost the whole day, in the homes of the wives of Muhammad (PBUH) the stoves were lit only very occasionally. They spent but little time cooking, for their habits were simple, and they and the Prophet subsisted largely on dates and water for months, while sometimes an Ansar of Medina would send some milk to them as a present *(hadiya)*. Even this milk, he notes, was drunk without having to be boiled. Likewise, marriages in the days of the Prophet were conducted with almost no expense, unlike today when the bride's family must spend a great deal of money, often having to land in deep debt (*Ibid.*, 29-31). In line with this great stress on simplicity and austere frugality, at large *tablighi* gatherings it is common for mass marriages to be arranged at little cost to either side, and sometimes dispensing with the customary dowry which, in South Asia, can be seen as a crucial symbol of the devaluation of female worth.

Conclusion

Probably the most widespread Islamic movement in the world today, the TJ has its roots in the reformist tradition that emerged in South Asia in the wake of Muslim political decline and the rise of British power in the region. In the absence of Muslim political authority, for the reformist *'ulama* who emerged in this period, every Muslim, man as well as woman, now had the onerous responsibility of 'preserving' and 'protecting' Islam. Growing out of the Deobandi concern for the 'proper' Islamization of Muslim women, who were seen as the bastion of 'superstition' and 'un-Islamic', 'Hinduistic' traditions, the TJ made women's active involvement an integral part of the reformist Islamization agenda.

The implications for Muslim women of the efforts of the TJ seem to send different signals for patriarchy. On the one hand, the TJ seeks to impose on Muslim society an extremely restricted and narrow gender regime as a response to the challenges of modernity. In this process, not only are the traditional sources of women's subordination sought to be reinforced, but even the limited spaces afforded to women within traditional custom-laden South Asian Islam, such as attendance at Sufi shrines, are fiercely attacked as 'un-Islamic' aberrations. Because of the importance that is placed on the regular reading of specific texts in *tablighi* circles one might expect involvement in the TJ to help promote literacy among women active in the movement. No firm statistical evidence can be cited in this regard, however. That enhanced *tablighi* activity may not necesarily lead to greater female literacy is evident from the fact that in Mewat, which is held by *tablighi* activists to be their most successful experimental ground, the female literacy rate is said to be no more than 5 per cent. On the other hand, the TJ provides women with new sources of mobility and a significant instrumentality within the family and the neighbourhood as active agents in the Islamization process. Furthermore, within the sternly patriarchal discourse of the TJ, one can discern a faint critique of certain traditional structures of male supremacy.

NOTES

1. At most we have at our disposal works containing general discussions of *tablighi* principles and beliefs, the most comprehensive of which are Nadwi 1983 and Anwar-ul Haq 1972. For a good summary of the basic principles of the TJ, see Metcalf 1994.
2. For selected portions of the book translated into English, see Metcalf 1990.
3. Waliul Islam 1996, 15. The length and frequency of *tablighi* tours for men differs in certain respects from this, however.
4. A mihram relative is one, such as a son or father, whom a woman is forbidden to marry under Islamic law.
5. Interview with Rukaiyya Begum, Barisal, 11 November 1996.
6. Interview with Gulshan Siddiqui, Dhaka, 15 November 1996.
7. Azmi 1993, 1-10. It is possible that some of these Hadiths could in fact be *mauzu* (fabricated) or *zaif* (weak) and not *sahih* (authentic), as several critics of the TJ have pointed out that the movement's books of *faza'il* can be faulted on the grounds of containing stories attributed to the Prophet that are actually concocted. Further, even in the case of *sahih* Hadiths, there is the possibility of their being interpreted in ways different from how they are seen in *tablighi* circles.
8. Bulandshahri, 70. A Bangladeshi *tablighi* activist writes that the *burqa* covering the entire body, including the face, is compulsory for all Muslim women because, he says, this it the 'age of *fitna* (disorder)' (*At-Turag*, No. 80, 1 January 1993, 12-13).

9. Bulandshari, 74-75. Thus Khan (n.d.,10) quotes a story, according to which the Prophet once asked his Companions to tell him which woman was the highest (*a'la*) in terms of qualities *(sifat)*. Hazrat 'Ali, on hearing this, went to his house. His wife, and the Prophet's daughter, Fatima, told him that that woman was superior to all who 'neither sees a *ghayr-mard* ('strange man') nor is seen by such a man'.
10. 'Abdul Matin's introduction to Palanpuri n.d., 8-9. Cf. Ferozepuri n.d.104.

REFERENCES

Akhtar-ul. 'Alam, Muhammad (1995): *Ma-bonder athti kaj* (Dhaka, Al-Amin Academy).

Anwar-ul, Haq, M. (1972): *The Faith Movement of Mawlana Muhammad Ilyas* (London, George Allen & Unwin).

Azmi, Majaz (1993): *Guidance for a Muslim Wife* (New Delhi, Idara Isha 'at-i-Diniyat).

Bulandshahri, Muhammad Ashiq Elahi (n.d.): *Muslim khawatin ke liye bees sabaq* (New Delhi, Idara-i- sha 'at-i-Diniyat).

Faruqi, Ziaur Rahman (1992): *'Ulama-i-Deoband: kaun hai, kya hai?* (Deoband, Dar-ul Kitab).

Ferozepuri, Muhammad Isa (n.d.): *Tabligh ka muqami kam* (Delhi, Rabbani Book Depot).

Hadiser aloke--*mahilader jonno hazrat maulana Saeed Ahmad Khan* sahiber (Bengali leaflet, no publication details).

Ikram, Shaikh Muhammad (1963): *Mauj-i-Kausar*, Vol. 3 (Karachi, Feroze Sons).

Khan, Saeed Ahmad (n.d.): *Khawatin ke liye rah-i-nijat* (New Delhi, Mushtaq Ahmad).

Metcalf, Barbara D. (1990): *Perfecting Women Maulana Ashraf 'Ali Thanawi's Bihishti Zewar* (Los Angeles and Oxford, University of California Press).

Metcalf, Barbara D. (1994): 'Islamic self-fashioning in a global movement of spiritual revival', in: M. E. Marty and R.S. Appleby (Eds), *Accounting for Fundamentalisms: the dynamic character of movements* (Chicago and London, University of Chicago Press), 706-725.

Nadwi, Sayyed Abul Hasan Ali (1983): *The Life and Mission of Maulana Muhammad Hyas* (Lucknow, Nadwat-ul-'Ulama).

Nizami, Muhammad Khalid (Ed.) (1993): *Paygham-i-falah* (Dhanbad, Dini Ta 'alimi Board).

Palanpuri, Muhammad Umar (n.d.): *Ma-behen-beti-bivi ki nijat ke liye rah-i-nijat* (New Delhi, Taj Book Depot).

Palanpuri, Umar Bin Muhammad Umar(1995): 'Auroton ne apna muqam ko kho diya', *Husn-i-Ikhlaq,* February.

Qasmi, Muhammad Azfar Jamal (Ed.) (1995): *London ki khawatin se maulana Ahmad lat sahib ka tablighi khitab* (Jalalpur, Paygham Book Depot).

Qasmi, Muhammad Rashid (n.d.): *Ghar ki ta 'alim* (Kamalpur, Daftar-i-Jami' a Arabi a Imdad-ul-Islam).

Shamsul Alam, A.Z.M. (1993): The *Message of Tableeg and Da 'wah* (Dhaka, Islamic Foundation, Bangladesh).

Waliul Islam (1996): *Tablighi Jama 'ater unpanchash koti shawab, mashturater mehnat o shadi poda namajer poriniti* (Dhaka, Sultanuddin Ahmad, Tat Turg Prokashini, Madrasa Dar-ul-Akram).

Zakariyya, Muhammad (1990): *Faza, il-i-'amal* (New Delhi, Idara-i-Isha at-i-Diniyat).

12

Gender and Reproductive Behaviour: A Comparative Study of Two Religious Communities in Delhi Slum

Sabiha Hussain

Introduction

Stereotypical explanations about the reproductive health, behaviour and practices of Muslims in India both by the popular and academician class is that Islamic prescriptions are against the small family. Therefore the assumption is that using any family planning devices is prohibited. Moreover, it is further argued that Muslims keep on having an increasing number of children with a view to outnumber the majority community. Such a view ignores not only the situation as it obtains at the ground level but also the prevailing diverse and heterogeneous practices among the Muslims.

There is very little comparative research on reproductive behaviour and practices of Hindus and Muslims specially migrants living in a slum of a metropolitan city. The reason as pointed out by Jeffery & Jeffery (1997:217) is that comparing Muslim and Hindu fertility is not an appropriate unit of comparison due to their diverse culture and because they don't share common-feature. I do agree that Muslims are a heterogeneous community but the stereotypical notions and propaganda of Hindu right wing elements does not consider the heterogeneity and class variation within the community and regional differences in population growth, rather the argument of these groups is based on "the philosophical postulates of a particular religion....constitiute the exclusive, unchanging organisational principle for an entire people across all kinds of spaces, times and historical changes" (Basu et.al. 1993:74). Hence, a comparative study in order to unravel some of the myth and stereotypical, explanation and propaganda related to reproductive pattern and practices of Muslims with that of the Hindus of same socio-economic strata who are living in a slum of Delhi (Seelampur). The issue is whether and to what extent Muslims in general and their women in particular are influenced by textual prescriptions regulating their reproductive behaviour or whether their reproductive behaviour and practices are determined by a complex mix of localised socio-cultural practices and their life situation in the same manner as women of other religious groups.

Secondly, most of the writings of seventies and early eighties on fertility differentials concluded that a strong religious element is involved in the higher fertility of Muslims than Hindus (Visaria, 1974; Srivastava, 1979; Ghosal, 1981; and Pakrasi and Halder, 1981). An example of this stereotypical notion can be seen among the general mass as one of the audio cassettes by Sadhvi Saraswati doing the round where she says, "For every five children the Hindus have, the Muslims have fifty. And who feeds the fifty children? Hindus do! After Muslim divorce, then the Waqf Boards support the children with taxes we pay... within twenty five years you will be living like a poor minority in this country. (Basu, 1996) In early nineties there was not much research on impact of religious prescription on fertility pattern which left most of the stereotypical notion alive in spite of falling religious differentiate in fertilty in many parts of the country, as I am going to substantiate this with my own findings.

However, in-mid nineties an attempt was made to re-examine the religious influence in fertility differential at macro level. Still there is dearth of micro data regarding the influence of religious prescriptions on reproductive behaviour and practices.

Statement of the Problem: Case Studies

It has generally been found that seeking health care specially reproductive health care and regulating the reproductive behaviour and practices are dependent on various structural and institutional factors such as cultural norms, values attached to motherhood, gender relations within the family and outside, negotiation with the partner, power dynamics within the household, cultural taboos and shame, employment status of women (i.e. home based worker or working outside), physical and financial cost of health services and its availability and accessibility etc. (Qadeer, 1996; Youssuf, 1993; Ravindra, 1993; Dwyen and Bruce, 1988, Jeffery et.al. 1988; Germain et.al., 1994; and Mukerjee, 1975. The preference of sterilisation is generally related to birth of a son (Rajan et. al. 1996; and Jain and Vasaria, 1988). The above mentioned are, to our mind, more important than mere religious prescriptions or explanations that regulate the reproductive behaviour and practices of any community.

Saira (41 years), a maid earning Rs. 1500 per month by working six hours in morning and two hours in the evening has six children and had two infant mortality (5 and 3 months). She did not want more children. So she asked her husband to use *Nirodh* but he vehemently refused by saying, *"Teri Himmat Kaise Huee Mujh Se kahne ki* How Dare you Said it to me". Since she was not interested in more pregnancies (which she explained in terms of financial loss, weakness and inability for managing more number of children) she went to health centre with her neighbour and inserted an IUD (Copper T) without her husband's knowledge. Once during inter-course her husband came to know about the device. She was beaten up and forced to take it out. Within few months she conceived. She wanted to abort the child but given the warning by her husband that if she aborts the foetus, she will be driven out of the house. She gave birth to a baby girl. She was blamed for using IUD which resulted in the birth of baby girl and was given ultimatum that in future if she uses any device she would be divorced. This resulted in two subsequent abortions and finally without telling her husband she got tubectomy done.

Renu (35) a piece rate worker earning Rs.1000-1500 per month has six children (5 daughters and one son). Her husband is a casual worker in a garment factory and is an alcoholic, whatever money he earns is spent in drinking. After four children she suggested to her husband that he should use "Nirodh" to prevent further pregnancies. Her suggestion sparked off a quarrel which resulted in physical abuse. She was given warning not to repeat it again.

Meri Marzi Hai Maih Estemal Karun Ya Na Karun aur Tu Bhi Goli Nahi Khae Gi. Tera Kam Baccha Paida Karna Hai, Mujhe Salah Den a Nahee. (It is up to me whether to use contraceptive or not and you also better not use pills. Your duty is to have children and not to give me any suggestion).

She was forced to have sex. As a result she had two more children. After six children, she consulted one of her co-workers who suggested her to insert IUD. She did that but due to several complications like heavy bleeding, irregular period etc. she had to take it out. Again she conceived for three times but without telling her husband she got the foetuses aborted, which resulted in weakness and other gynaecological complications. She with the consultation of her friend started taking the pill. When asked about the abortion she said *"In Bacchan Ko Ek Samay Ka Khana Bhi Pura Naheen Hota Aadmi ko Kuch Kahne Se Mar Khati Hun. Aur Bacche Main Chati Nahi Hoon. Aap Hi Batao Bacche Ki Saffai Na Karaoon To Kya Karaoon".* (These children are not even getting food for one time. If I say something to my husband, I am beaten up; and I don't want more children; now you tell me what should I do).

There are hundreds and thousands of Sairas and Renus who are living at the most uncertain level of human existence where concepts like "reproductive right" and choice have no meaning. Religious prescriptions also do not figure anywhere. They come from poor families, live in slum and work in the unorganised sector. After working for six to eight hours a day, they have to put up with the sexual encounters with their husbands.

The second important question that arises specially from Saira's story is: to what extent does faith in a particular religion affect the reproductive rights, choice and behaviour of a woman? Saira and Renu were forced to have children not because of their faith in particular religion but rather due to the power dynamics in the household and domination of males.

By citing both the case studies, my purpose is to raise a few questions within the framework of prevailing general stereotypical notion about Muslims which gives the impression that their faith encourages them to have more children and secondly, how the politics of power dynamics and male domination (notion of patriarchy) both at the household and societal and state level at large affects the women of both the communities in regulating the reproductive behaviour and practices with the support of my qualitative and quantitative data. I would also like to emphasize the least focussed determinants which I think as an important determinant in the regulation of reproductive behaviour of any community, i.e., the gender roles and gender relations and how it works within the broader framework of patriarchy than the stereotypical religious explanation. Thus the basic questions are: Is there anything like Muslim reproductive behaviour? Does the propagation of Muslim religious orthodoxy affect the reproductive behaviour, practices and pattern of Indian Muslims? (supported by qualitative and quantitative data). What is the nature of gender articulation and material resources allocation and control in the household within which women assert their sexual and reproductive rights and choice?

Can women exercise their rights freely where there is strong hold of patriarchy and politics of power dynamics within the household? In other words do really Indian women have any choice in reproductive matter? How, why and under what situations and with what consequences do women in general perceive and pursue their rights in asserting their sexuality and reproductive rights?

Reproductive Behaviour : Politics of Gender Relation

With the rise of women's movements during 70's and throughout 80's "the women's question" became the debated issue in the political discourse, in cultural arena and in state policies and programmes. But before the discussion on the politics of gender relation within the household and the hold of patriarchy in regulating the reproductive behaviour, a brief account of shifting focus in the field of demographic research in India with the rise of women's movement is given.

For the last three decades the focus of mainstream demographic research in India about the determinant of fertility pattern was mainly on the rationalisation for expanded family size. (Mamdani, 1973; Michaelson, 1981), social structural aspects of fertility behaviour (Caldwell et.al. 1988; Zacharia, Jejeebhoy, 1991; Savitri, 1994; Mitra, 1973; Kalifa, 1973; Chaudhary, 1977; and Becker 1991), and demographic correlates (Pakrasi and Malakar, 1967; Agrawal, 1962; Murthy, 1986; Manna, 1998, Sathor et. al. 1988 and Sandhu 1996). What seems to be commonly ignored by these studies are the heterogeneity in the household composition both in terms of desires and experiences of the household members specially women's agency in the reproductive process and the power dynamics. As pointed out by (Seal 2000) that although the dynamics of sexual behaviour are closely related to childbearing, the population studies have hardly shown their concern about "how women in particular class and gender context negotiates sexual domain; what they think and feel about love, physical affection, sexual initiation and sexual satisfaction."

This was the period when women's development approach came into being. In nineties the focus was shifted from social structure and demographic determinants of reproductive pattern to household dynamics which brought the issues of gender and class into the centre. (Seal, 2000). Through this approach the reproductive behaviour was looked as a gender disaggregated phenomenon within the household. With regard to the power dimension of the household structure Mazumdar and Sharma (1990) pointed out that this aspect has got little place in the writings on status of women in India although this aspect of power dynamics largely affects the allocation of labour, time and other resources within the family that has tremendous impact on the lives of women specially the working class.

Again I would like to go back to the case studies mentioned earlier to explain how this dimension worked within patriarchal structure in the case of Saira and Renu. Although, both the women managed to stop having more children, but the way they had exercised their choice, 're-establishes' their subordination in spite of their being economically independent. Their economic independence did help them in exercising their reproductive right and choice but within the broad frame of patriarchal structure. Thus, this aspect of women's life is largely controlled and shaped by social structure through which patriarchy operates. Most important among them are gender related factors such as gender roles. These gender roles are determined and shaped by societal values. These values in turn influence the gender gaps in various spheres of women's life, in terms of gender and class rather than faith in particular religion.

Patriarchal Society

In almost all societies, in some form or the other gender system and gender hierarchies are found (Moghadam, 1992). I would like to view my study in this framework and see how different roles are assigned to men and women and also to see how various agencies under patriarchal structure leading to power relations between them in regulating reproductive behaviour and practices of women under study influence them. I would also like to focus on how this gender relation is constructed at micro and macro levels related to health issues in general and reproductive health in particular. Patriarchy as defined by Walby (1999:20) refers to "a system of social structure and practices in which men dominate, oppress and exploit women". She emphasizes the term social structure and rejects both the biological determinism and the notion of every man as dominant and every woman as subordinate. Further she says that there are two abstract levels through which patriarchy has to be understood: at the most abstract level it refers to a system of relation and at the less abstract level, it is comprised of six structures. They are patriarchal mode of production, patriarchal relations in paid work, state, sexuality, cultural institutions and male violence. These six structures according to her are core of patriarchy and are necessary to capture the variations in gender relations. Kandiyoti (1988) uses the term 'classic patriarchy' which is explained in terms of gender relations and position of women. Mann (1986) defining patriarchy in the historical and cross cultural perspective says, "patriarchal society is defined as one in which power is held by male heads of household. There is also a clear separation between the 'public' and 'private' spheres of life. In public sphere, power is shared by male patriarch, no female holds any formal public position of economic, ideological, military or political power."

Reproductive Behaviour: Does religion really matter?

Here I will restrict myself to Islamist interpretation related to reproductive issues to explain Islamist-feminist approach of patriarchal interpretation of Islamic doctrine related to the regulation of reproductive behaviour and birth control. The intention to see whether Islamic prescription are against small family, birth control as perceived by academia class, in political arena as well as the general impression. In almost all ages religious ideologies have been determined by the interplay of economic, political and social forces. Religion proved to be the best way to combat both the political and domestic-threats. And women were chosen to be sacrificed on the altar of Muslim identity. Therefore, on the pretext of preserving Islamic identity women are made to have a large number of children and live in seclusion (Bhatty, 1999).

Traditional Islamists place greater importance to domesticity and motherhood after that they can explore other avenues of their liking. islamist-reformist and feminists have some differences on these established patriarchal norms and have contested this established version of Shari'ah. For showing their differences, they have chosen many instances from the Qur'an and Hadith where no difference is made among believers. They argue that there is basically egalitarian ethos in Islam that was distorted by patriarchal forces (Ahmad, 1986, 1992). For example one of the preconditions to marriage and procreation under Islam is that parents particularly husband must have the ability to provide for the upbringing and welfare of children. The Prophet says, " Nothing is more gruelling than the trial of being impoverished and having to provide for a large family." (Allaudin, 1992). A number of statements of the scriptures reveal that God does not wish to burden man, and suggests that quality is as important as quantity in children. In addition to this, there is found to be a clear recognition of women's right to sexual enjoyment (Obermeyer, 1994). For preserving wife's health and allay anxiety over numerous children, the Qur'an has justified Coitus interruptus (Yossuf, 1978). The Islamic Jurists have reasoned that to avoid the economic hardship, individual may adopt family planning methods. The Grand Mufti of Egypt, after reviewing the Islamic law about family planning concluded, "It is permissible for either husband or wife by mutual consent to take any measure to prevent semen entering into uterus in order to prevent conception." (Yossuf, 1978). Regarding abortion, most Islamic Jurists agree that the soul enters the foetus at about 120 days after the conception. Different schools of thoughts have different opinion, yet everyone agree upon entering of soul in foetus not before 40 days (Obermeyer, 1994). Sterilisation poses a greater difficulty, because the finality of the method is seen as interfering with divine will and therefore, Muslim authorities have not condoned its use." (Bowen, 1991 Obermeyer, 1992; Amran, 1992). On the basis of these above statement of Shari'ah the Islamist feminists and reformists argue that the constraints on reproductive choice amongst the Muslims are not inherently Islamic and therefore, they suggest that "the egalitarian elements of the religious texts should be the guide to a reinterpretation of the doctrine that would be fully compatible with ideas of human rights and reproductive choice." (Obermeyer, 1994).

The pertinent question to be asked is: Is Fertility differential an outcome of religious prescriptions? After the Princeton European Fertility Project, the economic' explanation of fertility differential shifted to 'culture' in a more general term and 'religion' in a specific sense in Europe, Africa and Asia (Kertzer, 1995; Mazrui, 1994; Caldwell & Caldwell, 1984). Few demograhers in India also have explained difference in fertility pattern on the basis of religion (Jeffery & Jeffery, 1997). The communalisation of population debate by the right wing Hindu politics is based on the claim that "the philosophical postulates of a particular religion.....constitute the exclusive, unchanging organisational principle for an entire people across all kinds of spaces, times and historical change" (Basu et. al. 1993). Could this just be a basis to justify the higher and lower fertility growth of any community? To our mind, fertility pattern of any community can't be dealt in religious framework for that matter in any single perspective. Religion could be one of the variables in determining the reproductive behaviour. This statement can be substantiated by the population growth of Muslims in India for the last three decades. In 1971 the total Muslim population was 11.2 per cent that increased marginally to 11.4 per cent in 1981 and in 1991 it was 12.1per cent. Another illustration could be seen in the state of Kerala where the increase in percentage of Hindu and Muslim population is almost the same, i.e., 2.46, per cent Hindu and 2.48 per cent Muslim. Similarly in the State of J & K Muslims have lower fertility (1981 census) than the Hindus (Goyal, 1990). Other factors like political stability confirmed by not being a minority, the feeling of stability instilled in a less hostile environment may also be important (Kaushik, Basu, 1996). The study of these three states shows that the fertility gap by religion is higher in Maharashtra than in Uttar Pradesh. My argument is that if it is religious prescription which encourage the Muslims to have more children, there would have been the same trend of population growth both inside the country and across the country. The recent demographic trend of Bangladesh reveals growth in use of contraception since 1971 (3 per sent) to 1991 (40 per sent) which negates the stereotypical notion about South Asian Muslims that they are against family planning methods and as a result they have faster population growth rate. (Kabeer, 1995; Krishna Kumar, 1991; Wright 1983; and Van der Veer 1994). Here I would like to add that the population of SC and ST has also gone up from 23.6 in 1981 to 24.7 per cent in 1991 but the population growth of this section is not brought into discussion by the political parties specially the right wing Hindu political leaders.

Politics of Fertility: Changing Perspective

Politics of fertility operates at various macro and micro levels within the broader patriarchal structure. The Role of State is an important agency of the politics of fertility control. As pointed out by Jain (1998) "this starts with the government's involvement in policies to alter human behaviour related to reproduction and sexuality." The role of international donor agencies is another important factor that is influenced by the political climate within their own country which designs the policies to reduce fertility of the developing countries. Most importantly, the politics of fertility control is about the gender relations within and beyond the household. India's Population Policy and Programme started with the formation of Planning Commission in 1950. The Planning Commission's Panel on Health Programmes set up a committee on Population Growth and F.P. The report of the committee came out in 1951 with its recommendation that "Population Policy is essential to planning" and family planning is "a step" towards "improvement" in health, specially of mother and children." (Vasaria and Vasaria, 1998). The committee also recommended to raise the age of marriage, along with an investigation on non-contraceptive methods of family limitation.

In the first three five year plans, the objective of family planning programme was on health and welfare of mother and children. The Government was supposed to provide services according to the choice of couples. But from the 4th plan onwards there was a clear shift in the Family Planning Programme. "The shift was from a Programme of health and Welfare of the Population to a Programme of Population control, which was time and target oriented. (Karkal and Pandey, 1998). National government had decided to keep FP as a centrally sponsored scheme and the outlay was raised from Rs.3.0 billion to Rs.3.15 billion (Planning Commission, 1969b.)

Gender Implications of the five year Planning and Policies

From gender perspective, it seems that the Government of India in its FPP has given less importance to women's health, autonomy and empowerment. In the first three five year plans at least, women's health remained an important issue within the Family Planning Programme. The major shift from its initial objective of health and welfare of the mother and children of the Programme of Population control shows Government's little concern about women. The target approach and the coercive nature of programmes inherent in the incentives and disincentives given for limiting the family size were also not in the interest of women. Continuous deterioration in the quality of mother and child health care services has worsened the situation. The report on the status of women in India reveals the (GOI, 1974) miserable state of Indian women and the declining sex ratio (Gupta, 2000).

India 's FPP has largely been women centered wherein major responsibility of birth control lies on women. Thus, women have always been considered as reproductive agents who can reduce the population growth rate (Channa, 1989; Manna, 1998; and Agnihotri and Gupta, 1996). "While for the most part, programmes related to food production, income generation and education lost sight of them; policies for 'population control' easily identified poor women as target group" (Seal, 2000).

In spite of the criticism from scholars and practitioners and its adverse effect on the health of women, female sterilisation has been the most used and growing form of birth control in India (Mukhopadhya and Savithri, 1998; Aslam, 1992). This trend of policy makers and planers as pointed out by a few scholars is a culturally ingrained mindset that operate within a patriarchal system. If men have to be vasectomised it will affect their superiority or virility. Secondly, men are more concerned with sexual gratification than the use of contraception. Thirdly, male sterilisation proved to be volatile for the government. These are few of the reasons why the policy makers and the medical community have very little interest in developing male contraceptives (Banerjee, 1971; Dutt et. al 1992 and Joseph, 1992).

However, here the evaluation of FPP and policies are not within the perview of our study. Rather, the aim is to furnish a general information about constraints women face in using family planning methods and the follow up if any complication starts. Further, by briefing the programme and policies intention was to bring into light the ethos of patriarchy in the use of contraception and curtailment of essential social support threates the health of women even more. (Sabai and Kran, 1995). With the introduction of Structural Adjustment Policy (SAP), Government is under tremendous pressure from outside to control population. The reason is that the developed countries perceive large population size as the root of all problems and not the unequal distribution of resources. The privatisation of health care system is adding the fuel to the fire. As a result whatever health support for women and poor existed earlier are now being undermined and dismantled. "with reduced expenditure on health, dismantling the public distribution system, and increasing impoverishment, social conditions are being created which will cause rise in infant mortality and a rise in unemployment. More young persons in unorganised sector and loss of social security all these factors contribute to high fertility which further affects the health of women" (Sabai and Krann, 1995). With regard to foreign aids and grants, all the aids and development loans are conditional specially in the name of improving health loans are given to meet the target of Family Planning. During 1990-93 the share of foreign aid spent on family planning programme rose.

Economic Status of the Respondents' Family

In the two localities 75 per cent of the people of both the communities had their own houses. 50 per cent had their own machines, (32 per cent Muslim and 18 per cent Hindus). Fridge, air cooler and television are owned by 35 per cent of the Muslim and 40 per sent of the Hindus. Washing machine (manual/semi automatic) owed by 10 per cent of Hindus and 6 per cent of Muslim families. The possession of two wheeler among Muslim was approximately 30 per cent and 5 per cent were having Maruti car or van. Among Hindus, the number of 2 wheeler was approximately 35 per cent followed by 6 per cent who had four wheeler. The family income of both the communities vary from Rs. 2000-15000 per month approximately. (This approximation was done on the basis of occupation and electric and electronic assets owned by the respondents family). Similarly, the income which has been divided into two categories of stable, unstable is based mainly on the nature of occupation of the respondents and their husbands.

Age Profile

If we looked at age profile of the respondents we find that majority of the women (75 per cent) of both the communities are between the age group of 20 to 35 years. As far as age gap between the spouses is concerned we can see that four categories are significant, i.e., none of the Muslim spouses were of equal age whereas among Hindus it is 4 per cent. Similarly two years age gap was found among 22 per cent of the Hindus while it was 8 per cent among Muslims. Another significant difference between the two communities about the age gap is of 10 years. (Muslim 11 per cent, Hindus 1 per cent).

Occupation

On looking at the occupation of both the communities in that particular locality we find that majority of them are self-employed. But the difference is that Muslims of that area are basically manufacturers, whereas Hindus are traders who had their own shops like grocery, general stores, chemists, sweets, electricals, foods, stationary shops, ice cream factory, readymade germents, dairy etc. Muslims are mainly in the manufacturing of small motor parts, of sewing machines, cooler body, plastic toys, garment stitching and embroidary mainly for export purpose, manufacturers of trunks, jeans and leather jackets etc. The business, especially the garments, which they get, is mainly from Hindus of Gandhi Nagar. They bring the material and stitch it on their own machines. About 65 per cent of the manufacturers of garments, motor parts, swing machines had their own machines. The labourers get payment weekly at the rate of 5-6 rupees per piece depending upon the material manufactured. The manufacturers, specially those of the garments expressed that in 1992 riots had adversely affected their business, because they had been getting business mainly from Hindus who were the wholesalers of readymade garments. Some 10 families were engaged in Rajasthani and Moradabadi handicraft business which they export through Hindu businessmen and they get share of profit. Thus self employed category consists of manufacturers (readymade garments, Jeans, leather jackets plastic toys, hardware, motor parts etc.) and for those running small hotels or tea stalls, embroidery works, kabari shops, thread making and dyers, vendors who either had their own carts on which they sold fruits and vegetables or used rented place.

Most of the Muslim women are piece rate workers engaged in stitching and embroidery while Hindu women are in bindi pasting, making polypacks and nailing the file covers.

Caste Profile

The caste of the respondents had been divided into two broad categories: the backward castes comprising: Ansari, Kasab, Darzee, Nai, Carpenter, Kabari, Rangrez (dyer), Ghosi etc. while the 55 per cent forward castes are Sheikh Siddiqi, Pathan, Syed (very few). Among Hindus 56 per cent of the respondents belong to backward communies comprising Teli, Barber, Yadava (milkman), Sunar, Chamar and Lohar etc. while 44 per cent are forward castes.

In a sample of two hundred households 57 per cent are migrants. Among Muslims majority of the migrants are from Western UP, like Muzzafarnagar, Bijnor, Muradabad, Bahraich, Bareilly, Agra, Bulandsahar, Meerut, Saharanpur, Sakini. Very few migrants are from Bihar, Eastern UP, MP, HP and Haryana. Two to Three per cent migrants are from Rajasthan who are engaged in their traditional occupation of tie and dye and handicrafts.

The peculiar thing about these migrants is that they still prefer to marry in Rajasthan. Early marriage 15-16 years is common among them, education of girls is not preferred. When asked about the reason for preference to this kind of marriage, they explained it in terms of maintaining traditional art and craft.

As far as Hindu migrants are concerned they are mainly from Haryana, Punjab, HP and Western UP. Gujjars from Haryana are economically sound and are self-employed (dairy and export). They run their own school and health club in BP.

Among locals Muslim people are from Yamuna Bazar Jhuggi, Delhi Gate, Turkman Gate, Daryaganj, and Ballimaran. Similarly the Hindus are from Chandni Chawk, Sadar Bazar, and Tees Hazari.

Reasons for migration were mainly employment opportunities, low profit in traditional occupation, lower wages at their places, and distribution of land among siblings. Majority of the people from Muradabad and Meerut migrated during 80s especially after communal riots which had adverse effect on their business. The export orders for their goods especially from Saudi Arabia and Middle East went to Pakistan. Most of the *karigars* (craftsmen) started facing the problem of unemployment and irregular wages.

Although, overall educational level of both the communities is low, it is even lower among the Muslims (both male and female) especially in the realm of higher education.

This can be seen in the form of their low representation in jobs specially those in government. This trend of lower education can still be seen in respondents' own children which is termed as of low functional value in case of boys. Out of 100 Muslim families it has been found that the rate of dropout among boys is higher (29 per cent) than the girls (16 per cent). The reason for high dropout rate among boys even of economically better of families was that there is discrimination against Muslims in government jobs and that early entry into family business is better. For them it makes sound economic sense. It is common to both the communities.

The drop-out rate among Hindu children is also high. But those who can afford, wanted their sons to complete their schooling. Here poverty was found to be the main reason for dropout rather than benefitting family business. Among Hindus, the drop-out rate of sons and daughters is 20 per cent and 18 per cent respectively.

The reason for dropout among girls was mainly economic and unsafe environment. Most of the children of the respondents go to government schools in the same locality. Those who can afford send their children in private schools also. It is seen that in some families, youngest child (boy/girl) is attending private schools basically due to fascination for English language which they consider a language of modern and advanced people. Most of the girls receiving higher education among Muslims belong to the first generation.

Marriage and Family

Among Muslims consanguineous marriage was found to be very common-- 50 per cent especially among migrants. A few cases of inter caste marriage, i.e., Sheikh boy married to an Ansari girl or an Ansair boy married to Sheikh girl were also found. Two cases of inter-religious marriage and two cases of polygamous marriage (one self-employed Ashraf, one non-Ashraf), one case of divorce and remarriage were also found in that area. Among Hindus 8 per cent marriages took place with distant relatives mostly migrants. Most of the marriages are endogamous. Two cases of separated women, one case of polygamy and one case of adoption (son) were found among the Hindus. This trend of consanguineous marriage was shown by the finding of Rao et al (1972) and Khlal & Khoury (1991) that 27 per cent of Muslim women were married to a blood relative due to the concentration of Muslims in urban areas.

Family Size

The average number of surviving children among Muslims is 3.78 per couple while it was 6.07 in the previous generation. Similarly, the average number of surviving children among Hindus is 2.72 per couple which was 5.56 in previous generation.

If we compare the number of siblings of the respondents of both the communities with that of their own children, we find that in previous generation 36.5 per cent couples had up to four children, 49.0 per cent had four to eight children and 14.5 per cent had eight and above. While in respondents' generation 83.0 per cent are having up to four children and 17 per cent have four to eight children. If we analyze our data communitywise, we find that 73 per cent Muslim couples have up to four children, 17 per cent have four to six and 10 per cent have six to eight children while among Hindus 91 per cent are having up to four children, eight per cent have four to six and the couple having six and above children was found to be nil.

It was interesting to note that in previous generation of both the community none of the couples had 0-2 children.

Political Profile

The respondents of both the communities were found to be quite aware of their political rights However, the voting pattern is largely decided by the male members. Majority of the women had used their franchise in the last assembly and Lok Sabha Elections. Majority of Muslims had given vote in support of independent candidate in last assembly elections while majority of Hindus are BJP voters for both the elections. While talking to Muslim men about voting preference and pattern, it was found that they do not have preference for any particular party. Their preference is based on individual candidates and work done for the development of the area. When asked, if they impose their decision on their women for casting their votes, most of them said yes. The reason (a) since they remain at home, they do not know about the candidate and his work; (b) they themselves ask us whom to vote. (c) they do not know difference between not Congress (I) and BJP and are completely unaware of the changing environment (safe/unsafe).

When the same question was asked to Hindu men and women, majority of them promptly said we have been casting our votes for BJP and will continue to do so. But few women (including elderly) in absence of men did say that sometimes they vote for Congress (I) even if their husbands had preference for other parties.

Conclusion

On the basis of the comparative analysis of reproductive behaviour few points have emerged:

There is nothing like Muslim fertility or reproductive behaviour as seen by the response on motivation for having more children. Although the number of pregnancies and children is higher among Muslims, reasons seems to be mainly:

(i) Lower age at marriage and early pregnancies increasing reproductive span of Muslim women;
(ii) late use of contraception;
(iii) lower level of education;
(iv) occupational background; and
(v) some misconception about the use of contraception which is more cultural in nature than religious.

Contraception is widely used by the Muslim community (74 per cent) to prevent more child birth but the difference is they are the late and irregular users. On the basis of the discussions with the women specially with the Muslims, it is found that the use of contraception is affected by personal circumstances and communication between the spouses, her reproductive age; presence of married sons and daughters in the house, etc. than the religious prescription.

Tubectomy is not an approved form of birth control by majority of migrant Muslims. But the younger women did show intention to go for operation rather than having more children in future.

There is very little impact of religious orthodoxy in regulating reproductive behaviour. Although the preference for son was found among both the communities but the difference is, Muslims want them for cultural and economic reasons while Hindus for religious.

Men specially in case of Muslims often use religious explanation as a tool to control the fertility of women.

Real factors however, are occupation, income, education of both husband and wife and interference of family members.

Gender bias in health care and food is not related to religion. Most deliveries still take place at home by untrained *dai* irrespective of religion. Women irrespective of religion had very little say in regulating their reproductive behaviour with regard to when and how many children they want, use of contraception and other reproductive health issues.

13

Relative Economic and Social Deprivation in India

Abusaleh Shariff[1]

Introduction

The declaration of Indian Repubic as a secular state, after independence, explains the religious and ethnic diversity imbibed in its socio-cultural and political ethos since time immemorial. The caste, religious and regional differentials in economic, social and political spheres in India have a historical basis and are deeply influenced by the feudal relationship which have persisted for centuries. Indian socio-economic fabric is more complex than ordinarily believed because of various layers and segmentations the society is divided and subdivided into, due to factors unique to India. Compared with many other parts of the world, India as a whole is a less developed economy and society. In spite of many forces to the contrary it is a democracy in the making which is reassuring.

In India, the per capita GNP in 1995 was only $340 (ppp$1,400) as compared to USA with $ 26,980, Switzerland with $40,630 (ppp$25,860), Indonesia with $980 (ppp$3,800) and China with $ 620 (ppp$2,920). The Human Development Index value was only 0.446 and it ranked 138 among the 175 countries of the world in 1997. A large majority of people in India suffer from abject poverty. Poverty has two dimensions: an absolute and a relative dimension. India has over 330 million people belonging to all faiths, religions and regions who live a miserable life of absolute poverty suffering from extreme degree of human deprivation. In spite of falling levels of poverty in terms of proportion, the absolute number is hovering around 300 million since independence. Those belonging to this head count have command over resources which can barely replenish the energy/calories needed for human survival on a daily basis. If one expands the definition of poverty to incorporate the human development parameters, the population so classified will be much more. Given this massive, absolute dimension of poverty aspects of relative poverty gets obscure. Nonetheless, there are two essential reasons for understanding relative poverty profile. Firstly, reduction in relative proverty is a pre-condition in alleviating absolute poverty in any society. Secondly, it is important for any government to track the variations in relative poverty gap between various types of population groups so as to ensure equity in opportunity as a mechanism of poverty alleviation.

While studying relative differentials another statistical fact needs consideration. The actual gap in a measurement has to be understood in association with the level at which differentials occur. For example, a 10 percentage point difference at say a 50 per cent overall level of literacy is too serious an issue to be ignored by planners and policymakers compared with 80 per cent literacy rate. Similarly, a 50 to 100 per cent differential in the incidence or prevalence rate at less than 10 per cent of over all occurrence should be a matter of deep concern, a case in point, for example, of metric level education in India.

Thus far a study of relative deprivation in India and its many states was difficult to perform due to want of data. Although the Indian Censuses and NSSO Surveys do collect data on selected human development parameters they are not made available even to academicians for reasons best known to the respective departments and key politicians. However, of late a few independent data sources have come into existence which help in both estimating and redefining the parameters of poverty in its absolute and relative dimensions. A survey of 33,000 nationally representative rural sample, conducted by the National Council of Applied Economic Research in 1994 provides data on household income and a range of human development parameters which can be cross-classified according to a number of population groups. These data have been used to estimate levels of poverty according to selected population groups. In the following, I present a discussion of the relative position in economic, educational and health areas according to poverty line classification[2] and according to caste and religion for rural India, the two of the eight population groups analysed in the main report[3]. I also draw upon the 16 state level reports and 28 village studies which have been completed by the NCAER during 1995-98.

Income and Levels of Living

Household income and selected levels of living parameters according to poverty line categorization are in Table 1. The last 16 per cent of population classified as 'Lower Segment Below the Poverty Line' have reported an annual income of Rs 6,950 and a per capita income of Rs.1,095; compare this with those classified as 'Upper Segment Above the Poverty Line' (about 20 per cent of population) with income as high as Rs.58,100 and 11,396 respectively. Thus the poorest of the poor have access to only about 10 to 12 per cent level of income of the rich. This high disparity in levels of income among the overall population can be summarised in the Gini Ratio which is 0.43 for all India. More alarming fact however is the absolute level of income of the bottom 16 per cent who have per capita per day access to only Rs. 3, next about 20 per cent have an access to Rs. 5.5 per day per capita. Being the land owners, the richer households draw incomes largely from agriculture followed by salaried jobs. The share of income from salaries increases four to five folds for those above the poverty line and in absolute terms the difference is much more. Those below the poverty line draw their income largely from agricultural and non-agricultural wage labour. There is also a high incidence of non-working adult male population among the poor. This points to a high incidence of unemployment among those below the poverty line. The female

WPRs are fairly uniform across population groups. Excepting for the utilization of the public distribution system (PDS) access to basic needs such as housing, electricity, tap water and toilets are very low for those below the poverty line.

A startling finding is the relationship between the incidence of Poverty Head Count and Capability Poverty. While the last two categories are all poor and the remaining are all above the poverty line the percentage of households showing capability poverty declines only marginally from a high of 58 per cent to 42 per cent.

TABLE 1

Income, Asset and Material Wellbeing of Households According to Poverty Criteria

		Lower Segment Below	*Upper Segment Below*	*Lower Segment Above*	*Upper Segment Above*	*All*
Household Income (Rs.)		6950	12379	22138	58100	25653
Per Capita Income (Rs.)		1095	2026	3931	11396	4485
Work Participation Rate	Male	45.1	48.8	53.7	56.9	51.9
	Female	16.8	17.8	20.2	16.4	18.4
Source of Income	Agriculture	38.8	38.5	48.3	64.6	55.0
	Artisanship	6.2	7.4	6.1	2.6	4.5
	Salaried	4.4	6.5	15.1	20.4	16.5
Land Holding/ Reporting Household		2.4	2.6	3.9	7.6	4.5
percentage Kutcha Houses		70.8	68.8	53.0	37.3	55.4
percentage Electric		27.7	30.6	44.8	60.7	42.9
percentage Protected		67.0	69.9	72.9	75.6	72.0

Water					
percentage Piped Water	22.7	21.6	25.4	28.1	24.8
percentage Having Toliet	9.6	9.9	14.4	26.2	15.3
percentage Using PDS	30.1	29.5	37.1	30.6	33.2
Poverty Head Count per cent	100	100	-	-	39.0
Capability Poverty per cent	58.2	56.3	50.9	42.3	52.0

Source: India: Human Development Report of the 1990s (forthcoming, Oxford University Press).

The above key indicators according to caste and religion are in Table 2. One would find a very high incidence of poverty among the Scheduled Castes and the Scheduled Tribes followed by the Muslims compared with the all India average. The percentage of population below the poverty line is about 50 for the SCs and STs and 43 for Muslims compared with 39 for the whole population (32 per cent among the Hindus excluding SCs and STs). If the household and per capita income are considered a scenario emerges where the SCs, the STs and the Muslims can be considered as the economically deprived population groups. The respective incomes are 32 per cent, 24 per cent and 11 per cent lower than the national average. The income differentials widen when the per capita income is considered mainly because of relatively larger family size among the poorer groups. This brings to the fore the lack of access to productive assets, employment and wage stability for the Scheduled groups and the Muslims. Land is the most preferred and valued asset across India and the SCs and Muslims are relatively more deprived in terms of land ownership across India. Hindus as a whole have a relative advantage of owning land in larger proportion and in large size class, for example, while one-fifth of Hindus own five acres or more of land, only one-tenth of Muslims belong to this category. This points to the need for creating new instruments which may provide an alternative for land as the main source of security among the rural households.

Agriculture is the main source of income among the STs and

all Hindus; all Hindus and SCs also receive relatively higher share of income from salaried positions. Agricultural wage is an important source of income to the SCs and STs and artisanship for Muslims. The proportion of income derived from agriculture and allied activities among the Muslims is much lower than the Hindus; whereas their share of income is disproportionately large from artisan and industiral work. This at the outset appears a positive feature, but in fact it is not. In rural areas stable and higher level of income is derived from land and agriculture matched only by those with salaried regular income.

The work participation rate among the Muslims is the least both for males and females suggesting relatively higher unemployment rate. WPR among the Muslim women is as low as 10 per cent compared with an all India average of 18. Access to selected basic needs are below the national average for the SCs, the STs and the Muslims, particularly in electricity and piped water supply. Muslims particularly have lower PDS utilization compared with all other castes and religious categories.

TABLE 2

Income, Asset and Material Well-being of Households According to Caste and Religion

	Scheduled Tribe	Scheduled Caste	Hindus	Muslims	All
Household Income(Rs.)	19556	17465	25713	22807	25653
Per Capita Income(Rs.)	3504	3237	4514	3678	4485
Work Participation Rate:					
Male	51.6	52.8	52.3	48.0	51.9
Female	27.7	23.0	19.3	9.6	18.4

Source of Income:					
Agriculture	55.6	37.7	56.1	44.1	55.0
Artisanship	2.7	5.7	4.3	8.3	4.5
Salaried	14.8	15.2	16.4	14.7	16.5
Land Holding/ Reporting Household (acres)	4.3	2.8	4.6	3.6	4.5
percentage Kutcha House	74.0	66.6	55.2	65.9	55.4
percentage Electric	29.7	30.7	43.2	30.0	42.9
percentage Protected Water	61.6	72.8	71.1	78.1	72.0
percentage Piped Water	17.2	22.6	25.3	19.4	24.8
percentage Having Toilet	12.2	8.3	13.2	26.7	15.3
percentage Using PDS	37.5	32.1	34.1	21.8	33.2
Poverty Head Count	51.0	50.0	39	43.0	39.0
Capability Poverty per cent	68.0	60.0	-	56.0	52.0

Source: India: Human Development Report of the 1990s (forthcoming, Oxford University Press).

Note: Hindus includes the SCs and the STs.

Literacy and Schooling

Literacy, school enrolment, type of schools and cost of schooling are presented in Tables 3 and 4. It is clear that both literacy and enrolment rates increase substantially as levels of poverty decline. The relative improvements in these rates are similar both for literacy and enrolment. The discontinuation on the other hand increases a little before declining steeply among the richer households. The contrast is in respect of percentage of population above 17 years of age who have passed matriculation. The richer households have disproportionately large advantage over the poorer households. This is one aspect which needs substantial attention by the participants of this seminar. Persisting gender disparity in literacy and enrolment rates is a matter of concern as well. It has been found that relatively larger proportion of children belonging to better offs go to the private schools and the annual household expenditure is also higher although as a proportion to household income the expenditures will be relatively low for the richer. Thus the pinch of educating children is felt more by those who are living below poverty line.

TABLE 3
Levels of Literacy and Schooling According to Poverty Criteria

		Lower Segment Below	*Upper Segment Below*	*Lower Segment Above*	*Upper Segment Above*	*All*
Literacy Rate 7+age	Total	43.5	45.9	54.4	67.1	53.5
	Male	55.5	57.8	66.6	78.4	65.6
	Female	31.1	33.1	40.7	53.7	40.1
Enrolment Rate	Total	61.1	64.3	75.7	83.8	71.4
	Male	69.1	70.5	81.0	86.6	77.1
	Female	52.6	57.2	69.7	80.4	64.8
Discon-tinuation Rate (Average for 6-14 years)	Total	6.1	7.2	6.4	3.6	6.0
	Male	-	-	-	-	4.8
	Female	-	-	-	-	7.6
Percentage Matriculates 17+Years	**Total**	**4.5**	**5.4**	**8.7**	**13.9**	**8.6**
Per cent	Total	7.6	8.1	9.3	14.9	9.8

Students aged 6-14 year in Private Schools	Male	8.7	9.5	10.0	16.3	10.8
	Female	6.1	6.0	8.2	13.0	8.3
Annual Household Expenditure on Schooling	Govt. School	450	492	540	680	539
	Aided School	487	541	675	936	665

Source: India: Human Development Report of the 1990s (forthcoming, Oxford University Press).

The SCs and STs are least literate in India, followed by the Muslims compared with rest of population (Table 4). Only about 40 per cent of SCs and STs and 50 per cent of Muslims are literate compared with about 54 per cent over all average (60 per cent for Hindus excluding SCs and STs). Literacy is a stock measure and it changes slowly over time. But a matter of concern is that the enrolment rate among the Muslims is only 62 per cent almost at parity with the SCs and STs as compared with about 72 per cent for all India and 77 per cent for Hindus (other than SCs and STs). The enrolment is a flow variable and can be improved within a relatively shorter period of time. But a larger inter-group disparity in enrolment compared with the disparity in levels of literacy suggests that enrolment rate in elementary schooling among the Muslims has been falling in the immediate past especially so in case of females. This also suggest that some sections of the Muslims are unable to utilize the schooling and educational opportunities provided by the respective state governments. While there is considerable difference in terms of level of literacy, the gender differentials measured in terms of the female-male ratios are marginal between communities.

TABLE 4
Levels of Literacy and Schooling According to Caste and Religion

		Scheduled Tribe	Scheduled Caste	Hindus	Muslims	All
Literacy Rate 7+ age	Total	39.3	41.5	53.3	49.9	53.5
	Male	51.4	53.4	65.9	59.5	65.6
	Female	26.0	28.2	39.2	38.0	40.1
Enrolment Rate	Total	60.3	62.5	72.0	61.6	71.4
	Male	67.6	69.6	78.1	66.2	77.1
	Female	51.5	54.7	65.1	56.6	64.8
Discontinuation Rate (Averge for 6-14 years)	Total	7.2	7.0	5.9	6.9	6.0
	Male	6.6	5.7	-	6.4	4.8
	Female	8.0	8.8	-	7.7	7.6
Percentage Matriculates 15+ years	Total	4.9	4.9	8.5	5.9	8.6
Per cent Students aged 6-14 years in Private Schools	Total	3.2	5.8	9.3	13.3	9.8
	Male	3.8	6.9	10.4	14.4	10.8
	Female	2.3	4.2	7.7	11.9	8.3
Annual Household Expenditure on Schooling	Govt. Schools	397	450	531	515	539
	Ailded Schools	664	544	671	542	665

Source: India: Human Development Report of the 1990s (forthcoming, Oxford University Press).

Another important fact to highlight is the onset of private schooling across India, more so in Uttar Pradesh, Punjab, Haryana, Bihar, Andhra Pradesh and Kerala. Muslims send their children relatively more to the private elementary schools compared with all other communities. There appears to be some sort of resentment on the part of Muslims to send their children to government schools. Since, schooling and education is a state subject important policy initiatives have to be taken by the states to set right this anomaly in providing equal opportunities and appropriate education at least at the primary and elementary levels. National efforts should be initiated to find out as to why the Muslim children are being withdrawn from the publicly provided free schooling in India. Allowing this trend to continue is also likely to affect female education among the Muslims much more. Considering education as one of the main parameters of human development. Clearly the SCs, the STs and the Muslims lag in most of the output indicators such as the literacy, enrolment, discontinuation and percentage of population (aged 17+years) completing matriculation. A relatively greater dependence on private schooling of Muslims, which is disproportionately expensive, and especially given the low economic conditions, seems to be due to compulsions emerging out of inappropriate education. There is an urgent need to take a serious note of the above facts to design appropriate public policy interventions and implement them in due earnest taking help from multi-national agencies such as the United Nations and the World Bank if needed.

Health and Demography

The short duration morbidity is negatively related with levels of living, whereas, major morbidity is positively related. The lower incidence of major morbidity among the poor is likely to be due to low diagnosis[4] on the one hand and selectivity caused by high deaths as a result to such morbidity. The infant mortality rate is also substantially higher among those below the poverty line. A considerably higher incidence of physical disability is found among the poorer households for children 5-12 years old. Severe degree of malnutrition especially in younger ages is considerably high among the poor.

The crude birth rate among the poor is significantly large for households reporting below poverty level incomes. It seems high fertility is a direct response to high degree of insecurity faced by the poor due to lack of a durable source of income, lack of immovable assets and saving portfolio. As expected contraceptive practice improves by levels of income. The poverty levels are also positively related to utilization of health care services such as institutional deliveries and immunizations.

TABLE 5

Health Care Utilization According to Poverty Criteria

	Lower Segment Below	*Upper Segment Below*	*Lower Segment Above*	*Upper Segment Above*	*All*
Short Duration Morbidity ('000)	125	128	120	117	122
Major Morbidity (Per)	4183	4216	4615	5231	4578
Percentage receiving ANC Care	10.7	10.2	9.3	9.6	9.8
Percentage Delivery Attended Trained Person	32.4	35.2	43.7	53.1	40.0
Percentage Children Immunized (All 8 doses)	40.8	45.4	52.0	54.6	48.5
Disabilities:					
0-4 years/lakh	1836	2258	2045	2000	2042
5-12 years/lakh	2861	3521	2823	2195	2896

Sever Malnutrition					
0-4 years per cent	38.1	38.2	37.3	33.8	37.2
5-12 years per cent	30.6	30.0	28.2	27.3	29.0
Crude Birth Rate	45	41	28	21	32
Total Fertility Rate	6.4	5.5	3.6	2.7	4.3
Infant Mortality Rate	88	95	83	70	84
Contraception	33	34	37	39	36
per cent Spacing Methods	4.6	5.2	5.5	7.7	5.6

Source: India: Human Development Report of the 1990s (forthcoming, 1998, Oxford University Press).

Besides, high fertility rates among the Muslims, the SCs and the STs, overall birth rate of 32 per thousand population for rural India as a whole should be a cause of concern. The mortality and morbidity rates are relatively high among the SCs and STs and low among the Muslims. The physical disability rates are relatively higher among all the three communities focused in this presentation. The contraceptive practice is low for Muslims followed by the Scheduled groups. However, a dynamic look at the changes in all these factors over time suggests that relative differentials in fertility, mortality and family planning practice are declining over the past four decades and the differentials found recently are the lowest. In fact the rate of increase in contraception has begun to be more than the general population among the Muslims an evidence emerging from intensive studies on contraception. Muslims prefer to use spacing methods relatively more than all other communities which is cause for optimism for the programme implementations. This scenario suggests that Muslims have begun to accept family planning measures in large numbers in the preceding two decades or so. Research has also conclusively proved that an improvement in human development parameters depress fertility and mortality and improve choice based contraception. Therefore there is a great prospect that various states in India enter the third and fourth level of demographic transition in the early first decade of the next century and Muslims will be not lacking in contributing to this important achievement. While it is encouraging that the population group differentials are narrowing down in demographic parameters, the utilization of government provided health care services is relatively low among the SCs, STs and especially the Muslims. For example the number of deliveries conducted under the care of trained professionals such as the Auxiliary Nurse Midwives and the child immunization rates among the Muslims are low. There is thus an urgent need that Muslims come forward in a big way to harness the benefits of public programmes.

TABLE 6

Health Care Utilization According to Caste and Religion

	Scheduled Tribe	*Scheduled Caste*	*Hindus*	*Muslims*	*All*
Short Duration Morbidity ('000)	130	124	123	106	122
Major Morbidity (Per Lakh)	3377	4527	4503	4441	4578
Percentage receiving ANC Care	5.7	11.6	9.9	8.0	9.8
Percentage Delivery Attended Trained Person	31.9	37.6	40.5	31.5	40.0
Percentage Children Immunized (All 8 doses)	39.5	42.6	49.7	34.5	48.5

Disabilities:					
0-4 years/lakh	1881	2058	1983	2409	2042
5-12 years/lakh	2406	3325	2771	3792	2896
Sever Malnutrition					
0-4 years per cent	38.0	40.3	37.4	37.7	37.2
5-12 years per cent	30.2	30.3	28.7	33.5	29.0
Crude Birth Rate	35	35	32	39	32
Total Fertility Rate	4.4	4.7	4.2	5.8	4.3
Infant Mortality Rate	98	99	86	75	84
Contraception	34	31	36	25	36
per cent Spacing Methods	4.4	4.7	4.9	8.2	5.6

Source: India: Human Development Report of the 1990s (forthcoming, Oxford University Press).

Hope for the Future

On the whole compared with the dominant Hindus, the SCs, the STs and Muslims seem to be characteristically marginalised due to social and physical distancing from the social, economic and political nucleus. They also have low personal esteem. The process and mechanisms of exclusion could take mundane and subtle routes that often go unnoticed. Most of the downtrodden are illiterate, maintain endogamous social relations, work as wage labour and artisans. They have a high (age) dependency due to high fertility and, low economic dependency ratio because almost every one has to work including children. Low employment and wage stability, relatively more nuclear and fractured families, high mortality and low health care utilization. Their participation in public programmes and utilization of publicly provided goods and services is substantially lower than the population as a whole. They have been unable to find adequate proportion of positions in the government machinery, and in public and political policy making.

The reasons for relative backwardness of the SCs, STs and Muslims is only partly due to historical reasons. All these communities have a poor asset base especially in terms of ownership of immovable assets, such as cultivable land. Partly, the reasons for relative backwardness are social—the relative bargaining power in the local social and political system has always been low. Rural to urban migration of the SCs, and Muslims since Independence may have also contibuted to this state of affair. Concurrently the particular and unique problems emerging from the caste system and multi-religious population composition were not accorded adequate attention in public debates, public allocations and program implementation, notwithstanding the reservation for the SCs, the STs and OBCs. Most programmes aimed at alleviating the problems of poor and minorities are symbolic and un-sustainable due to want of implementation and adequate public commitment. There should be public efforts to create enduring opportunities, and carefully conceived affirmative actions, at least in the short run, to alleviate the relative backwardness especially in the areas of education, employment and training, productive credit and political participation.

Ensuring that India remains a multi-cultural, multi-ethnic, diverse and dynamic society is imperative both for national integrity and strength. While these attributes are India's strength a reformed legal system should evolve which can penalize vested interests that misuse these characteristics regardless of whether they be individuals, communities or the political parties. There has been considerable progress in this direction, but much has to be done. The Indian legal system has not been fully harnessed to address these issues. It is essential that the Indian policy clearly distinguish between the religious minorities and ethnic minorities.

The forces of globalization and a new deal world economic order can create opportunities to overcome many a crisis faced by the downtrodden only if the fruits of new economic order are accessible to all and are fairly distributed. The economic forces of liberalization and globalization should essentially be the most secular forces sweeping India in the recent past.Yet, however, the peculiar way of adaptation of these forces may not entirely be free from subjective decision making, thus excluding selected population groups and regions from accessing the ensuing benefits. The present day private and to some extent the corporate sector seem to still rely on traditional social systems which needs to change.

Promoting mainstream participation of the SCs, STs and Muslims in social, economic and political spheres should be one of the important objectives of the state governments. This will imbibe the feeling of propriety and ownership which brings along with it responsibility to save, protect and promote. In this regard it is essential to conceptualize programmes and to generate a sense of agency and trusteeship among all but more so among the community leadership irrespective of religion and caste. Participation in secular education is a necessary but not sufficient condition. Education should impart values emphasizing the multi-cultural nature of Indian society, tolerance and mutual respect of basic human values rather than propagation of procedures, rituals and unconformable historical events. Choice based education system should be evolved in which different religions and communities should have opportunities to choose their language of instruction and topics of interest. Importance in providing education and schooling in English should be reviewed, along with priority in computer literacy. This reemphasis in education is in the interest of all the future generations in India.

There are certain responsibilities that the respective communities should share. These communities should be senstitive to local issues and should identify first with the local population and then to the larger population identities of states, nation and international communities. The 73rd and 74th Constitutional Amendments do not automatically address these issues. Yet they provide a good platform. The hitherto marginalized communities should participate in large numbers in the

Panchayati Raj system and the urban local self-governments. The respective communities which often suffer from urban middle class stereotype should come out of it as soon as possible. Besides, there is a need to recognize diversity within communities, including those in the minority communities. Creating homogeneity is not the answer. Locate where community lives and integrate. Ensure gender equity and enable female participation in market activities. These should be effected both in the intra-household as well as community context.

There should be institutions and structures that encourage individuals and community to realize the benefits of social services provided by the government. It needs social mobilization not necessarily of the communities alone. The SCs, STs and Muslims should come out in a large way to realize the benefits provided by a large number of public programmes. Special programmes for the downtrodden are yet not fully implemented. Pressure groups and lobbying may help improve programme implementation. Administrative, rather than delimited boundaries for electoral purposes, should be used for planning. Special trade fairs and display of unique skill that the Indian SCs, STs and Muslims have deserves special encouragement. Private and corporate sectors should open avenues for employment for all communities based on the principles of efficiency and competition.

ANNEXURE TABLE

TABLE A1

Percentage Distribution of Households by Poverty Groups in States (Rural India)

Region/ State	*Lower Segment Below*	*Upper Segment Below*	*Lower Segment Above*	*Upper Segment Avove*
North				
Haryana	10.1	13.0	48.7	28.2
Himachal Pradesh	18.5	20.1	37.9	23.4

Punjab	13.6	14.6	47.7	24.1
Upper Central				
Bihar	17.1	22.2	41.4	19.3
Uttar Pradesh	18.8	20.6	40.2	20.3
Lower Central				
Madhya Pradesh	14.9	18.6	45.3	21.1
Orissa	23.8	23.5	33.4	17.5
Rajasthan	18.2	21.3	40.3	20.2
East				
North-Eastern Rg.	13.5	15.5	41.8	29.1
West Bengal	23.7	29.3	30.3	16.7
West				
Gujarat	15.1	17.5	48.8	18.6
Maharashtra	13.1	15.5	50.3	21.2
South				
Andhra Pradesh	7.4	9.9	56.7	26.0
Karnataka	16.3	18.8	45.1	19.8
Kerala	11.8	14.2	50.5	23.5
Tamil Nadu	13.0	14.6	45.3	27.1
Rural India	**15.9**	**18.8**	**43.8**	**21.6**

TABLE A2

Percentage Distribution of Households by Poverty Groups in Social Groups

Social/Groups	*Lower Segment Below*	*Upper Segment Below*	*Lower Segment Above*	*Upper Segment Above*
Caste				
STs	20.2	24.3	41.6	14.0
SCs	22.1	23.6	42.4	12.0

Other Hindus	12.6	15.6	44.8	27.0
Religions				
Hindus				
Muslims	17.5	23.7	42.6	16.3
Christians	12.9	11.8	46.7	28.7
Other Minorities	18.9	18.0	42.8	20.3
All Groups	**15.9**	**18.8**	**43.8**	**21.6**

REFERENCES

1. I acknowledge the research assistance provided by Veena Kulkarni, Prabir Ghosh and secretarial support, by Jaya Kumari.
2. The poverty line and the estimates of poverty were undertaken using the new methodology suggested by the Planning Commission now popularly known as the Expert Group Method of Estimation.
3. The key findings of the above cited survey will be available in August 1998, entitled, India: Human Development Report of the 1990s, New Delhi: Oxford University Press (forthcoming). The Study itself was jointly funded by the UNDP, UNICEF, UNFPA and IDRC.
4. The major morbidity prevalence reported in this paper refers to individuals reporting current medication for an identifiable chronic disease at the time of survey.

14

Economic Problems of Muslim Women in India

Malika B. Mistry

Introduction

Muslims are the largest minority in India constituting 12 per cent of the total population of India in 1991. In terms of absolute numbers, India has the largest Muslim population of 120 million only next to Indonesia, Pakistan and Bangladesh. Compared to Hindus, the majority community (24 per cent), a greater proportion of Muslims live in urban areas (36 per cent). Indian economy has made remarkable progress in the last 50 years. Yet, for various reasons, Muslims in India, have been unable to enjoy the fruits of development and so belong to the weaker sections of society. With the trend of globalization and liberalization, the conditions of Muslims are expected to worsen because only highly competitive and skilled individuals and industries are expected to survive in such atmosphere. So there is an urgent need for their socio-economic upliftment.

Nearly half of the 120 million Muslim population of India is of Muslim women (sex ratio, 930 females per 1000 males, 1991 census). Thus, Muslim women form a sizeable chunk of Indian population. Economic independence for Muslim women, like for women from any other community, is very important to lead a dignified life. As such, it is necessary to study the economic problems faced by Muslim women. However, the problems of Muslim women cannot be studied in isolation from the socio-economic backwardness faced by the community as a whole. Therefore, in this paper, an attempt is made first to assess the level of socio-economic backwardness among Muslims in general and later we try to find the same among Muslim women. Thereafter we move over to identify the factors responsible for their economic problems and finally try to find solutions for the same. Thus the objectives of this paper have been: (i) to assess the level of socio-economic backwardness among Muslims in general and Muslim women in particular; (ii) to identify the factors that account for the economic backwardness of Muslim women; and (iii) to suggest solutions for these problems.

Socio-economic Backwardness among Muslims

Before we talk about upliftment, it is necessary to know the extent of socio-economic backwardness among Muslims as compared to the other religious groups. Census data could be the best source of information for ascertaining the socio-economic backwardness of Muslims but unfortunately Indian census authorities do not publish the same. Yet data available from different sample surveys conducted in different parts of the country reveal that the Muslims have been left out of the development process. In 1983, N.C. Saxena, Secretary to the Minorities Commission, stated: "Over 70 per cent of Muslims in India live in the rural areas and are marginal and small farmers or self-employed artisans. Of the remaining 30 per cent who live in the towns, roughly 80 to 85 per cent are skilled workers, tailors, retailers, petty businessmen, small manufacturers or are engaged in traditional industries like bidi-making, perfumery, block-making etc." (1983: 120). Thus more than 90 per cent of Muslims are small and marginal farmers, artisans and workers. The occupational structure of Muslims makes them poor, for their educational backwardness and lack of skills do not allow them to enter high-income occupations. In modern industry and trade, except for rare instances, Muslims have not owned large-scale industry or business and generally lack high entrepreneurial skills. There is not a single Muslim industrial house among the fifty existing in India while at the lower end of the scale, most Muslims are poor and backward. Another scholar, Rashiduddin Khan states:

> "there is no denying that Muslims have been at the lowest rung of the ladder in terms of the basic categories of the socio-economic indicators of development." (1978:1515).

NSSO Survey

The latest published data on socio-economic indicators by religion at the national level has been made available for the first time by the National Sample Survey Organisation (NSSO), through its 43rd round survey conducted during 1987-88. The indicators considered are: occupation, work participation, ownership of land and relative standards of living, all of which are presented below (NSSO, 1990).

Occupation and work participation

Distribution of persons by household type (occupation) and religion for rural and urban areas are given in Tables 1 and 2 respectively. (Distribution of population who are included under a certain category, is based on the household type

TABLE 1
Distribution of Persons by Household Type (Occupation) and Religion, Rural India, 1987-88

(Per cent)

Occupation	*Hindus*	*Muslims*	*Christians*	*Others*
Agriculture	43.9	36.3	37.9	38.6
Non-agriculture	11.7	21.2	10.9	22.9
Agricultural labour	28.3	24.4	28.4	21.7
Other labour	8.3	9.9	10.9	4.6
Other occupation	7.9	8.1	11.9	12.3

Source: NSSO, 43rd Round, 1987-88, Table 27R (p. S-56).

TABLE 2
Distribution of Persons by Household Type (Occupation) and Religion, Urban India, 1987-88

(Per cent)

Occupation	*Hindus*	*Muslims*	*Christians*	*Others*
Self-employed	35.9	53.4	21.4	44.6
Regular wage/ salaried	46.7	28.9	56.1	38.3
Casual Labour	12.1	13.4	12.3	10.5
Others	5.4	4.3	10.2	6.6

Source: NSSO, 43rd Round, 1987-88, Table 27U, (p. S-57).

of income of the household to which they belong. These percentages do not present employment levels). In rural India, 44 per cent of Hindus and 38 per cent of Christians undertake agricultural occupations, as opposed to only 36 per cent of Muslims. However, 22 per cent of rural Muslims are engaged in non-agricultural and non-labour occupations, as opposed to only 12 per cent Hindus and 11 per cent Christians. In urban areas whereas 47 per cent of Hindus and 56 per cent of Christians are employed in regular jobs (that is wage/salaried occupations in organized sector), only 29 per cent of Muslims are thus employed. Furthermore, 53 per cent of urban Muslims are self-employed as opposed to 36 per cent Hindus and 21 per cent Christians.

Data by type of employment by religion and residence is given in Table 3. A look at the distribution of males by type of employment reveals that over 53 per cent of urban Muslim males are self-employed. This percentage is substantially lower for both Hindu (39 per cent) and Christian (30 per cent) males. On the contrary, the proportion of Hindus (46 per cent) and Christians (53 per cent) in the category of regular workers is substantially higher than among Muslims (30 per cent). In rural areas, the differentials between different religious groups in the above categories of employment are less. Still, highest proportion of Muslims are self-employed and the lowest proportion of Muslims work as regular workers.

Type of Employment Among Muslim Females

Proportions of females employed in different categories in the NSSO survey are also given in Table 3. A examination of these

TABLE 3

Type of Employment by Religion and Residence, India 1987-88

(Per cent)

Residence/Sex and Religion	*Self-Employed*	*Regular Workers*	*Casual Workers*	*All*	*Work Participation Rate*
Urban Males					
Hindus	39.1	46.4	14.5	100.0	52.0
Muslims	53.3	29.9	16.7	100.0	49.1
Christians	29.7	53.4	17.0	100.0	48.9
Rural Males					
Hindus	58.5	10.1	31.4	100.0	54.2
Muslims	59.0	7.5	33.5	100.0	50.5
Christians	52.1	12.0	35.9	100.0	
Urban Females					
Hindus	45.0	27.7	26.4	100.0	15.9
Muslims	60.0	15.7	24.3	100.0	11.4
Christians	34.3	51.5	14.2	100.0	23.6
Rural Females					
Hindus	59.9	3.6	36.5	100.0	33.7
Muslims	67.9	3.0	29.1	100.0	19.6
Christians	57.6	9.9	32.4	100.0	37.3

Source: NSSO, 43rd Round, 1987-88 (Scheduled-10).

proportions reveals that the pattern of employment is similar for Muslim females as for Muslim males. In urban areas, the proportion of self-employed is the highest and the proportion of regular workers is the lowest among Muslim women and the differentials between Muslim females and females of other religious groups are substantial. In rural areas too, the same pattern is observed, but differentials between Hindus and Muslims are not large.

Ownership of Land and Overall Living Standards

As opposed to only 28 per cent of Hindus, 35 per cent of Muslims are landless. Hindus also have a relative advantage in owning land, in the large size class. For example, while one-fifth of Hindus own five acres of land, only one-tenth of Muslims fit into this category.

There are substantial differences in standards of living between rural and urban areas and among the different religions in urban India. In rural areas, the relative difference between Hindus and Muslims is marginal while the Christians are better off. The difference between Muslims and other religious groups is considerable in urban areas. For example, while 53 per cent of Muslims fall into the category of spending less than Rs. 160 monthly per capita, this percentage is only 36 among Hindus and 28 per cent among Christians. In the highest expenditure class (per capita more than Rs. 300), the proportion of Hindus (23 per cent) and Christians (36 per cent) is substantially larger than among Muslims (11 per cent).

Summarizing the above data based on the 43rd round survey of NSSO, Shariff states:

> "Muslims are mostly self-employed and their share in regular paid jobs is low. The Hindu population is relatively better employed in regular salary-paying jobs in urban areas. The work participation of Muslim females is extremely low. The land holding is better among Hindus than Muslims, and Muslims work on non-agricultural occupation in substantial proportions in rural part of India. Muslims, are , by far, the least educated when compared with Hindus and Christians populations in India. The scenario is the same if one studies the student

population both in rural and urban areas as well. Muslim women are the least educated. Although monthly per capita expenditure compares well between the Hindus and Muslims in rural areas, it is highly lopsided (favouring Hindus) in urban areas. On the whole, Muslims are socio-economically worse off in all parts of the country." (Shariff, 1995:2951).

NCAER Survey

In 1994, the National Council of Applied Economic Research (NCAER), Delhi, as part of *INDIA: Human Development Report* collected data from 33,000 nationally representative rural households spread over all parts of India. Religion was one of the variables in this category. This is the most recently released data.

Data on level of income and material well-being by religion, caste and tribe for rural India, are provided in Table 4. An examination of the table reveals the following: Over all, the Head Count Poverty and Capability Poverty ratios are considerably higher for the Muslims compared with all India (rural) average and the caste-Hindus. The percentage of population below the poverty line is 43 for Muslims compared with only 32 for cast-Hindus and 39 for the whole population. Muslims on the whole are worse off than their Hindu counterparts. Not only is the household income of Muslims only Rs. 22,807, twenty-three per cent lower compared with Rs. 29, 786 for the high caste-Hindus, but also it is eleven per cent less than the national average for rural India that is Rs. 25,653 in 1993-94. The differentials in fact get widened when the per capita income is considered mainly because of relatively large family size among the Muslims. This brings forth the lack of access to asset and other types of employment and wage stability for the Muslims. Land is the most preferred and valued asset across India; but 43 per cent to Muslim households are landless compared with only 30 per cent among Hindus. Hindus also have a relative advantage of owning land in larger size class.

On an average, the high-caste Hindus own 5.1 acres of land compared with only 3.6 acres for Muslims.

The proportion of income derived from agriculture and allied activities for the Muslims is much lower than the Hindus; whereas

TABLE 4
Levels on Incomes and Material Well-being

	Scheduled Tribe	*Scheduled Caste*	*High Caste Hindus*	*Muslims*	*All*
Household Income (Rs.)	19556	17465	29786	22807	25653
Per Capita Income (Rs.)	3504	3237	5113	3678	4485
Work Participation Rate:					
Male	51.6	52.8	52.2	48.0	51.9
Female	27.7	23.0	16.6	9.6	18.4
Source of Income:					
Agriculture	55.6	37.7	60.0	44.1	55.0
Artisanship	2.7	5.7	4.2	8.3	4.5
Salaried	14.8	15.2	16.3	14.7	16.5
Land Holding/Reporting Household (acres)	4.3	2.8	5.1	3.6	4.5
Percentage Kutcha Houses	47.0	66.6	47.7	65.9	55.4
Percentage Electric Connections	29.7	30.7	50.1	30.0	42.9
Electric Protected Water	61.6	72.8	72.2	78.1	72.0
Percentage Having Toilet	12.2	8.3	15.2	26.7	15.3

Percentage Using PDS	37.5	32.1	34.2	21.8	33.2
Povety Head Count Ratio per cent	51.0	50.0	32.0	43.0	39.0
Capability Poverty per cent	68.0	60.0	49.0	56.0	52.0

NCAER/HDI Survey, 1994.

their share of income is disproportionately large from artisan and industrial work. This at the outset appears to be a positive feature, but in fact it is not. In rural areas, stable and higher level of income is derived from land and agriculture followed only by the salaried class. It is also found that the Muslims in rural areas depend relatively more on wage labour and the number of days of wage employment is also lower, more so in case of women. The work participation rate of Muslims is much lower suggesting relatively higher unemployment rate. Employment of Muslim women is extremely low.

Once again, Shariff, after comparing the data from the NCAER survey for Muslims and other religious groups on economic, social and demographic variables has concluded:

> "On the whole Muslims seem to be characteristically obscure due to social and physical distancing from the social, economic and political nucleus. They also have low personal esteem. The process of and mechanisms of exclusion could take mundane and subtle routes that often go unnoticed. Most of the Muslims are illiterate, they are mostly, endogamous, wage labour and artisanship are the main source of income, apparently low dependency ratios because almost every one have to work including children, relatively more nuclear and fractured families, high fertility and mortality, low health care utilization, low employment and wage stability. Their participation in public programmes and utilization of publicly provided goods and services are substantially lower than the population as a whole. Muslims have been unable to find adequate proportion of

positions in government machinery, and in public and political policy making." (Shariff, 1998:12).

Malegaon Survey

The data produced above are from the national surveys. It is also important to study the socio-economic backwardness of Muslims by conducting micro surveys. One such survey was conducted by Mistry (1998) in 1994 in Malegaon city in Nasik district of Maharashtra, which is a Muslim majority area with 73 per cent of its population being Muslim in 1991. In this survey 800 Muslim households from Muslim majority wards and 961 women in the age group 15-49 were interviewed. Though it was a demographic survey, a good deal of information was collected from the Muslim households regarding socio-economic conditions of Malegon Muslims.

Malegaon is an important power-loom centre in western India. Weaving is the major occupation among Malegeon Muslims. Most of these weavers live at subsistence level. A distressing feature of Malegaon city is that a considerable proportion of its population lives in slums. It has poor medical facilities. The streets in Malegaon are narrow and congested with uncleared garbage heaps after every three or four houses and open drains being a common sight. Water is supplied through common connections at street corners and the toilets are community toilets located at distant corners of the Municipal wards.

In 1996, according to Powerloom Federation of Malegaon, about 1,10,000 registered and about 10,000 unregistered power looms existed in Malegaon. Also there were more than 100 sizing units. Along with men, women and children work on the loom to undertake associated operations. The weavers continue to suffer for several reasons. The textile policy is unfavorable to them. They cannot afford buying of yarn, and marketing of cloth is not in their hands. The middle men exploit the weavers as they lack organization. Since no other economic opportunities exist, many of the weavers continue in the occupation even though it provides them only with a subsistence level of living. In spite of their hardships, Malegaon

Muslim weavers are simple, innocent and happy-go-lucky people.

It has also been observed that Malegaon Muslims are characterized by low level of modernization as revealed by their following characteristics: (i) their major industry; viz. Powerloom weaving industry, is decentralized and unorganized; (ii) for their credit requirements, the weavers borrow from the yarn and cloth merchants who exploit them rather than from the banks; (iii) they do not realize the power of collective bargaining and are unwilling to form co-operatives; (iv) they are oblivious of the connection between economics and politics; (v) they are fearful and resentful of the government and try to maintain maximum distance from it; (vi) they prefer traditional channels of justice; (vii) the gap between he weavers and the state level politicians is striking; (viii) they seem to ignore the numerous public spirited campaigns that occupy provincial polity of Maharashtra from time to time; and (ix) social interaction in Malegaon is mainly restricted to the city itself which excludes not only the immediate surroundings but also the larger world outside. Further, they seem to lack awareness about civil liberties that an individual can enjoy in a modern democratic society. Thus, Rajeevlochan, (1996), a civil servant who worked among Muslims in Malegaon city, observes that the Muslims in Malegaon exist "in a framework where the scale of society has not expanded beyond the confines of a small town or village and the behavioural patterns, habits and the attitudes of the weavers resemble those of the small time 19th century peasants much more closely than those of the middle class trader, small industrialists or entrepreneures. Thus they see no need to participate competitively in a democratic polity and do not see that this is necessary to secure scarce funds and help. Thereby they closed off important avenues for improvement".

Socio-economic Development Indicators of Malegaon

Per capita income, housing characteristics, ownership of consumer durables and occupation could be some of the important indicators of socio-economic development of a community. Distribution of Malegaon Muslim households by per capita monthly income is given in Table 5. A look at the table shows that three quarters of the household earn only upto Rs. 200 per month. It would be more revealing to examine the per capita monthly income of the household by family size. The per capita monthly income for the Muslim population in the survey was only Rs.2000. Further in the income group upto Rs.1000, the per capita monthly income was less than Rs.100. As the per capita monthly income increases, the average family size also increases indicating that there was no real increase in the welfare of the family.

TABLE 5

Distribution of Malegaon Muslim Households by Per Capita Monthly Income

Income group (Rs.)	*Number of households*	*Percentage of households*	*Persons*	*Per capita income (Rs.)*	*Average household size*
Less than 1000	295	36.9	1792	82.3	6.1
1000-1999	297	37.1	2382	187.0	8.0
2000-2999	129	16.1	1252	257.6	9.9
3000 and above	79	9.9	816	446.7	10.4

Note. Since exact figures were not collected, the per capita income is computed at group level using midpoints of class intervals.

Source: Mistry (1998c), p. 217.

Percentage distribution of households by housing characteristics and by ownership of consumer durables is given in Tables 6 and 7 respectively. A perusal of the Table 6 shows that around half of the Muslim households in Malegaon live in one room houses, two-thirds of them do not have a separate kitchen, and only 17 per cent have toilets attached to their houses. Also by type of house, around half of the households live in kutcha houses. This reveals that most of the

Muslim households in Malegaon belong to the lower stratum of the society. Ownership of consumer durables (Table 7) too supports the above conclusion.

TABLE 6
Percentage Distribution of Households by Housing Characteristics

Characteristics	*Numbers of households*	*Percentage of households*
Number of rooms		
One	388	48.5
Two	281	35.1
Three	97	12.1
Four	28	3.5
Five	3	0.4
Six	3	0.4
Kitchen		
Separate	273	34.1
Common	527	65.9
Toilet		
Separate	134	16.7
Common	666	83.3
Source of Water		
Public tap	441	55.2
Own tap	334	41.7
Public hand pump	12	1.5
Own hand pump	13	1.6
Electricity		
Yes	663	82.9
No	137	17.1
House ownership		
Owned house	706	88.3
Rented house	94	11.7
Type of house		
Kutcha	374	46.7
Semi-Pucca	290	36.3
Pucca	136	17.0
Total	800	100.0

Source: Same as Table 5, p. 218.

TABLE 7

Distribution of Households by Ownership of Consumer Durables

Consumer durables	*Percentage of Owning Household*
Stove	98.75
Cooker	87.13
Cooking gas	12.75
Cot	65.38
Chair	60.63
Cupboard	47.75
Sewing machine	27.37
Charkha	7.25
Power loom	11.00
Cycle	72.50
Scooter	7.75
Fan	46.00
Radio	32.75
T.V.	16.75
Fridge	6.63

Scurce: Same as Table 5, p. 220.

Occupation is one of the most important indicators of socio-economic development of a community. Distribution of household population by occupation for male and female is given in Table 8. It is observed that majority of the males (41 per cent) fall in the category of 'others' viz. students, retired persons, unemployed etc. About 27 and 10 per cent of Muslim males are engaged in loom and labour category respectively. Thus, a little above one-third of the males are engaged in low income occupations. The percentages of males engaged in 'profession' and 'service' categories are very low (3 and 1 respectively). Majority of females (60 per cent) were not working outside home. Another 32 per cent of the females were in the category of 'others' viz. students, handicapped, too old etc. Five per cent of females were working on loom. In general the female participation in important occupations is negligible.

The work participation rate (percentage of total workers to total population) in the study area for males was 44 and for females 8. According to 1991 census the work participation rate in Malegaon city (all communities) is 45 for males and 7 for females. These rates compare well with those of the study area.

Occupation of Every-married Women

Among the 961 every-married eligible women in the age group 15-49, more than four-fifths of them were housewives. About 6 per cent had reported working on charkh a as their occupation and 5 per cent were engaged in paid jobs. Less than half-a-per cent are engaged

TABLE 8
Percentage Distribution of Population by Sex and Occupation amongst the Household

Type of occupation	*Male*	*Female*
Profession	3.0	0.6
Service	1.3	0.5
Business	6.6	0.3
Technical	3.6	0.4
Loom	27.2	4.5
Labourer	10.3	1.3
House-work	6.5	60.3
Religious	0.2	0.1
Others	41.3	32.0
Total Perccntage	100.0	100.0
Number	2,690	2,591

Source: Some as Table 5, p. 222.

in services related to religion. Thus the proportion of women engaged in gainful employment among married Muslim women in Malegaon is very low.

What is true of Malegaon, one can safely assume that a would be true of a majority of Muslims anywhere in India, because socio-economic conditions in Muslim majority areas everywhere in India seem to be similar.

The data on Muslims from the two national survey and from a micro study of Malegaon Muslims suggest that Muslims are much behind other communities in their socio-economic development. What is true of Muslim males seems to be more true of Muslim females. It is disheartening to see that the work participation rate among Muslim women are low and the lowest compared to Hindu and Christian women. In the next section, let us try to identify the factors responsible for their low participation.

Factors Responsible for Low Work Participation of Muslim Women

The following factors, to a large extent, account for low work participation rates among Muslim women in India.

Low Levels of Education

The first and foremost reason for the low level of work participation among Muslim women in India is their low level of education. At least passing of High School is necessary for qualifying for jobs in the organized sector. Data from the NSSO 43rd round survey and also from the NCAER survey reveal that Muslim men as well women are the least educated compared to other communities.

Regarding the levels of literacy and education, detailed data are available from the National Family Health Survey carried out by the Ministry of Health and Family Welfare, Government of India and International Institute for Population Sciences, Bombay. In this survey, interviews were conducted with a nationally representative sample of 89,677 every-married women in the age group of 13-49, from 24 states (in Jammu and Kashmir, only in the region of Jammu) and National Capital Territory of Delhi (which later became a state) from April 1992 to September 1993 with the main objective of collecting reliable and up-to-date information on fertility, family planning, mortality and maternal and child health. It used uniform questionnaires and uniform methods of sampling, data collection and analysis in different states. This was one of the most complete household surveys of its kind ever conducted in India. In the above survey, for the first time data on education and exposure to media have also been collected for women belonging to major religious groups in all the states in India except the small states of north-eastern region where the populations are small. (IIPS, 1995).

The levels of education among women by religion for India and also for rural and urban areas are provided in Table 9. At all India level the largest proportion of illiterate women is found among Muslims. In the categories of High School Complete and Above High School, again the lowest percentages are those of Muslims. Some pattern is observed in general both in rural and urban areas. But the differentials in educational levels between Muslim women and women from other communities are wider in urban areas.

Even in Malegaon, it was observed that even though their literacy levels are high, their educational levels, both among males and females, are low. (Table 10).

Thus, if we want to increase the work participation rate of Muslim women, we need to increase the educational levels among Muslim females. Also lower socio-economic status of Muslims could be one of the reasons for their lower literacy levels. In such a case this vicious circle of lower socio-economic status leading to lower literacy and educational level leading to lower socio-economic status has to be broken somewhere.

TABLE 9

Levels of Education among Women by Religion and Residence for India National Family Health Survey, 1992-93

Level of education of every married women age 13-49

Religion	Illiterate	Literate primary complete	Primary school complete	Middle school complete	High school complete	Above high school	Total percent	Number of women
				URBAN				
INDIA								
Muslim	52.1	11.1	16.4	8.5	9.2	2.7	100.0	3902
Hindu	34.7	6.7	15.3	12.6	18.9	11.7	100.0	17730
Christian	17.6	7.3	13.1	15.0	30.2	16.8	100.0	692
Sikh	25.3	1.7	16.8	11.8	28.0	16.6	100.0	419
Jain	7.8	5.1	13.1	9.3	34.2	30.5	100.0	311
Buddhist	50.8	9.8	14.9	12.4	9.1	3.0	100.0	342
				RURAL				
INDIA								
Muslim	74.0	9.4	9.9	4.5	1.8	0.4	100.0	6905
Hindu	73.5	5.9	10.0	5.4	4.4	0.8	100.0	55919
Christian	40.5	12.0	15.9	14.4	13.8	3.4	100.0	1450
Sikh	59.0	3.6	19.8	7.0	9.2	1.5	100.0	1254
Jain	16.8	13.0	14.4	18.5	31.4	6.0	100.0	117
Buddhist	67.0	12.7	10.7	6.5	3.1	-	100.0	392
				TOTAL				
INDIA								
Muslim	66.1	10.0	12.2	5.9	4.5	1.2	100.0	10806
Hindu	64.1	6.1	11.3	7.2	7.9	3.4	100.0	73648
Christian	33.1	10.5	15.0	14.6	19.1	7.8	100.0	2142
Sikh	50.5	3.1	19.0	8.2	13.9	5.3	100.0	1673
Jain	10.3	7.2	13.5	11.8	33.4	23.8	100.0	428
Buddhist	59.4	11.3	12.7	9.3	5.9	1.4	100.0	784

Source: IIPS, 1995.

TABLE 10

Percentage Distribution of Population of five years and Above Age Gruop by Sex and Level of Education

Level of education	*Males*	*Females*
Illiterate	18.2	24.6
Upto 4th Std	28.3	26.1
5th-9th	43.6	42.7
S.S.C.	3.3	2.2
Above S.S.C.	5.7	3.7
Religious	0.9	0.7
Total: Percentage	100.0	100.0
Number	2,690	2,591

Source: Same as Table 5, p. 221.

Low Exposure to Media

One can attain informal education and also know about economic opportunities by being expcsed to media. National Family Health Survey gives percentage of every-married women age 13-49 who usually watch television or listen to radio at least once a week or visit a cinema at least once a month orwho are not regularly exposed to any of these mass media by religion for India and different states. (IIPS, 1995).

The data on exposure to media for Muslim women and women of other communities is given in Table 11. A look at the table reveals that the exposure of Muslim women in any category of media is the least except in the cinema going category (Here least proportion of Sikh women visit cinema theatre). Therefore the proportion of women not regularly exposed to any media is the highest among Muslims. Thus it is necessary to increase the levels of exposure among Muslim

TABLE 11
Levels of Exposure to Mass Media among Women by Religion for India National Family Health Survey, 1992-93

Religion	*Watches Television at least once a week*	*Listens to radio at least once a week*	*Visits cinema theatre at least once a week*	*Not regularly exposed to any media*	*Number of women*
INDIA					
Muslim	27.6	40.4	11.0	51.4	10806
Hindu	31.2	43.3	15.7	47.7	73648
Christian	41.3	57.4	18.9	32.4	2142
Sikh	54.7	41.9	3.1	37.1	1673
Jain	85.0	78.0	28.4	8.6	428
Buddhist	46.6	50.4	15.6	36.4	734

Source: Same as Table 9.

women to make them modern and aware of various existing economic opportunities.

Pardah System

The *pardah* system as practised among Muslims may be a hindrance for the Muslim women to go outside home and participate in the market activities. In India, total seclusion of Muslim women in present times is neither possible nor feasible. Still the *pardah* in the form of *burqa* or *chadar* too can instill certain inhibitions and prevent Muslim women from participating in all kinds of work. For example, in Malegaon two-thirds of all the women were wearing *burqa*. (Ministry, 1996). The most favoured professions by Muslim women in Malegaon were those of medicine and teaching. Further most of the working women were teachers. Not a single Muslim woman could be found working in a shop or a bank.

Poor Organization

Poor Organization is another factor accounting for the low economic participation among Muslim women. Quite a few studies have reported that Muslim women do want to educate themselves and attain economic independence. But they did not know how to go about it. (Lateef, 1990; Minstry, 1996). In Malegaon, the Muslim women are good tailors and good embroidery makers. Because they are not organized, they have neither bargaining power nor a regular income. There are hardly any NGOs of Muslim women. Whenever they are organized, they have been able to function efficiently and earn enough profits to develop further., e.g., India Women's Trust of Bombay.

Also since most of the Muslims are of artisan, marginal farming and petty business background, their women do help their menfolk in their work. It is unpaid labour and unorganized and so has no economic value.

Lack of Awareness

Lack of awareness about existing financial schemes to help women become economically independent is another factor which hinders Muslim women's economic participation.

After identifying the factors accounting for the economic problems of Muslim women, now let us try to find solutions, which is done in the next section.

Solutions to Economic Problems of Muslim Women

The following measures may be helpful in solving the economic problems of Muslim women:

Spread Awareness and Organize Muslim Women

Educated Muslim women with aptitude for social work should set up NGOs in Muslim localities to spread awareness about the economic opportunities available to the Muslim women. Also these NGOs with the help of secular organizations, both general and of women, should organize the Muslim women with skills to form co-operatives so as to enable them to get benefits of the organized sector.

Provide Credit

Credit creation facilities among Muslim women should be encouraged so as to enable them to have enough finance to carry on their economic activities. For example, Kokan Mahila Co-operative Credit Society is doing good work among Muslim women in Bombay. Also financial institutions based on Islamic banking principle of sharing profits/losses should be set up to provide finance to Muslim women.

Reduce Family Size by Increasing Family Planning Acceptance

Large family size as a result of lower family planning acceptance adds to the economic problems of Muslim women. It is not that Muslim women do not favour family planning. Many a time, Muslim areas do not have proper family planning facilities and health facilities. Quite often there is a wilful negligence of Muslim localities on the part of the government officials assuming that Muslims are not interested in family planning. Thus there is an urgent need to provide counselling, health and family planning services of good quality in Muslim areas.

Provide Vocational and Other Types of Training

More and more Muslim women should be encouraged to take up jobs in organized sector. For this, they should be provided with vocational training and other types of training. They should also be encouraged to learn local languages besides Urdu, which is their mother tongue. Above all, educational levels among Muslim women need to be raised. For this, drop-out rates among Muslim girls at lower levels of education need to be reduced substantially. Also changes in the attitudes of Muslim parents in general and Muslim men in particular need to be brought about. Specially among the Muslims from lower economic class, motivation to educate their daughters, has to be strengthened. At the same time, a universal literacy programme assumed urgency when we look at states like Haryana where only 2 per cent of the Muslim women are literate (IIPS, 1995).

Reservation

Reservations for Muslim women in jobs, if there are reservations for women in general, may be another measure to empower Muslim women economically.

Social Measures

Also at social level, certain measures can help Muslim women attain economic well-being. *Shariat* does give a right to women to inherit property. Usually, male members appropriate the share of the women in the family. If Muslim women can fight for their inheritance right, it can surely uplift them economically. Secondly, in a Muslim marriage, like in other communities, dowry is given to the bridegroom (though it is *haram,* i.e., illegal) and marriages are celebrated with pomp. Instead, the dowry amount should be given to the bride/ daughter in her name. Also, simple marriages should be made the order of the day and the money thus saved should be given to the bride/ daughter for acquiring skills or investing in business or to be just kept in the bank in the form of savings, after marriage. Thirdly, Mehr amount, which is solely the right of the bride/wife should be fixed in accordance with the economic status of the husband and should be delivered to her at the time of marriage. This measure too can uplift the Muslim women economically. These social measures are difficult to be implemented but worth trying. Muslim elite families/leaders can take lead in giving property share to their daughters, performing simple marriages and fixing Mehr in accordance with the husband's economic status.

Upliftment of Socio-economic Status of Muslim Community

Above all, we have to remember that the Muslim women's economic problems cannot be solved and their economic status cannot be improved in isolation from the economic status of the Muslim community. This necessitates that the socio-economic status of the Muslim community as a whole has to be raised. To achieve this, all efforts should be made to make the benefits of various development programmes meant for weaker sections reach the Muslim community too. For this, educated Muslims, NGOs and Muslim leaders have to work very hard and selflessly, with patience and vision. Greater and more intensified efforts are necessary as proportionately more Muslims reside in urban areas. Another important measure to prevent the Muslim community from further economic deterioration, is to prevent the recurring communal riots. This requires strong will on the part of the Indian state and understanding on the part of the majority community. All those sympathizers of Muslims can do great service to the Muslim community by fighting for prevention of communal riots.

Conclusion

Nearly half of the 120 million Muslim population in India is of Muslim women, thus forming a sizable chunk of Indian population. Economic independence for Muslim women, like women from any other community, is very important to lead a dignified life.

The data from NSSO survey, 43rd round, and from NCAER's survey reveal a very low work force participation rate for Muslim women both in urban and rural areas. Compared to Hindu and Christian women, the work participation rates are the lowest for Muslim women.

Low levels of education, low exposure to media, prevalence of *purdah* system, poor organization and lack of awareness about existing financial schemes are some of the factors which account for the low workforce participation rate of Muslim women.

Educated Muslim women should form NGOs in Muslim localities to spread awareness about availability of economic opportunities and also organize Muslims with skills to form co-operatives. Credit creation facilities should also be provided. Further, quality counselling, health and family planning services should be provided in Muslim areas so as to reduce their family size which adds to the economic woes of Muslim women. More and more Muslim women should be encouraged to take up jobs in organized sector by providing them with vocational and other types of training. Above all, educational levels among Muslim women need to be raised. For this, drop-out rates at lower levels of education need to be reduced substantially. To achieve this, changes in the attitudes of Muslim parents in general and Muslim men in particular have to be brought about. Besides, social measures such as ensuring the implementation of Muslim women's right to inheritance, performance of simple marriage and thereby giving the savings to the daughter, and ensuring that the Mehr amount is in accordance with the husband's economic status and delivering it at the time of marriage itself, can empower Muslim women economically. Furthermore, raising the socio-economic status of Muslim community in general is necessary for upliftment of the Muslim women. All this requires that the NGOs, both Muslim and non-Muslim, educated Muslims, Muslim leaders, both men and women, work very hard selflessly with patience and vision.

REFERENCES

International Institute for Population Sciences (IIPS), (1995): *National Family Health Survey (MCH and Family Planning) India* 1992-93, IIPS, Bombay.

Khan, Rashiduddin, (1978): *Economic and Political Weekly*, p.1515.

Lateef, Shahida, (1990): *Muslim Women in India, Political and Private Realities,* 1890s-1980s, Kali for Women.

Mistry, Malika (1996): *Fertility and Family Planning Behaviour among Muslims in India: Evidence from a Survey in Malegaon City, Maharashtra,* Gokhale institute of Politics and Economics and Poona University. (Ph. D. thesis).

------------ (1998a): "How can the Muslims be uplifted?" *Radiance Views Weekly,* 3-9 May, pp.11-13.

----------------------(1998b): *Fact Sheet on the Levels of Education to Media among Muslim Women in India,* Centre for Study of Society and Secularism, Bombay.

---------------------(1998c): "Quality of Life of Muslims in Urban Localities: A Case Study of Malegaon City (Maharashtra)". In

M.H. Qureshi (ed.) *Muslims in India since Independence: A Regional Perspective,* Institute of Objective Studies, New Delhi, pp. 213-226.

--------------------(1998d): "The Minority Status of Muslims in the Development Process from the Point of View of Equality in India", *Life and Religions,* November, 1.4, pp. 13-17.

---------------------(1999a): "High Fertility, Low Family Planning Practice and Unsafe Motherhood: Challenges to Muslim Women" paper presented at the National Seminar on *The Challenges before Women in the 21st Century* held on 29-31 March. by S.P. Mahila Visvavidyalayam, Tirupati.

-------------------(1999b): "Muslims in India: Prospects for Islamic Banking in 21st Century" paper prepared for the Conference on "Islamic University, Malyasia, in April 1999.

Saxena, N.C. (1983): "Public Employment and Educational Backwardness among Muslims in India," *Political Science Review* Vol. 22, No. 2,3, April-September.

Shariff, Abusaleh, (1995): "Socio-economic and Demographic Differentials between Hindus and Muslims", *Economic and Political Weekly*, Vol. 30, No. 46, November, 18, pp. 2947-2953.

---------------(1998): "Relative Economic and Social Deprivation of Indian Muslims", paper presented at the seminar on *Muslims in India since Independence* organized by the Institute of Objective Studies, New Delhi on 28-29 March.

National Sample Survey Organization, (1990): *Sarvekshana: Results of the Fourth Quinquennial Survey on Employment and Unemployment,* (NSSO), Ministry of Planning, Govt. of India, N. Delhi.

Rajeevlochan, Meeta, (1996), "The Past in the Present: The Weavers of Malegaon", *Economic and Political Weekly*, Vol. 21, No. 11, pp. 673-678.

15

Bandheriya of Jaipur: A Study of Muslim Home Based Women Workers

Mandakini Pant

Introduction

Discussions on the subject of Muslim women's employment generally highlight the statistics, which point to their lower economic participation. Much less attention has been paid to the realities behind the statistics. Why are Muslim women under-represented in the labour market? What are the factors that limit their fuller participation in the formal labour market? What factors lead them to seek home-based income generating work in the informal sector? The aim of the present study is to provide a theoretical framework, which attempts to theorize Muslim women's relation to the labour market. It has three dimensions, which critically explain the nature, extent and patterns of their participation in labour market. These are as follows:

(i) The nature and the context of labour market in the historical perspective. This dimension describes the terrain on which Muslim women's relation to the labour market is negotiated.

(ii) The social construction of 'woman's labour. This dimension highlights the extent and ways the social representations construct women as a category and how such stereotypes structure their positions in the labour market.

(iii) *Role identity*. This dimension aims to understand women's perception of themselves, their employment and the labour market.

The case of home-based women workers in the tie and dye handicraft production has been examined in the light of these perspectives. The tie and dye handicraft is one of the most celebrated cottage industries of Jaipur. The artisans are predominantly Muslim. Women who are colloquially known as *bandheriya* mostly do the tying work. The study analyses how the labour of these women is:

(a) Constituted by the labour market;
(b) Socially constructed; and
(c) Framed within personal narratives.

Although this paper suggests a framework, which explains the labour market issues as they relate to Muslim women. Yet this can be applied to wider ethnic categories of home based women workers.

Socio-Economic Profile of Home-Based Muslim Women Workers

The informal home-based sector is a major source of employment for poor Muslim women in Jaipur. It enables them to support their households financially. The ensuing socio-economic profile of Muslim women workers, engaged in home-based income generating tieing work, will help in understanding the forces and factors that keep them under a state of poverty.

(i) A substantial section of worker were widows, divorçees, and separated. Bandhej was their only source of livelihood.
(ii) Majority of the workers were illiterate.
(iii) Women of all age groups from 20 to 40 years were involved in tieing work.

An overwhelming section of women workers belonged to low-income households. Their husband had irregular employment in petty informal trades, crafts and casual work.

Women workers often supported the households. It was mostly on account of widowhood, separation, or desertion. In many cases they could not rely on their husband's income because the contribution by spouses were irregular and inadequate.

Bandheriya from slum-areas lacked basic amenities such as water and electricity. They spent much of their time in such trivial yet essential chores as fetching drinking water (whose supply too was infrequent). A large number of these workers lived in dilapidated one-room tenements that served as their dwelling unit, kitchen, bathroom, etc. all rolled in to one. These tenements were invariably unhygienic. It had limited access to even fresh air and clear light. This had concomittant effect over the health and psyche of women workers, which further compounded lags in their productivity and consequential economic misery.

Some of the principal Muslim groupings in Jaipur city may be classified as:

(a) Ashraf such as Sheikh, Pathan, Mughal, Afghan.
(b) Muslim Rajput include Kayamkhani, Bhati etc.
(c) Occupational categories such as Bhisti, Chipa, Manihar, Darzi, Nilgar, Palladar, Luhar etc.

Kayamkhani Rajput women formed the major stratum of the workers. Kayamkhani Rajput belong to Sekhawati region of Rajasthan where tie and dye is a traditional handicraft. But there has been infiltration in traditional bandhej craft from other occupational groupings. Notable amongst the non-traditional workers are Ashraf Muslims—Sheikh and Pathan who consider themselves superior. Their participation in bandhej work has been probably because of steady deterioration in their socio-economic conditions.

The Nature and Context of Labour Market in Historical Perspective

Subsistence Labour and Home Based Activities of Women

A historical perspective of the home based informal sector helps in focusing the conditions under which women's subsistence labour is integrated into the capitalist market production. Earlier women were part of subsistence production system. They were involved in a variety of tasks, which simultaneously were part of the market economy and of the production of goods and services directly for consumption within household. With the growth of capitalist market economy, men became part of industrial labour force. Capitalist production system isolated women from economically productive work. Segregation from productive activities and economic dependence on men limited their access to income, property and other crucial resources such as education. Socio-economic crisis, inadequate incomes and lack of education and technical skills led some women to become part of low waged informal home based income generating activities such as, cooking, washing, cleaning, papad making, pickle making, grinding of masala, handicraft etc. Though these informal home based activities are parts of market economy as they stimulate the capital growth, yet in capitalist production system it has no value. They are marginal activities, which are outside the boundary of legal rules. Consequently, women remained invisible.

There was fundamental restructuring of the economies of the advanced industrial societies from the 1970's and the developing countries from 1980's. The recognition of export-led growth as the only viable development strategy, ushered in the economies with trade liberalisation and de-regulation. Liberalisation and de-regulation changed the structure of labour market making it more flexible than in the past. The decline in the old manufacturing sector led to a large-scale job loss. Simultaneously there was growth of jobs in the service sector This transition entailed a rise of 'flexible specialisation' leading to more decentralised forms of labour process and greater emphasis on contracting out of functions and services. There was an increase in low status, part-time work and a variety of forms of home based work. The ready availability of paid work that could be carried out from home appeared a realistic option to many poor women.

Structural Features of Bandhej Industry

A brief discussion of the structural features of bandhej industry will help in understanding conditions of employment of Muslim women primarily engaged in the tieing work in Jaipur. They generally receive work at home and are paid on piece-rate basis. The trade is organised along the "putting out" system. The trader/exporter does not directly employ the workers, he subcontracts the work either to the wholesaler or to *nilgarh* (dyer) on commission basis. Nilgarh is also the master craftsman who recruits workers, distributes the work, organises entire production process, and finally delivers the finished product to the wholesaler or to the trader directly. Production units are either home based, or are in the form of small-scale workshops. Dyeing is done mainly in workshops, which is usually located within the residential premises of nilgarh. This work is done in group with functions being flexibly allocated among workers. Male *karigar* (workers) are employed on daily wage basis. For home based production units, nilgarh either personally recruits the workers (mostly women) or partially subcontracts the work of distribution and collection to *bicholiya* (mostly women intermediaries) on commission basis. Women workers receive the work at home and are paid on piece rate basis. Tieing work is spread to many bandheriya. A single piece is passed through different hands for tieing various types of knots at different stages. There is no fixed channel of distribution of work to bandheriya and disposal of work to nilgarh. Bandheriya are free to work with any number of nilgarh. They received assignments either from *bicholiya* or nilgarh or both of them. Bandheriya are atomised producers. In their desperate need to earn extra money, they accept work from as many sources as possible with little control over their wage structure. In a working atmosphere marked by extreme competition and jealousy. Nilgarh/*bicholiya* take advantage of this fragmented labour force. Though nilgarh could not coerce women to work and deliver the product in time, yet he could control these workers by means of cuts and rejection. Hence, bandheriya are careful not to tie themselves in knots in "tieing the knots", they do sincerely try to finish the work in time and not fall fowl of nilgarh to remain in circulation. Wages are based on piece rates—more intricate the design (requiring finer skills), higher is the piece rate. There is, however, little uniformity in fixing these rates: these are essentially decided by nilgarh. Nilgarh are essentially middlemen. They further undercut the already low wages payable to *bandheriya/ bicholiya* and pocket the difference. There is no uniform method of payment; often, Nilgarh, *bicholiya* withhold workers dues, to retain his hold over them. Bandheriya has no direct access to the market. The traders and exporters constitute the link to the market. They control the capital, market channels as well as production process. Costs of production are also very low. They extract labour and products from the workers at wages much below the production costs. The relation between them and bandheriya is invisible. Bandheriya has contact with the market through nilgarh. Their relation is invisible. It is with him that they bargain for better rates of payment. Nilgarh in turn often presents their case to the wholesaler or traders and exporters. The contradiction between bandheriya and traders manifests itself in the tussle between nilgarh and bandheriya. Bandheriyas are sympathetic to *bicholiya*. They feel that input of *bicholiya* is more particularly when one considers the time they take in coming and going from nilgarh to them. Both nilgarh and *bicholiya* belong to the same ethnic group of workers. The relationship between them is entirely based on personal discretion. They are their benefactors. This informal dependency ensures their survival in the labour market. Both nilgarh and bicholiya operate in such a way that worker's gratitude for service is forever ensured. That is why, some workers do not ever question them. They often prefer to keep their wages with them and obtain it when in need. Due to this primordial loyalty workers are in a weak bargaining position.

The socio-economic marginality of bandheriya also influences their bargainig power. They have urgent need for work, but have no formal qualifications, working capital and influential patron or friends. Consequently, they have no option other than working for low remuneration with no job security. They are dependent on nilgarh, and *bicholiya*, particularly in matters relating to their occupation like collection of raw materials and wages. Such dependence on employers, suppliers, and subcontractors makes them susceptible to various forms of exploitation. Traders and dyers control the price as well as the quality and quantity of the product. Through the mechanism of putting out system and subcontracting they extract and monopolise the surplus produced by the workers. Thus, the traders and exporters acquire and accumulate profit, created by the workers. They deliberately tap needy and secluded workers because they are willing to work for a pittance.

The Social Construction of Women's Labour

Waged labour by itself does not explain the labour market position of Muslim women. This issue in fact falls under the realm of gender system, which is deeply embedded, in the social structure. It is the most pervasive and widespread organisation that affects all aspects of social functioning. Patriarchy forms the core of gender system. In a patriarchy roles are allocated not only in accordance with the biological functions (procreation), but also according to the values prescribed to males and females. Dominating and controlling social functions are prescribed to males whereas the supportive functions are the preview of females. Role allocations, certain norms such as the norms of motherhood and domesticity, values such as chastity, fidelity, and practices such as *pardah* lead to stereotyping of female roles. In addition to these, predominant social institutions like Islam and family institutionalise the social placements according to the norms of gender system. Both of these institutions socialize its members to gender differential functioning. Consequently women are confined to the tasks of the household and rearing of children. Female chastity and seclusion/*purdah* become important for protecting religious and ethnic purity.

Traditional role of Muslim women, as wife-mother, centres on household tasks and household productive activities. Conditions of economic depression impaired men's ability to perform role of a breadwinner and led to changes in familial reciprocities. Consequently, new roles emerged that combined wife-mother responsibilities with that of the breadwinner. While occupational pursuits by Muslim women acquired de facto legitimacy, there has been little change in the ideological structure of the society. This situation is particularly precarious for poor working women. They are trapped into two opposite role structures. They must conform to traditional subservient role, and yet, at the same time, toil for household subsistence. They face double burden of a dual role of a wife-mother and of a wage earner. Economic compulsions and demands of incompatible roles narrow down their choice of occupation. Due to constraints of patriarchal norms they are driven to the home-based employment. Since they combine their remunerative work with domestic work, their economic participation is only intermittent and casual. They become part of the floating labour pool, which is tapped and purchased at minimal costs. But their employment is crucial for them and their household. It is an integral part of their survival strategies to cope with the situations of poverty. Their incomes, howsoever low, are crucial for household subsistence without which a number of households would plunge further deep into the abyss of poverty.

A Muslim woman is socially defined as housewife. This implies that she is dependent on male breadwinner for her survival. Such a definition renders the work of women both within the house and in the labour market, invisible. Women, perceived as (dependent) housewife, are seldom fully integrated into the labour market. The norms of domesticity and seclusion kept bandheriya atomised. They were looked upon as housewives who were utilising their leisure time to supplement the household income. Workers themselves considered their remunerative tieing work as a leisure time activity. They undervalued their work because they did not attach monetary values to time. They frequently defined handicraft work as an incidental spare-time activity. They had difficulty in reporting the accurate time devoted to tieing work. The work organisation of tieing was such that there was no clear-cut demarcation between housework and income generating work. Women worked whenever they had free time. When we look at the total time which they devoted to the tieing work (approximately 6 to 9 hours), we find that they were true labourers. They worked hard to complete within a stipulated period, particularly when there was extra demand of work. In such cases they worked even longer hours per day. Still they did not look upon themselves as full time workers. Any remuneration was acceptable to them. Such assumptions however obscure the true relations of production. It relegates them to a status of a disguised wageworker that is readily available and easily dispensable. Labour time of home based women workers does not appear as cost factor for traders and exporters. They manipulate it according to the exigencies of the situation. They tap the unlimited supply of cheap female labour and labour time without any risk. Uncrupulous employers exploit them and deny them fair wages for their labour.

Thus, patriarchal ideologies influence women's participation in the labour market. Patriarchy confines women to household roles. They are only housewives. Capitalist system utilises such patriarchal ideologies for capital generation. It purchases women's work at lowest price. Since women's household work affects their participation in the productive activities for the market, capitalist production system regards them as subsidiary wage earners. Market accepts them as surplus labour force, which is utilised whenever the demands arise.

Role Identity

Identity, the knowledge of who one is and where one belongs, is a powerful denominator of selfhood. A reflexive awareness about oneself and others is anchored to day to day activities, which produce and reproduce appropriate behaviours. The descriptions about appropriate behaviours combine individuals' thoughts and feelings, their presuppositions of the 'significant others' expectations and their relative statuses. Muslim women worker's cognitive orientations about themselves, work opportunities, and choice of work alternatives are the resultant of interaction between three factors:

- their pre-existing norm commitment;
- their perception and evaluation of role situation; and the esteem and disesteem with which the peripheral social networks or the reference group would respond to their role performance.

The social norms of male bread winner/dependent female reinforce in women a subordinate image. Home-based working women adhere to the role as 'wife and mother'. They are caught in a dilemma between two-role expectation viz. ascription and achievement role expectations. They must conform to the traditional roles, and at the same time work for household subsistence. Consequently they incorporate into their self-conception the compliant roles. They deliberately limit themseleves to distinct set of parttime home-based occupations where they are able to focus their primary attention on their family. They could also fulfil their economic needs without the loss of self-esteem within their community. The 'significant others' (reference group) also take part in home-based women workers manipulation of role structure since they are linked with their actual social position.

Women's commitment to normative stereotyped conceptions is so deep that they deliberately select the congenial roles, which are compatible with their ascribed roles. Bandheriya, for instance, perceived themselves as housewives. The normatively prescribed familial role for woman influenced them as that of any other women in wife-mother social position. Though they were primary earners, yet they felt that their primary role was that of childcare and housework. They accepted male dominance. Spouse was still the breadwinner of family. Home-based tieing work was preferred because it did not clash with their traditional role conceptions. It was compatible with the wife-mother role. There was relative insulation from non-family male contact. Their community upheld the seclusion ethic for them and did not permit social interaction outside the home. By engaging in home-based handicraft production, they could support their families without losing their community's respect. It did not entail any loss of self-esteem within the community. Their occupation generated income. It did not greatly interfere with their domestc chores because of flexible working conditions. It had the approval of influential members of the immediate family and the larger society, that is, the community. Hence, the perceptions and patriarchal evaluations of community influenced their manipulation of living.

Bandheriya entered wage labour because male wage earners could not support their households. The economic marginality of the worker's household, gender role constraints and workers cognitive orientations about themselves as housewife and their work as leisure time activity propelled them to work under exploitative conditions, such as, low wages and no job security. Needy and desperate workers were deliberately recruited, as they were available at fairly low level of pay. While women workers had the satisfaction of getting a suitable employment, the traders minimised both the recruitment and wage costs. The relationship between the home-based women workers and the traders are de facto market relationships where workers lack of access to the surplus leads to the accumulation of profit by the traders. Despite disadvantaged earning conditions, they are contributing substantially at times more than their spouses. Their time contribution to an income generating work as well as to a complex range of unpaid tasks such as fetching, cooking, conserving, building of kin network, usually go unnoticed. These are crucial for the family's survival at the time of crisis. Poverty stricken households depend on the subsistence or survival production of women workers.

Conclusion

Informal home-based sector largely draws upon the labour of women workers who are poor, has had no/little access to formal educational training. Economic compulsions drive them to informal occupations, which though lowly paid at least gives some kind of sustenance. Bandheriya are no exception to this rule. The invisibility of home-based production process leads to the exploitation of female labour.

Deprivations are largely due to gender belief systems, which support the assumption that women are dependent on men. Societal emphasis on domestic-child centred role leads them to seek home based employment. The home-based work satisfies their urgent need of work without the loss of social esteem within their milieu. The working conditions of home-based work, however, have negative implications particularly for the workers. It supports the belief on the peripheral nature of their employment. It reinforces their home based and child-centred status. They are perceived as housewives, who are utilising leisure time for market production. Income thus earned is very low. They are actually disguised and semi-domesticate wage-workers. Their labour power is tapped for production in the market. The traditional sexual division of labour assigns them larger amount of household related work. They are unable to devote much time to market oriented work. Their participation is intermittent and casual. Their labour power therefore, has low value.

Gender belief system condition women's perception of role identity. They select congenial role structure for themselves that combine both familial and extra-familial roles. It is one of the important coping strategies to reduce role strain and to ensure survival. The dual roles with equally strong legitimate expectations often result in ambivalence. Their ambivalence about their role as a wage worker makes them function as surplus labour reserve who is drawn into or expelled from work forces any time.

Thus, women's relation to the labour market is structured by economic and ideological structures such as the impact of global and national economy on the labour market; ideologies about women's role in relation to caring responsibilities and paid work. Women's own perspectives about themselves also influence their labour market positions. They are all integrated to the framework of analysis as outlined.

REFERENCES

1. Afshar Haleh (ed): *Dynamics of Race and Gender-Some Feminist Interventions*, London, Taylor & Francis, 1994.
2. Lateef Shahida: *Muslim Women in India,* New Delhi, Concept Publishing Company, 1990.
3. Mies Maria: *Indian Women and Patriarchy,* New Delhi, Concept Publishing Company, 1980.
4. Palariwala Rajani and Dube Leela (ed): *Structure and Strategies: Women, Work and Family*, New Delhi, Sage Publications, 1991.
5. Singh A.M.et. al (ed): *Invisble Hands, Women in Home-Based Productions,* New Delhi, Sage Publications, 1987.

16
Vocational Training of Muslim Women in Maharashtra to Solve Economic Problems

Ramala M. Baxamusa

Introduction

A careful review of the literature available on Muslim women in India indicated that the data were very insufficient and most studies had avoided to mention the economic problems faced by Muslim women. Muslim women today, like Hindu women of their class, participate in economic productive work but are classified as not working and thus become invisible in the economy.

This study investigates into the economic conditions of Muslim women in Maharashtra. Work participation rate of Muslim Women is low but they have always shown desire to be economically active. Case studies of two educational institutes are presented which have tried to involve Muslim women in vocational training to develop skills to better their economic conditions.

The first report of the Government of India analyzing the status of women of India was published in Dec. 1974. *Towards Equality* published by the committee on the status of women expressed that Muslim women like other women of India faced poverty and they too wanted to be economically active. Since Muslims were the largest minority community, a separate report of the status of Muslim women in nine states was prepared.

Some Major Findings

Muslim women did not know any written language. Their knowledge of religion, i.e., Islamic rights was limited. Educated or career women did not use *purdah*. Women in general were opposed to mixed marriages but in Delhi and Maharashtra there was partial acceptance.

Muslim women despite *purdah* and other constraints participated in their husband's lives? Their interaction with outside community was limited and their benefit from the social welfare schemes was negligible. Only a few career women participated with other community women.

Women did not consider the issue of *purdah* nor equal rights with men as important demands. Most women emphasized that they needed education and job opportunities. This indicates that they wanted employment opportunities for economic upliftment of their community. (Government of India, 1974).

Implementation of the Five Year Plans and various Government Schemes affected the socio-economic conditions of women. Therefore using the Government data of the 1991 Census and the NSSO 43rd round of 1987-1988, and 50th round of 1993-1994 an attempt is made to draw a profile of Muslim women in Maharashtra. To understand the Muslim women properly the data is compared with that of Hindus who are in the majority, and with the Buddhists whose conditions are almost similar to those of Muslims. For analysis only the unpublished Government data are used.

The Profile of Muslim Women

The 1991 Census data indicated that in Maharashtra there was 8 per cent Muslim population. Mumbai, the biggest city, had 14 per cent Muslims. In cities the Muslim women's population was less but there was nobig difference; sex ratio was 925: 1000. Unlike majority of the States in India Maharashtra has more urban Muslim population. Thus 60 per cent of Muslim women live in urban areas. [Census 1991]

As the Census does not provide any other type of data one has to look into data provided by various Govt., semi Government, and

NGOs . Since "small survey methodology" was not common, it was difficult to compare the data to get a socio-economic picture of Muslim women. One has therefore to use the National Sample Surveys conducted by the state.

The codes and the sampling design used at central and state level NSSO are international as these estimates are utilized by World Statistical Organisation, ILO, World Bank, UNO etc. to prepare their international reports to get a picture of the socio-ecnomic conditions. The Maharashtra picture of Muslim women was different in many ways from the all India Muslims data. As genderwise classification of two rounds was available one can visualize changes within the last five years.

Socio-economic Characteristics (Hindu, Muslim, Buddhist)

Size of Landholding. Looking at the data for land ownership in the 43rd round, the landless Muslims were 56.8 per cent and the marginal landholders are 13.4 per cent. [Table 1] Therefore agriculture was not important to Muslims. The Hindus were 30.1 per cent landless, Buddhists 18.6 per cent. Among the 30 per cent Muslim farmers nearly 24.6 per cent were small and semi-medium farmers. Large farmers among them were very few. Taking into consideration the all India data Muslims had less land than the Hindus had. But they had more land than the Buddhists had (Sarvekshana Sept. 1990).

Economic Profile: Expenditure-per capita: The income data were not provided by the NSSO, however it provided data on per capita monthly expenditure which is usually a better indicator of the standard of living of the people. Looking at the 43rd round rural and urban data we find that per capita expenditure was more for urban areas than for rural, as here earning capacity was more.

In the rural area, 69.8 per cent Muslims had expenditure of less than Rs. 160 while in the urban area, 39.8 per cent, had expenditure below Rs. 185. In urban area, 59.0 per cent Muslims had expenditure below Rs. 700, and only 2.5 per cent of Muslims had expenditure above Rs. 700. In the rural area, 26.5 per cent, had expenditure below Rs. 310, and 3.3 per cent, had expenditure of Rs. 370 and above. Most of the Muslims were self-employed and hence their income was not regular. Since British period they have been petty artisans. Very few had cultivable lands. In villages they were weavers, goat rearers, ironsmiths, potters, etc. Their earnings were not high thus they generally fell in the low expenditure group.

Comparing the data on religionwise, expenditure, one finds that in rural areas 77.2 per cent and in urban areas 50.3 per cent of the Buddhists were in the lower expenditure category i.e., below Rs.160 & Rs. 185 respectively. Due to small landholding, casual work, both in rural and urban areas, many Buddhists were hardly literate and were drawing very less income. (Table 1).

TABLE 1

Some Socio-Economic Characteristics on Religious Groups 43rd round and 50th round

Household Characteristics			*43rd round*			*50th round*		
			Hindu	*Muslim*	*Buddhist*	*Hindu*	*Muslim*	*Buddhist*
1. Rural Household by Size of Land Holding								
No land			301	568	186	207	326	171
Marginal	0.1-1.0	hectare	225	134	250	399	312	552
Small	1.1-2.0	hectare	172	124	235	316	208	181
Semi-Med.	2.1-4.0	hectare	152	122	134	133	81	79
Medium	4.1-8.0	hectare	87	30	124	75	73	17
Large	8.81	hectare & above	63	22	71	not reported		
2. Rural Household by monthly per capita expenditure in Rs.								
Less than 80			66	80	62			
80-160			530	604	710			
160-310			352	265	211	not calculated		
370 & above			45	33	16			
NA			7	18	1			

3. Urban household by monthly per capita expenditure class in Rs..

Less than 90	19	52	55	
90-185	253	326	448	
185-310	329	259	338	not calculated
310-700	322	331	151	
700 & above	68	25	8	
NA	9	7	8	

Source: Unpublished data of the Maharashtra State NSSO data: Government of Maharashtra, Bombay.

Draft Report on Employment and Unemployment. Based on National Sample Survey 43rd Round (July 1987-June 1988) and 50th Round (July 1993-June 1994). Prepared by Directorate of Economic and Statistics.

In rural areas 4.5 per cent of Hindus were in higher expenditure group, i.e., Rs. 700 and above. Only 3.3 per cent Muslims and 1.6 per cent Buddhists were in this expenditure group. Whilst in urban areas the gap was much wider, 6.6 per cent of urban Hindus had higher expenditure than Rs. 700 and above whilst the Muslims in this bracket were only 2.5 per cent and the Buddhists only 0.8 per cent. These data indicate that the Muslim population were poor, the Buddhist were much poorer. Shariff's study in rural areas also conforms to the above data that 43 per cent Muslims were below poverty line, then followed by 50 per cent Buddhist and 39 per cent Hindus. (Shariff, 1995).

Buddhist get reservation in jobs. However, 6.0 per cent of regular jobs were not salaried work but the wages work. A study of reservation of seats for Schedule Caste has shown that many of the Buddhists lacked training, therefore they were unable to compete and take up higher post. (VIKALAP, 1997).

The analysis of the 50th round did not have a table on religion-wise expenditure this may be due to deterioration of the economic condition as due to inflation. (R.M. Baxamusa, 1997).

Occupation Characteristics

The occupational differences were clearly observed among the religious groups in the two rounds. In rural areas, Table 2, among all

TABLE 2

Occupation Characteristics of Rural and Urban (Religious Groups) 43rd Round and 50th Round

	43rd round			*50th round*			
	Hindu	*Muslim*	*Buddhist*	*Hindu*	*Muslim*	*Buddhist*	
Rural Female Worker							
Self-employed total	21.3	8.6	11.4	18.8	10.9	8.4	
Self-employed helper	1.6	2.6	1.4	1.5	2.7	0.8	
Regular worker wage/salary	4.5	0.4	0.5	0.0	0.0	0.0	
Casual worker Public work	13.6	20.5	30.3	20.4	16.8	30.8	
Casual worker Private work	0.8	1.0	2.2	0.7	.0	1	
Workers Total	42.5	30.5	48.7	40.7	29.4	41.1	
Non workers Total	57.5	695	51.3	59.3	70.6	58.9	
Rural Male Worker							
Self-employed	28.5	24.4	11.8	26.9	21.3	12.9	9.5
Self-employed helper	4.1	12.9	1.7	4.6	7.4	3.4	
Regular Worker Wages/Salary	5.3	3.5	3.7	.2	0.6	0.2	
Casual worker Public work	18.1	21.5	37.9	20.0	21.1	34.8	
Casual worker Private work	2.1	4.2	3.5	1.7	3.1	2.3	
Workers total	54.9	54.3	53.9	53.4	53.8	52.1	
Non Workers Total	45.1	45.7	46.1	44.6	46.2	47.9	

religious groups Buddhists had the highest number of female workers. The Muslim had the least number of workers. The Buddhist and the Hindus workers were less in the 50th round but there was not much difference for the Muslims between the two rounds. The study on "Liberalization Policy after 1991 indicated that mechanization in rural areas resulted in reduction in employment of women". (Baxamusa, 1997).

The picture of the urban female workers was almost opposite of the rural female worker's. In rural areas there were more workers than in urban areas. This was true among all the religious groups. In the 50th round there were more workers. In 43rd round the Buddhists were 15.2 per cent, the Muslims 7.9, and in 50th round the Buddhists were 26.6 per cent and the Muslims 9.6 per cent. Muslim females work participation rate in rural India was very low compared to Buddhist and Hindus workers. (Shariff, 1990).

In rural as well as urban areas casual work was highest among the Buddhists, than among the Hindus and the Muslims. As Maharashtra was the pioneer in most of the Government Employment Guarantee Schemes in rural areas, many poor women worked in it. After 1991 when the government, because of the new policy, stopped the schemes there was a fall in casual workers in the villages. In urban areas as there were no government schemes functioning earlier, casual work was not affected. Here one notices an increase in number of workers due to inflation, when things become expensive more women were pushed to work and earn a livelihood for the family.

In rural areas self-employment was highest among 21.3 per cent Hindus according to the 43rd, and 18.8 per cent according to the 50th rounds respectively. The Muslim women in self-employment were only 8.6 per cent in 43rd round and 10.9 per cent in the 50th rounds respectively. The Buddhists in the 43rd round were more in self-employment but in 50th round their figure was less than that of Muslims.

In the rural areas Hindus and Buddhists were engaged in nearly 6 per cent of regular jobs. Perhaps they had entered work very early.

Some Buddhists benefited due to reservation of jobs. The Muslims entered into job market late, therefore very few of them had regular jobs.

Comparing the occupation (Table 2) of the urban and rural male workers to the female workers, one realizes that there were more male workers in Maharashtra among all religious groups. According to the all India data the Muslims were highly engaged in self-employment [Sarvekshana Sept. 1990]. But in Maharashtra the self-employment is the higher among the Hindus than the Muslims. This may be due to the fact that mere Hindus of Maharashtra were artisans than the Muslims. The Buddhists were not artisans, therefore they too, were less in this category. Muslim male workers, i.e., 28.8 per cent, the highest number in the 43rd round, were casual workers and 22.2 per cent of them were self-employed. In the 50th round 19.9 per cent male workers were self employed and only 1.4 per cent casual workers. This picture was not similar for the Hindus and the Buddhists both in rural and urban areas according to 43rd round among Hindus majority 20.5 per cent was engaged in self-employment and according to the 50th round the figure decreased, but the Buddhists (22.3 per cent) were self-employed.

Casual employment in public work was highest among the Buddhists, as most of them do menial work. The other important thing one notices that females were mostly casual workers. Both Buddhists and Muslims as they were having very low percentage of regular employment, their percentage as casual workers was more. Hindus from urban and rural areas generally take up jobs in bank's or Government organisation. The Buddhist and the Muslims came late in the labour market without much training, therefore they did not get jobs. They generally took casual work which was not regular, and was only seasonal for small duration, thus they remained unemployed for longer periods.

Muslim women/men having no alternative are forced to enter the employment market, only through self-employment. Thus, training programmes were needed to develop skills to better their earning capacity. Developing their artisan skills which could make them independent. There was a need for credit facility being made available, and Government should create market for goods produced by them.

Educational Characteristics

Even after 50 years of independence, looking at the data on literacy level of women, we find that in all the religious groups more women were illiterate. The 43th round indicated that in rural area 73 per cent Muslim women, 67 per cent Hindu women, and 72.5 per cent Buddhist women were illiterate. (Table 3). Emphasis on girl child and

TABLE 3
Educational Characteristics of Religious Groups
43th round and 50th round

Household Education	*43rd round*			*50th round*		
	Hindu	*Muslim*	*Buddhist*	*Hindu*	*Muslim*	*Buddhist*
Urban Female Education						
Illiterate	339	427	465	234	373	325
Literate Below Primary	170	210	173	82	142	153
Primary and Middle	312	203	193	279	312	135
Secondary	133	57	186	224	130	371
Graduate and above	46	03	3	81	12	16
Urban Male Education						
Illiterate	136	323	270	91	148	239
Literate Below Primary	233	254	235	83	144	117
Primary and Middle	352	307	345	314	480	331
Secondary	210	94	116	383	186	262
Graduate and above	89	22	34	129	42	51
Rural Female Education						
Illiterate	670	730	726	604	610	638
Literate Below Primary	152	145	244	116	117	104

Primary and Middle	154	109	31	216	183	201
Secondary	22	16	19	65	87	57
Graduate and above	2	0	0	9	3	0
Rural Male Educational						
Illiterate	412	458	429	299	291	291
Literate Below Primary	216	208	214	148	160	207
Primary and Middle	283	274	292	348	346	315
Secondary	77	52	62	172	161	162
Graduate and above	12	8	3	33	32	25

Source: Government of Maharashtra, 43rd and 50th NSSO round un-published.

several adult education programmes resulted slight reduction in the rate of illiteracy according to the 50th round. Compared to Hindu and the Buddhist the Muslim female education was still very low in rural area.

In urban areas where the facilities of education are comparatively of better quality than those available in villages, the illiterates in urban areas among all religious groups are less. Comparig the rates of illiteracy figures in the 43th round with the 50th round, one finds that in urban areas illiteracy has decreased by 10 per cent among all religious groups.

The figures of number of those who have covered middle school level were highest among almost all religious groups. However the females who had cleared the secondary school and the graduate level was very low.

The percentage of educated Muslim women, in the 43rd round showed that literate-middle school level female in urban area were 56.8 per cent, while in rural areas they were only 25.4 per cent. According to the 50th round there was a definite improvement in education and there was more women in each of these religious groups in both areas who had passed secondary or graduation. Generally the existing polytechnic and higher education courses take care of the graduates and secondary trained. It is necessary to start vocational training for the school dropouts as they are sitting idle as it is difficult for them to get work.

Looking minutely at the growth of education among all religious groups one finds the growth was still low among the Muslims. Most of the Muslim girls dropped out of the schools in rural and urban areas before puberty when at 5th to 8 stds. As a result of *purdah* many women were not permitted to go to far away schools. The Hindus were more educated than Muslims or Buddhists. In 43rd round there was no Muslim graduate in rural area but by 50th round there were 3 per cent graduates. In the 50th round the education of the Buddhists women grew faster than the Muslims as they had realized the need for it. That type of awareness needed to be cultivated also among the Muslims.

Comparing the education level of male with female in urban/ rural areas one finds that among each religious groups males were better educated than the females. In the 50th round the education had comparatively improved for both girls/boys, however the gap which existed between them did not decrease. As majority of school drop-outs were girls, there is need to concentrate in training this group.

Case Study of Training Programme Institutes

Evaluation of the post-riot situation of the Muslim females in Bombay in the *mohallas* and slums revealed they were not very much educated, mostly below SSC. They had no courage to face the situation and protect themselves. General price rise and changing socio-economic condition made all demand job oriented training to make them self-sufficient. Case studies of two institute are presented. Generally the polytechnics, ITI (Industrial Training Institutes) and other offer training to those who had passed secondary school, here the training is offered to the school dropouts.

Saboo Siddiq Open University Scheme

The Saboo Siddiq under the leadership of Ms. Uzma Nahid in 1997 started the Open University Scheme for school dropout, girls and women. The programmes were open to all literates and courses duration of 6 month to a year were started to equip them to start independent work or employment. There were courses of *mehendi* beautician, tailoring, embroidery, home science, fashion designing, textile designing, cooking and journalism. In these courses already more than 500 females were admitted 20 per cent of those admitted were elderly women but rest were adolescent young girls, below 20 years. Being a Muslim institute the majority were Muslims, but as there was a police training institute near the college; around 2 per cent Hindu girls of police had joined.

Through the analysis of students attending this programme it was learnt that the majority were from lower middle class families. Around 20 per cent were from upper class and around 20 per cent were from the very poor class. The fees for 6 months is around Rs. 700 to Rs. 1000 and for one year Rs. 1500 to Rs. 2000. The 20 per cent students coming from poor families who were not in a position to pay fees, were offered fellowship from the Saboo Siddiq. All Boys Association and rest of the needy were paid from funds collected from rich Muslims Zakat and other charity funds.

The course drew girls from all over Bombay. The majority of girls were from Byculla to Crawford Market, while 30 per cent come from suburbs as far as Kausa, Mumira, Vikhroli, Mira Road. A few, that is 10 per cent, were students who had passed secondary but the rest were school dropouts.

The courses opened opportunities for more than 10 per cent of them to get employment directly from the institution. As some Fashion designer who came to take lectures gave jobs to a few students. There were many exporters who needed women to do needle and sewing work, they contacted the vocational centre. Also the small sewing institute, who needed sewing teachers etc. they also approached the vocational training centre.

The aim of the course was also to give women employment through co-operatives, self-employment etc. However a beginning has still not been made as it is very difficult to arrange, credit and market for the finished products. Lately there is a feeling among the management that it shall also be difficult for them to run production units as management of the training centre is a big task: they feel that a voluntary organisation should take up the responsibility. This year emphasis is laid on holding exhibition and encouraging students to prepare items for sale. This activity of vocational training should expand, then only we can provide employment opportunity for them.

Department of P.G. Studies and Research, College of Home Science, SNDT Women's University

The P.G. Department, under the leadership of Dr. Mariamma Varghese, in 1991 started a Community Development Project in Gilbert Hill where there are 14,000 families with nearly 1,20,000 population. When work started this slum was known as notorious slum. Therefore neither Government nor any NGO had any welfare programme. This slum had predominantly 98 per cent of Muslims. Poor Muslims generally consider education as secondary. SNDT intervened to focus the programme on women and children for their holistic development in the areas of health, education, sanitation, clean drinking water supply and capacity building.

In the first year with the help of 238 volunteers representing various pockets of the slums, 17 balwadis were opened. There was difficulty to get trained personal, so training for *balwadi* teachers was organized and then this slum dwellers were given jobs.

With the help of *Mehndi* teachers from slum in exchange of fees, training was offered to some adolescent girls who later used this art to earn their livelihood in the slums.

By then the SNDT was able to get a contract from the BMC to supply nutritional food to 1000 primary school children. Training was offered to slum women, and today around 14 are engaged regularly in supplying food, and some slum dwellers who have provided space for cooking, are also earning.

As unemployment in the slum was the major problem most of them requested that the SNDT, beside running other programmes should concentrate on income generating programmes for the needy women.

A decision was taken that the SNDT will go on with its

programme of (i) *Education:* Adult literacy, Non-formal education centres, Children education trips, Summer camps, encourage reentry into schools; (ii) *Health and Nutrition:* Child spacing programme, Immunization, Medical camps, antenatal care; (iii) *Environmental Sanitation* and *Capacity Building and Leadership:* but now they are emphasizing more on *Skill Training, Vocational Guidance and Income Generation: and Entrepreneurship Training:*

Vocationnal Training. The school drop-outs and many young divorcels were not permitted to go out as a result of *purdah*. They did not have opportunity to express themselves, therefore the SNDT conducted around 10 *mehndi* classes, sewing centres, fabric painting, embroidery, flower making, card making, folder making, Diya making and crochets. The items manufactured were sold in the SNDT Juhu campus regularly. Items were also sold at exhibitions held in Mumbai. As a person was appointed to look after the sale this was possible. Women by this activity did not earn a sizeable income but in a small way were able to add to the family income. As women were not permitted to go outside the premises, small jobs were given to them in the area itself.

In the tailoring programme, women of the area were taught stitching of laboratory coats, aprons, scarves, petticoats. The units take the order and supply coats to colleges. Women are paid money per coat stitched. Around 10 of these trained women were taken to the neighbourhood garment industry and were given jobs.

Now a few women are taught weaving. Looms are set at the college and in the slum. The women are paid according to the *work done*.

Some women were taught how to make snacks and these eatables were prepared in the slum and brought to SNDT campus and sold to the student and the staff.

Another very important skill taught was flower-making. This work has good demand and they are able to sell small pots. These women are able to earn nearly Rs. 2500 in 15 days.

The other important thing done was organisation of the

entrepreneurship course at the SNDT university. The course opened up their eyes, and 30 women opened their accounts, a few get loans and they started their independent business. These 5 women are regularly paying back their loans and making a good earning.

The SNDT has made a beginning but still they have a long way to go substantially to give all women some income.

Conclusion

Since the Report on the Status of Women India of 1974 there was great urge among Muslim women, to improve their skills, so they could better their economic position. A beginning has been made after the 90's by the two academic institutes to teach skills. Efforts by Muslim and non-Muslim institutes mark a beginning to train the middle and the lower class women. As noticed in both areas the majority of the girls/women were dropouts at middle school level. The training programmes have opened doors to these school dropouts. One is aware that getting regular jobs is difficult. Now with the effort of the institutes self-employment is initiated. This needs to be encouraged by the Government. There is need for the Government to start schemes like the IRDP which will give credit facilities to this to start their self-employment work. It is very difficult for these women to sell their products, therefore the states government should purchase their products. The States of Gujarat and Punjab are since many years purchasing things from women and selling them in their showrooms.

If more and more of such training programmes are held other urban and rural areas, one will be able to improve the lot of female workers and especially that of the Muslims. The beginning has been made and this should be encouraged.

TABLE 4
Occupation of Urban Workers

Occupation	43rd round			50th round		
	Hindu	*Muslim*	*Buddhist*	*Hindu*	*Muslim*	*Buddhist*
Urban Female Workers						
Self-employed total	4.6	3.6	1.7	4.8	3.8	1.5
Self-employed helper	3.4	3.4	1.3	3.2	2.8	1.3
Regular salary/wages	4.9	1.6	6.0	0.0	0.0	0.0
Casual worker public	1.5	1.1	2.0	0.0	0.3	3.3
Casual worker private	2.4	1.1	4.0	1.6	1.1	6.5
Workers Total	14.3	7.9	15.2	14.0	9.6	26.6
Non workers total	85.7	92.1	85.8	86.0	90.4	73.4
Urban Male Occupation						
Self-employed	16.3	22.2	4.6	17.4	19.9	8.9
Self-employed helper	14.1	21.2	4.3	15.1	19.5	8.1
Regular salary/wages	29.4	20.6	28.9	0.1	0.1	0.1
Casual worker public	1.1	20.3	12.9	0.2	.5	8.5
Casual worker private	4.5	6.5	10.0	1.4	0.3	5.6
Workers Total	54.1	52.3	50.7	54.7	49.4	52.4
Non workers Total	45.9	47.7	49.3	45.3	50.6	47.6

Source: 43rd round and 50th round NSSO. Government Data unpublished.

REFERENCES

Baxamusa R.M. (1997): Impact of the New Economic Policy on the Life of the Muslims presented in the conference of Indian Association of Women's Studies. VII Jaipur. (mimeograph).

Census of India, 1991 Series No. 10 Religion published in 1995

Maharashtra Religion - Director of Census Operation, Maharashtra.

Census of India, 1991 quoted in A. Sen and J. Dreze, Oxford University Press, 1996.

Govt. of India, 1974: "Towards Equality", Department of Social Welfare, Ministry of Education and Social Welfare.

Shariff, Ahusaleh, 1995: "Socio-economic and Demographic Differentials between Hindus and Muslims", *Economic and Political Weekly*. Vol. 30 No. 46, November, 18: p. 2947-2953.

_______, (1998): "Relative Economic and Social Deprivation of Muslims" paper presented at the seminar on *Muslims in India Since Independence,* organised by the Institute of Objective Studies, New Delhi on 28-29 March.

National Sample Survey Organisation, (1990): *Sarvekshana: Results of the Fourth Quinquiennial Survey on Employment and Unemployment* (NSSO) Ministry of Planning, Govt. of India, New Delhi.

National Sample Survey Organisation, (Unpublished): *Results of the Fourth Quinquinnial and the Fifth Survey on Employment and Unemployment* (NSSO), Directorate of Economic and Statistic, Government of Maharashtra.

Vikalp, (1998): *Issue; Globalisation and Dalits,* Vol. 5. No. 3 Vikas Adhyanyan Kendra, Bombay.

_______. (1998). *Perspective on Dalit Question and Dalit Politics,* Vol. No.2. Vikas Adhyanyan Kendra, Bombay.

17

Education Among Varanasi Muslims: A Study in the Perspective of National Integration

Muniza Rafiq Khan

Some recent findings related to education among the Muslims indicate that modern education is yet to catch the imagination of the Muslim masses. Modern education, particularly occupational and technical education is yet to appear indispensable to Muslims. Many of them consider it expensive, others complain of lack of facilities and the vast majority regards it as irrelevant. Since the vast majority of the Muslims in most pieces in India consists of occupational castes and artisan classes it is quite understandable that in general education imparted in colleges and universities is of little use to them. Only that education which is related to their traditional professiom can be of some use to them. They openly say that even after earning a first class graduate or postgraduate degree they cannot expect their children to make as much as they would while remaining illiterate but engaged in their particular ancestral occupation. It is only a thin layer of the Muslim elite which finds education both profitable and prestigious.

It has been seen that the vast majority of Muslims being from the occupational and artisan communities find little economic value in education—even in the technical education imparted in the lower technical institutes. The economic aspect of education appears to them the most important aspect if not the only important aspect, and the prospects of economic advantage do not appear very bright. Many Muslim weavers, fruit merchants, bangle makers, dealers in meat, *zari* workers, etc. have became millionarie despite remaining illiterate or having any education worth the name. It is not easy to convince them of the various intangible advantages of education.

The aim of the present study is to develop insights into the state of Modern Education Among Muslims of Varanasi and to find out attitudes, avenues, prospects and problems that exist in relation to modern education. The coverage of the sample was fairly wide to ensure that as far as possible no occupational, educational, age, sex and caste group was left unrepresented. In addition to tapping the attitude and opinion in relation to the specific aspects of modern education, we collected information regarding facilities of educational help and support expected or available from the non-Muslim communities of the town or from the government. One of the aim was to find out the form and depth of the feeling of persecution, isolation, alienation, close mindedness and insecurity from which the Muslim community has been suffering.

Modern education have both advantages and disadvantages. Table 1 presents opinion regarding modern education.

TABLE 1

Opinion with regard to Modern Education

S. No.	*Responses*	*Total N=278*
1.	Useless, creates moral crises and counter to Islam, and lacking sense of direction	30 (10.79)
2.	Non-oriented towards professional organisation	47 (16.90)
3.	Examination system is faulty	5 (1.8)

4.	Education is delinked with indigenous culture and creats trends towards material benefits	5 (1.8)
5.	It alienates from society which endangers national unity	5 (1.8)
6.	This create ambivalence and imbalance in attitude and approach	3 (1.08)
7.	Inadequacy in the present system caters to the needs of the present day society.	
8.	D.K.	9 (3.24)
9.	N.R.	22 (7.91)
10.	Not at all	152 (54.68)

In the present study out of 278 respondents, 54.68 per cent were of the opinion that there is no disadvantage of modern education. It indicates that respondents were very well aware about the modern education. On the other side 10.79 per cent said that modern education is useless, creates moral crises, is counter to Islam and lacking sense of direction. 10.9 per cent maintained that, it is non-oriented towards professional work.

To know the opinion regarding modern education, respondents were asked to give their opinion separately regarding Muslim youth going in for technical/engineering/medical/professional/business management and other types of education (Table 2). It was found that a large percentage, i.e., above 90 per cent respondent were of the opinion that Muslim youth should go for the modern education. Here the percentage of girls in comparison to boys were slightly less. In comparison to other subcategories respondents said that best education for girls is medical.

TABLE 2
Opinion Regarding Technological Education

Sl. No.	Technological Education	Should go Boys	Should go Girls	Should not go Boys	Should not go Girls	D.K. Boys	D.K. Girls
1.	Higher level	260	237	1	24	17	17
	Tech. edu.	(93.52)	(85.25)	(.36)	(8.63)	(6.12)	(6.12)
2.	Medical	258	243	3	18	17	17
	Education	(92.8)	(87.41)	(1.08)	(6.47)	(6.12)	(6.12)
3.	Journalism	257	233	2	25	19	20
		(92.45)	(83.8)	(.72)	(9.00)	(6.83)	(7.20)
4.	Business	256	233	2	25	20	20
	management	(92.08)	(83.80)	(.72)	(9.00)	(7.20)	(7.20)
5.	Law	258	236	2	24	18	18
		(92.80)	(84.90)	(.72)	(8.62)	(6.48)	(6.48)

The respondents were asked whether they think that Muslim boys and girls who join professional courses are in adequate numbers in comparison to other communities. Table 3 suggests that a majority 93.16 per cent thought that they did not join professional courses.

TABLE 3

Opinion about Joining Professional Courses by Muslims in Adequate Numbers

Sl. No.	*Responses*	*Number percentage N=278*
1.	Yes	6 (2.16)
2.	No	259 (93.16)
3.	Can't say	13 (4.68)

The reasons for not joining the professional courses by Muslims in terms of various relevant factors are economic, social, political, and traditonal. 83.4 per cent were of the opinion that due to financial backwardness Muslims are not joining professional course. As far as social factor is concerned 33.78 per cent respondents said that tradition and social status is incompatible with demands of education and 25.87 per cent said that due to illiteracy among the Muslim families they did not join these courses as they do not know the importance of these courses. It was interesting that Muslims were very well aware about the impact of *purdah* (veil) system. 37.84 per cent said that due to *purdah* system girls did not join professional courses. But the respondents did not know much about the political and communal factors.

Therefore nearly fifty per cent gave no answer. Among the rest of the respondents 25.86 per cent said, that Muslims are discriminated on the basis of religion and they were rejected in the interviews. Due to fear of discrimination Muslims are not joining the professional courses. And as far as tradition in the community is concerned less than 50 per cent respondents who responded, 30.5 per cent were of the opinion that higher education or professional courses are not in conformity with prevailing traditions. Muslims prefer their traditional occupations in comparison to professional courses. It was found that their main source of earning was their traditional occupations. Girls were also engaged in saree weaving.

According to Table 4 generally Muslims have a good opinion with regard to modern education as out of 278 respondents only 16.55 per cent said that modern education alienates from traditional occupations. They gave suggestion for remedying the situation by introducing some changes in the educational curricula. According to them the needs and requirements of a community must be kept in mind while preparing the syllabi.

TABLE 4

Opinion about the Modern Education Whether it Alienates from the Traditional Occupations

Sl. No.	*Responses*	*Number and Percentage*
1.	Yes	46 (16.55)
2.	No	181 (65.11)
3.	Can't say	51 (18.34)

Respondents were also asked whether they are aware of any problems that Muslim boys or girls face in educational institutions managed by non-Muslims? Table 5 indicates that a majority of the respondents were not aware of any problems that Muslim students face there.

TABLE 5

Knowledge about the Problems Faced by the Muslim Students in the Institutions Run by Non-Muslims

Sl. No.	*Responses*	*Number and Percentage*
1.	Yes	87 (31.29)
2.	No	158 (56.84)
3.	Can't say	33 (11.87)

In fact, 87 (31.29 per cent) respondents reported that Muslim students are facing problems in the educational institutions run for all. The problems differ from level to level in the institutions. On the basis of the levels in institutions four levels were developed:

(I) *Primary and Junior high school* —Out of 87, (74,71) per cent were of the opinion that discrimination at the time of admission and final results is practised at this level.

(II) *Higher Secondary and Intermediate*—At this level 42 per cent respondents said that text books are anti-Muslim, which create communal feelings among the students. 39.08 per cent gave no reply. With regard to suggestions, they said, that syllabus should include information about Muslim, their religion and their culture and anti-Muslim contents should be removed. Apart from this they added that chapters containing character building must be added in social studies.

(III) *Degree Colleges and Universities*—Out of 87 respondents 53 (60.92 per cent) maintained that at this level discriminatory policy is practised against Muslims.

(IV) *Technological, Medical and other occupational Institutions*—At this level out of 87 respondents (55.17) per cent thought that Muslims faced discrimination.

TABLE 6

Knowledge about the Cases of Muslim Boys and Girls who could not Receive Higher Education and Thereof: Reasons

Sl. No.	*Reasons*	*Number and per cent*
1.	Non-availability of English schools in neighbourhood/locality	1 (.36)
2.	Due to family and traditional reasons	15 (5.39)
3.	Over attachment with politics	-
4.	Poor economic condition	37 (13.31)
5.	D.K.	225 (80.94)

Table 6 gives the actual cases of Muslim students who could not go for higher education due to some or other reasons. The table suggests that 80.94 per cent respondents were not aware of any such cases. Only 19.06 per cent knew the actual cases of Muslim students who could not persue higher education although they were interested and when asked about the reason 13.31 per cent said due to poor economic condition and 5.39 per cent said due to their family situation they could not go for higher education. Only one respondent said it was due to discrimination. Thus main reason why Muslim students did not persue higher education was economic backwardness and family tradition.

Educational Backwardness of Varanasi Muslims

Varanasi, one of the ancient cities and seat of learning in India is located on the left bank of the sacred river Ganges. Varanasi district had 3,701,006 population according to 1981 census. It has an estimated Muslim population of 20-25 per cent. Although the district has three universities, yet the literacy in the Varanasi district as per

1981 census is 31.05 per cent, 45.95 per cent among males and 16.25 per cent among females. The ratio of primary schools per ten thousand of urban population is 2.66 in the district. The ratio of Junior secondary and middle schools works out to 0.55 school per ten thousand of urban population of the district ranging between the maximum of 4.91 schools in Gangapur town and minimum of 0.29 in Varanasi city. The ratio for intermediate colleges per ten thousand of urban population works out to 0.54 college in the district. The highest ratio of 4.27 Inter College is observed in Gangapur while the minimum of 0.35 in Varanasi city. It is found through the present study that the number of institutions from the primary level upwards sponsored by Muslims is comparatively small in Varanasi. There are two Muslim high schools.

Problem Faced by the Muslim Institutions

Among the respondents, from the management committees or those taking active part to run the institutions, 55.03 per cent identified following problems:

(i) Want of financial and other resources
(ii) Generally prosperous Muslims are not interested in educational institutions
(iii) Groupism, casteism, sectarianism among Muslims
(iv) Good teachers and staff are not available.

It is observed that the standard of Muslim educational institution is not up to the mark, and due to lack of mutual cooperative attitude among them these institutions face severe problems.

Causes of Educational Backwardness

Economic Problems

In the present study out of 278 respondents, 82.43 per cent said that Muslim children do not attend schools and colleges on account of lack of financial resources. The community is generally poor and cannot afford to keep the children in institutions of higher learning as the time spent in school or college could be used for supplementing family income. The parents usually have to withdraw their sons from educational institutions to put them on some job that adds to the family income. Poverty is the main reason why the girls are also withdrawn from school and married off while still in their teens or early twenties.

Prejudices and Traditional Occupation

Muslim children in Varanasi do not attend schools for the simple reason that education of good quality which would help them in competing for a high level posts in government departments, public sector undertakings or private enterprises is not available and admissions to good institutions—general, professional or technical is extremely difficult. 25.86 per cent respondents reported that Muslims are discriminated on the basis of religion and they were rejected in the interviews. But 30.5 per cent are of the opinion that Muslims prefer their traditional occupations in comparison to professional courses. The easily available education in ordinary general schools and colleges turns the children worthless both for employment outside as well as for the traditional jobs at home. The same is true for the girls for the education they receive in ordinary institutions renders them useless for the domestic chore as well as for any other useful work outside. In other words, such an education is neither relevant to the traditional occupation of the family nor for employment in the various professions and enterprises of public and private nature.

Lack of Facilities and Ability

It is observed that one of the reasons why Muslim children have to remain deprived of the fruits of an occupational course is that access and admission to such suitable institutions are beyond the capacity of the Muslim parents. It is noteworthy that 16.47 per cent respondents reported that this is due to lack of interest in present system of education. With regard to employment 53.11 per cent said due to unfavourable educational environment and absence of proper guidance in the family. 12.03 per cent maintained, that Muslims do not compete due to their inability or incompetance. In other words the main reason why Muslim children remain uneducated and are rarely seen in medical and engineering colleges and other institutions is both lack of facilities as well as lack of ability.

Assurance of Jobs

In Varanasi quite a number of Muslims engaged in manufacture and commerce related to handicrafts also maintain that modern education including professional education does not necessarily assure the same income and independence that one can expect from traditional occupation. According to the respondents, the boy child may have to remain either unemployed or poorly employed after having a university degree which may have involved a good amount of expenditure, absence from traditional occupation of the family and, in many cases, alienation from the mores, values and culture of the family.

There are some other reasons also and each one of these appears to have a grain of truth.

The backwardness of the Muslim—social, economic and educational, like the backwardness of any other caste or community is a national problem. This must be recognised as a problem that should concern the whole nation and not the Muslims alone. The most crucial role, however, is our own. We should recognize that these are our problems and we have to solve them through our own unrelenting efforts, coordination and pooling of resources. Educational and social reform in the present circumstances can only be initiated by enlightened leadership from within the community. Unfortunately, Muslim leadership is obsessed with non-issues or mostly with success in politics. The task of reconstruction cannot be initiated unless the issues before the community are properly segregated from non-issues. The major thrust for Muslims' upliftment has to come from the community itself. The government however can help to promote education among the Muslims by enacting the following measures:

(i) Liberalising procedure for recognition of minority institutions.

(ii) Opening more educational/technical institutions in Muslim dominated areas.

(iii) Encouraging and giving liberal grants to training/coaching schools for preparation of Muslim youth for higher services.

(iv) Teaching in Government aided schools should become secular and non-communal so that Muslim apathy is overcame.

(v) Giving clear directions to all state governments/public undertakings/central government departments to furnish data with respect to representation of minorities to the Minorities Commission, so that the commission is able to promote sympathetic public opinion and to assist policy-makers in rectifying imbalances wherever they are found.

Apart from above measures, a forum should be created where government, voluntary organisations and Muslim intellectuals could meet periodically and review the educational, sociai and economic situation of the Muslims.

18
The Problems of Muslim Women in India with Special Focus on Kashmiri Women

Hamida Naeem

General Situation

Women have generally been subjected to stifling oppression and stultifying suppression, resulting in their mental suppression throughout human history irrespective of religious, economic, racial and socio-demographic differences. The inferior status assigned to women is a result of social evaluation of her biological activities of child-bearing and child-rearing as the only ones appropriate to her which give fulfilment in life. The stereotypes are formed on these bases which, being part of the cultural tradition, validate and justify their inferior status and account for their dependency, discrimination and degradation.

Islamic Position

The Prophet of Islam, Muhammad (PBUH) was the first crusader and vehement advocate of the human rights of women. He came to this world as a liberator, protector and guarantor of women's rights in order to rescue her from the depths of degradation, exploitation and humiliation, and admonished man in his farewell message, "You have rights over your women and your women have rights over you" which underlines the tremendous importance he assigned to his mission as a protector and guarantor of women's conjugal, legal, marital, social, economic and other rights to elevate her status and self-dignity.

But conversely, throughout the Muslim world, men have ignored one of the prime-moves of the Prophet's mission and have treated their women no better than other religious groups, races, communities and societies. In fact they have shattered others' records by suppressing and degrading their womenfolk, thereby they have given a ready whip in others hands to lash them with for their myopic vision viz-a-viz women.

The Prophet of Islam (PBUH) had also pointed to the essential and basic physiology and psychology of women as different from those of men, and thus emphasized that her femininity was a virtue, a strength and not a weakness.

Whereas, we see in the 20th Century, women's liberation movement has become almost fanatical claiming absolute equality between men and women in physical as well as psychological terms. In Euro-American tradition, Simone de Beavouir had been in the vanguard of this movement whose classic analysis of the situation of women denies the ontological validity of the concept of femininity. Her book, *The Second Sex*[1] insists that the notion of femininity is a notion created by men who tell woman that passivity and acceptance are her nature. It exhorts women to give the lie to this male fiction, to transcend the status of alterity or otherness or sex that men have imposed upon them. The position is not imposed of necessity by natural feminine characteristics but rather by strong environmental forces of educational and social tradition under the purposeful control of man. This has resulted in the general failure of women to occupy the place of human dignity as free and independent existents associated with men on a plane of intellectual and professional equality and has given rise to social evils and to a vitiating effect on the sexual relation between man and woman.

However, in exhorting women to deny their sexuality in order to transcend the definition men have assigned to them as 'the other sex', she is, in effect, rejecting all those values and virtues that arise from sanctified male-female contact—the very spring of life.

By stating and analysing the Western position on woman's rightful place in the world, I am simply trying to demonstrate that while the rest of the world is still consolidating its position on the states of woman and her rights, the Prophet of Islam had already offered her an honourable and dinified position in the 7th century A.D.

But in spite of that, Muslim women suffered and continue to suffer all over the world. One reason has been that the text or the Quran has been interpreted variously, rigidly and loosely according to the mind-set of the interpreters. Those who have interpreted retrogressively are the ones who feel insecure with women's power assigned to them by Qur'an. That is why we do not see in practice most of the rights granted to her by Qur'an or the honourable status accorded to her by Islam. And in some societies like ours, traditions and customs have been given a religious sanction whereas the religious injunctions have been buried many fathoms deep.

Indian Scene

Coming to the Indian scene which is pluralistic in every sense, surprisingly India has been more advanced and progressive in granting equal rights to women which have not been granted to them even now in some parts of the most advanced countries of the world, like USA and England. These countries pay less to women than to men for the same job. Mahatma Gandhi played a pivotal role in taking women out of the domestic confinements to the forefront of the national freedom struggle against British Raj. But socially, economically and even psychologically the majority of Indian women continue to suffer. Politically women have not been empowered to the extent to which they should have been. In the recent elections in South Africa, out of 400 and some odd seats, 120 women candidates have won the election whereas in Indian Parliament we have only a few women out of 545 seats.

Muslim Women

And since Muslims are in minority in India, their women's

position is even worse, because Muslim men have generally prevented their women from modern educational and social and economic progress. One manifestation of this is, as pointed out in one study, that the majority, i.e., 69.75 per cent Muslim women do not want to educate their daughters beyond the primary level. Further, many middle class women, who have requisite qualifications are not, allowed to seek employment because the patriarchal 'respectability' is likely to get smeared. This has resulted in the general backwardness of Muslim women in India which is aggravated by the discriminatory treatment as well as the feeling of the discrimination experienced by them in many parts of the country.

Problems of Kashmiri Women

Since it is difficult to discuss the problems of Muslim women in the entire country, I will specially focus first on the general problems of Muslim women in Kashmir and then move on to the problems they have been facing for the past one decade of turbulence. Ever since 1947, when India and Pakistan got their freedom Kashmiri women continued to suffer, earlier under autocratic rule, now under the sham of democracy. They continued to remain backward educationally, economically and politically. The stooge governments, one after another, did not encourage or initiate the emergence of strong popular governmental or non-governmental movements which could have brought about awareness of rights and duties of men towards women or could eradicate prevailing social evils. The percentage of women's education is abysmally low. It is 29 per cent in Jammu and Kashmir as against 86 per cent in Kerala and 39.42 per cent in the country.

For males it is 46 per cent as against 94 per cent in Kerala and 64 per cent in India. The total adult literacy rate is 38 per cent in Jammu and Kashmir while in the country it is 52 per cent (1991 census). Even though the schools have been opened in many parts of the state, drop-out rate has been almost 90 per cent in the villages. The schools are in a terrible mess. There is no accountability in Government schools for teachers or administrators which could goad them to better their performance or woo back the dropouts from the schools. There are no incentives or any disciplinary action taken to coax them back to the schools. Educational backwardness is also increased by the lure of money attached with carpet-weaving and other handicrafts in the valley. Poor parents prefer their children to earn money through short cuts without being encumbered by the long process of education. Besides, the economic condition, on the whole, is very bad which prevents the poor parents from educating their children especially if they happen to be girls.

Morever, women continue to suffer innumerable diseases arising out of ignorance and lack of awareness because no effort has been made so far to bring about health consciousness among women folk to improve their condition or the well-being of their children. A recent survey in the hospitals of Srinagar has shown that patients of breast cancer are deserted by their husbands. Economically too, most of the women, (around 80%, continue to depend on their husbands for their sustenance because work at home is considered no work at all. Of course, some middle class women about less than 30 per cent of the urban background have enjoyed a certain measure of personal freedom and a few women have been elevated and upgraded to higher positions in government jobs but this is an exception and not the norm. Most of them are teachers, few of them doctors and engineers, many of them clerks but majority of the women lead a sordid and degraded life in abject circumstances in the rural areas.

We do no t see women participating in the political process at any level as there is no encouragement in schools, colleges and universities to involve them in moreimportant roles like policy making for the developmental programme of the state. However, for the last fifty years she has struggled to evolve a distinct identity of her own and displayed exemplary courage in braving most of the problems, challenges and hurdles in her way, which she faces every day in he family and the society. She is paying a heavy price for the freedom she paradoxically enjoys. When the roles of women were defined within the sphere of home and hearth, there were no clashes within her or with the outer world. She resigned herself to a passive acceptance of her fate and was relatively happier with kids and the service of her husband and in-laws. But the collapse of the joint family system triggered off, among other things, by her education and work outside home, brought innumerable problems in its wake. Because once she is conscious and becomes aware of herself as an individual with countless dreams, desires and ambitions and a will of her own, she has felt increasingly claustrophobic in her traditionally assigned roles and is most of the times torn internally between two selves. She suffers intensely inwardly as there is a terrible conflict between her desires, dreams and will with those of her immediate family and the defined roles she is supposed to play. She rebels, sometimes successfully but most of the times even her rebellion shoots off further problems. This gives rise to a stressful life, full of agony and mental torment. To top it all, she has begun to expect too much of herself and when the expectations are not met, she feels guilty and suffers on that count as well. She craves for 'a form of her own' where she could reflect, relax and recharge herself, but this is constantly denied to her because neither her children nor her husband relinquish their claim on her time. She likes to play the roles in which she is creatively involved but feels gargantuan burden of the roles she is supposed to play by her family and the society. By obtaining an educational qualification and a job, she had presumed that she would get a respite from other roles and works she has been traditionally performing, and her husband would also share the burden of domestic work. But this has not happened.

There has been no easing of her burden or division of labour at home. Her husband and the famliy enjoy themselves her earnings but they also expect her to do everything else as well. Her husband feels threatened by her power and as a tortures and taunts her as well. I interviewed at least fifty (50) working women concerning the problems they faced at home. Among them 90 per cent were of the opinion that jobs only doubled their responsibilities and whenever they failed to come up to the expectations of their husbands, they beat them ruthlessly, refused to listen to them and treated them as if they were doormats, and the in laws refused to take care of their kids while they were away at the workplace.

All said and done, they did not want to reverse the process of change only wanted to bring about further changes where by division of work at home would take place so that their burden could be lessened and their husband could treat them at parity.

Some women opined that woman had unnecessarily burdened herself with additional responsibilities. Earlier on she used to do limited work, but now she worked outside home at least for 6 hours and yet she continued to do all the work at home. This made her life infernal, stressful and full of strain and denied her a peaceful and contented life.

Women's secondary status, ignorance, disease, economic dependence and her suffering can be alleviated if strong social and truly religious movements are initiated to bring about greater awareness about her human rights as guaranteed by Islam, and man's set notions about her supposed inferiority and secondary status are attacked, shattered and his misplaced obdurate dogmatic confidence in his own fictions about women is shaleen, punctured and finally undermined with a passionate concern for the most abused and oppressed sex in the history of mankind.

Problems Arising out of Conflict Situation

But what has brought about cataclysmic changes in Kashmiri women's life in the past decade, unprecedented so far, was the shots from the counter insurgency, suppressive and oppressive tactics employed by the Indian Establishment and her armed forces to crush and annihilate an entire population without any remorse under the facade of fighting back militants.

Ever since the eruption of armed conflict in Kashmir in 1989, after all civilized methods of resistance and protestation failed to secure justice and genuine democracy based on the exercise of the right to self-determination by the people of the state, all human rights are not only under threat but have been placed under 'suspended animation'. Massacres, disappearances and torture have become mere tactics; human rights are secondary to military advantage. Women have suffered enormously. They become the victims of reprisal killings and make up most of the refugees and displaced people. They are left to rear families by themselves.

They are raped and sexually abused with impunity, they are raped because their bodies are seen as the legitimate spoils of war. Rape by combatants is an act of torture and clearly prohibited by the rules of war and by international human rights law. Yet no steps have been taken by the Government of India or the armed groups to prevent crimes against humanity or to stop the gross violation of human rights.

In fact, India excels in glossing over the atrocities and the gradual extermination of Kashmiris under a hidden agenda with pious moralism. She is seriously believings in her own fictions about Kashmiris and uses blinkers to shut even the slightest of chinks into the stark reality. What is happening in Kashmir now is unbelievable for thought and odious to the soul, so withering to our belief in secularism and humanism. Deception is most sinister when it is self deception. They seem to achieve new refinements of horror which are new depths of degradation.

Kashmir Sitution Prevalent

Before I numerate the specific problems of women arising out of the turbulent situation let me give you a feel of the general situation prevalent in Kashmir for the last ten years. And while I try to build up the picture for you, I don't need to quote others because I am myself both a victim as well as withness of the current situation in Kashmir.

I cannot but state with a bruised sense of dignity and an agonised state of mind that for the last ten years my homeland has been passing through the worst period of its history. It has been gory and gruesome as never before. The heaven on earth, an abode of saints and sufis has been converted into a virtual inferno. The powers that be have crossed all limits in inflicting indescribable cruelties on innocent masses particularly women and children. The heinous atrocities include murder, rape, gangrape, arson, loot, custodial killings, crippling of youth both mentally and physically, shedding of pools of blood, chopping of those arrested at random, mutilating bodies of those killed, burning, cattle and property, setting fire on entire villages, localities and shopping complexes, torturing and humiliating non-combatants in all possible ways on the slightest, without any distinction of age or sex, piling massacre upon massacre, carnage upon carnage, third degree interrogation of those picked up at random diurnal and nocturnal crackdowns in which men are dragged out of the houses and women left alone at the forces beck and call, frequent parading of people before the hired-street urchins called informers, daily searches in any locality and house they choose for their wrath, insulting and molesting women, beating up people ruthlessly every now then—all this and much more have made the life of an average Kashmiri a horrendous and a horrifying nightmare. In short, "Blood-dimmed tide is loose, and everywhere the ceremony of innocence is drowned" (W.B. Yeats).

The sanctity of our religious places, hospitals, the delivery wards and labour rooms of pregnant women and institutions of learning have been defiled without any compunction. Even the University of Kashmir was surrounded many times by the forces at midnight. Professors and students—all were dragged out at gun-point like animals driven to a slaughter house and for the whole day paraded before hired agents of the armed forces. Some women colleagues and girl students were subjected to torture and humiliation in the hostels. Some male students were let off with fractured limbs and bleeding wounds. Boy's hostels have been raided countless times and the students have been brutally tortured many a time. Part of the campus has been converted into an army camp which has vitiated the atmosphere on the campus. Most of the private hotels and cinema halls have been converted into bunkers and pickets in a most dictatorial manner. The year-long seige of the holy shrine at Hazratbal 1994 is now no secret. The desecration and demolition of the famous Shrine of Noor-U-Din Wali, Alam Dar-Kashmir at Cherari-Sharief (1995) and Khangah of Shahi-Hamadar (1998) at Tral has dealt a severe blow to our collective psyche. All this runs counter to the professed and declared values and aspirations of the world community for a peaceful and dignified future for all mankind.

The forces have surpassed the world famous tyrannical regimes in annihilating and exterminating our people under a hidden agenda. We are thought of as a category, a class, a race and not human beings with certain rights. They have ordered a well-planned disorder and created an ordered darkness, an equality of misery and ensured justice in the sharing of that misery and darkness. That is why you have been misled about the real situation in Kashmir and our real aspirations. The disinformation campaign is carried out at all levels and facts are deliberately distorted to misin form you of our situation. The national media, in fact, plays the role of a predator rather than as a protector of human rights. So far it has never published any story of the suffering masses or a rape case except the news of the killings by militants.

I am not here to discuss or debate the right of self-determination of Kashmiris, but to ask why on earth women should bear the brunt of the forces for no fault of their's except their peaceful demand for the right of self-determination and for their indirect support for the upholders of this slogan. I am here in the capacity of an individual with no myopic-vision and a measure of detachment, one who feels terribly burnt and concerned by what is happening around me, the devastation of humans and human values especially by the fact that women's life, dignity, chastity, property, sanctity are dealt with fatal blows and her home is destroyed in our midst, and how helpless and powerless we are to avert all this. I began with a general description of the situation to enable us to arrive at the specific problems of women because in the ultimate analysis, we cannot separate women's problems from that of the society of which she forms a part.

Specific Problems of Women

1. Our women's, especially at the grassroots, very survival is at stake. Her battle for survival with dignity has shifted from home

and hearth to the road side, not with her traditional enemy-in-laws and the society but with armed forces and their agents who instead of providing her security, are ever ready to plunder her chastity, her property, her dignity in order to crush her spirit and strength. She has forgotten the old pangs of domestic confinement, she is now awfully scared of the confinement of bunkers, of pickets, of the custodial wards and torture cells and worst of all the bestial violence inflicted on their bodies by the forces. A good number of women have been kidnapped and then kept in confinements by members of the forces quenching their lust. Recently a huge scandal has been unveiled by the local media, giving heart-rending details of the women who have been kept in camps, bunkers and hotels under the forces and whose shrieks have been heard by the passers-by.

2. Rape is invariably being used both as a weapon of terror as was done by German army in the First World War, as well as weapon of revenge as was done by the Soviet army in the Second World War. It is also used as a weapon of oppression against women to subdue them to the level of abject degradation and humiliation so that not only women but their entire families are crushed down for ever with shame, never to raise their voice of dissent again. Beyond the brutality and trauma of the rape itself which often cause life-long psychological damage to the victims, sexual assault has also resulted in serious physical injuries, forced pregnancies diseases and even death. Most women do not recover from such shocking, traumatic experiences and those who do, live a disgraceful, miserable and tortuous life not because the society does not accept them but because they are unable to forgive themselves as if the vile experience has been of their own seeking. In China in 1990, a survey, on women's status was conducted; nearly 70 per cent of all respondents agreed with the statement that a women's virginity is more important than her life 20 per cent.[2] In Kashmir it could be over 95 per cent.

Some places where the gang rape has been committed have become synonymous with rape and ready symbols of reference for such cases like Chanapora, Kananposhpora, Pazipora, Dadsara, Kangan, Sopore, Shopian, Kupwara, Hundwara, Karna, Pulwama, Bijbihara etc. and the victims have been living with agonising memories.

3. The stigma and the social consequences of rape and sexual violations are such that speaking out may be totally against the dignityof women. Kashmiri society being a typically conservative particularly sensitive to social stigmas, exact numbers and details are not easily available. There is no end to a victim's suffering after speaking out as she loses all chances of respectful life. The rape initiates for her a whole process of depersonalisation and degradation as it estranges her from her immediate social context of near and dear ones. Even Amnesty International confirms that 'there is a strong evidence that members of the Indian Security Forces have used rape as a tactic in an increasingly violent suppression of the campaign for Kashmiri independence' in its 1995 publication called *Human Rights are Women's Right* [3] and has mentioned some cases of rape affirming that these incidents are a few in a continuing pattern.[4]

4. In Feb. 1991 at least 23 women were reportedly raped at gun point in their homes when soldiers raided the village. Some were said to have been gang raped, others have been raped in front of their children. The youngest victim was 13, the oldest was 80. (Anthony Woods.)

Around midnight on 10th Oct, 1992 an Indian army raided the village of Chak Saidapora, near Shopian. They carried out a house to house search, in the course of which at least six women were raped. Among them was a woman of 60 and 11 year old girl called Zait oon.

Over a year later, on 22nd Nov 1993, Indian soldiers entered the village of Warapora. Sara a young girl was out collecting firewood. Eye witness saw five soldiers approaching her. They found her dead body later that day. Her clothes had been torn off and the postmortem revealed....."marks of violence on neck, breasts, left knee,.......and extensive vaginal tear".

The fourth incident I am going to relate took place on 28th Nov. 1994 in Sopore. A daughter was stripped naked before her father, and father before his daughter, father could neither groan nor shout for help as his mouth was gagged. "Death was thousand times preferable to such disgrace and shame but at that time even death was not within my control," said the daughter. In fact, three young ladies Yasmeen, Parveen, and Rehana in the age group of 20 to 25 in Sopore were interrogated in the most barbaric manner to extract information about the whereabout of their husbands. Their households were totally destroyed, young kids mercilessly beaten, they were stripped off at gun point and then grilled through the most tortous third-degree interrogation a roller was rolled over their thighs and breasts, electric shocks were given to them, then they were gagged, sexually molested and raped in unconscious state as was confirmed by medical tests. This is the worst incident of its kind and happened after India's declared policy of transparency.

5. Recently a group of journalists revisited Kananposhora and came up with the finding that not a single girl has got married ever since the incident of 1991. These women have been suffering on all fronts.

6. With each passing day, the number of women being widowed in the current violence across Jammu and Kashmir State is appallingly increasing. Unoffical estimates put their number at around 15,000 in the six trouble-torn districts of Kashmir valley. And in the absence of any governmental or non-governmental rehabilitation programme, these widows have been left to their

fate. There is a dire need for noted non-governmental organisations in the country and abroad to launch rehabilitation projects here as the government's 'Rehabilitation Council' selectively offers nominal help to those whose husbands have been killed in militant fire, which are very few.

7. There are at least three villages where majority of the menfolk have been killed in the past decade of violence. And intriguingly, one among these villages, Sheikh Mohalla, falls in Chief Minister's constituency of Ganderbal, barely a few kilometres off from Srinagar City. The ten family strong hamlet has 11 widows, 31 orphans and just three men. They have yet to receive any *ex-gratia* relief as also a visit by their M.L.A., who also happens to be the Chief Minister of the state. Another village is in Bandipora where at least 70 per cent women have been widowed, 90 per cent orphaned and who feel so scared as the night approached that they leave their homes for safer abodes where there are men around. These women are forlorn and destitute.

8. Often adding to the plight of widows are the laws. According to Muslim personal law, if the father-in-law of the widow is alive neither she nor her children can claim for any share in the family property.

9. Then there are 'half-widows', who also suffer among other things at the hands of law.

They are wives of men who have gone missing during the decade long insurgency in Kashmir valley, some of them allegedly picked up by the members of the 'security forces', others by militants or by unidentified gunmen. Some simply never returned home. Unofficial estimates put the number of missing married men at around 900.
Amnesty International has reported 800 disappeared persons. one thousand (1000) have been documented by the Association

of the Parents of Disappeared Persons (APDP) in Kashmir. On the one hand, the wives, mothers and sisters of the disappeared live in constant pain of separation of loved ones and on the other, the wives do not know how long they have to wait before they get the religious sanction to marry again. According to religious scholars and the clergy, the waiting period varies from 4 years in one Muslim School of thought to even 90 years in another, although now even the Fiqh-i-Hanfia in India has decided to adopt the Maliki practice of allowing remarriage after four years. But they have to try to locate them during this period which is anuphill task. There is nobody to take care of these poor 'halfwidows' because even the nominal relief accrues only to those who are widows.

10. Hundreds of women have been and continue to get killed every day, devastating their families and depriving their young ones of the maternal solicitude, which nothing on earth can replace for them.

11. Even the daily life of women is full of risks and embarrassments as they too are frisked and searched wherever they go. They do not spend their time in shopping centres or entertainment clubs, but they feel terrorized as if birds in flight ever tense about their security and dignity. You will not find their children in playgrounds but you will withness vast graveyards in every village, town and city holding to their bosoms their dear ones. You will not find teen-agers in fun parks and health resorts but will hear their heart rending shrieks from third-degree interrogation centres all over Kashmir.

12. For the past decade, Kashmiri woman has been in the grip of debilitating cynicism, immobilizing depression and a state of paralysing mental torture and exhausting despair. The daily killings, arrests, search operations, crackdowns and denigrating parades and destruction of houses and property have made the entire population mentally sick. According to late Dr. A.A. Baig

and Dr. Mushtaq, the local psychiatrists, "practically the entire population suffers from psychological disorders, 'we get large number of patients who suffer from diseases ranging from mild depression, neurosis, phobias to serious psychotic probiems and post traumatic stress syndrome (PTS)—disorder in which the patients relive the trauma time and again". Even here the most affected section of the society are women, (nearly 70 per cent followed by youth. Most of them suffer from hysteria, drug-dependence and anxiety syndrome. Such patients are not only a drag on the modest means of a family but a constant instrument of torture for entire family. The vast destruction of houses and property across the valley has turned lakhs of people paupers over night and the women's privacy has been raided in an outrageous manner, which has on the one hand led to the loss of their mental balance and on the other has forced some women to become mendicants and even prostitutes to earn two time meals for the young ones. It has displaced them and forced their migration to places outside the state where they pass for strangers and try to escape the insult and ignominy brought about by their misery.

13. When a militant is killed his wife, who, to add salt to the injury, is often called to attend the camp. On the pretext of enquiring from her about the gun of her husband they harass her, molest her and sexually abuse her. This happens most of the times in the villages and border areas where the victims go unnoticed.

Instance: Two years back a militant was killed in Kupwara. This year an army camp was erected there and men in civies-renegades were sent to bring his wife to the camp. When she refused to go for the risks obviously involved in going, she was taken to custody and raped for many days. Again this is one instance of a continuing pattern which is aimed at terrorising an entire community.

14. The girls, education has been seriously affected because most of the parents especially in the village hesitate to send their

daughters to the school for fear of losing them to the continuing violence and hooliganism.

15. As elsewhere, exclusionary nationalism, in Kashmir tried to put down women in the beginning of the present armed struggle. Some groups tried to dictate terms to women and coerce them especially about the observance of *purdah* or more specifically Burqa and for some time women felt terrorized by them and got *burqas* and Abayas stiched. But gradually the fear evaporated and this has ceased to pose as a problem but was acutely felt for some time.

Conclusion

What I want to demonstrate is that without taking political positions, communal positions, regional positions, gender-dominated positions let us concentrate on the human aspect of the situation and press upon the powers that be, to change their attitude towards the women and wear at least a human face. These gross violations of human rights cannot be explained away by any logic or rationale of a scheme of things that pretends to be human and respecting human dignity. These cannot be explained away as pathological neurosis, sadism or masochism and hence can be condoned.

Let us remove the blinkers of parties, rigid ideologies, fanatic religiosity, communalism, gingoistic nationalism, and other parochial visions and view our condition as a human problem which is your concern and my concern, where 'I' and 'you' dissolve into collective 'we' as we rise above petty political postures and address ourselves to problems as we face them wherever we are lest history and humanism would have last laugh at us those who propagate and preach supremacy if human dignity and more particularly the dignity of women. Let us not succumb to power structure's manipulative methods and disinformation campaign and hence shrink from taking a stance against inhuman brutalities and draconian laws of the oppressors. Let us bend these structures of power to server the voice of humanity in us. We can bring down the curtain of oppression and repression by the sheer moral force of collective pressure that we can exert in various ways. Those who care for truth and for humanity, dismantle the man-made barriers and the walls of misunderstanding. The void created is too wide to be filled between the establishment and the people. There is no possibility of reconciliation after having done, what they have done. You don't degrade and torture your own people like that. You don't rob them of their dignity and property and home, self-respect in that most denigrating manner. Nowhere does the condition of women present a more saddening spectacle than in Kashmir given the fact that violations of their rights are carried out by none other than an establishment that claims the victims to be its own people. In most parts of the world crimes against women are committed by individuals for the gratification of their lascivious drives and urges and are meted out with punishment. Here it is most detestable as it is deliberately and calculatingly done by a particular establishment with the larger political ambition of suppressing and subjugating a whole people to disgraceful and miserable life. It is symbolically a whole collective psyche, which is raped, bruised, scrubbed, and ripped apart most violently. And then comes the plaint 'we are' not faithful. In the end let me tell you that I would have rather liked to talk about the pleasant things of life, things that would sooth you and entertain you rather than disturb you, I would have liked to talk about the variety of flowers, their sweet smells and how they enrich our poetic sensibility coming as I do from the vale of flowers. But for the last 10 years we have not seen the blossoming of flowers, but experienced only the erection of bunkers everywhere, thundering of shells, gingle of guns and what have you.

Even our dreams have deserted us. Hence talking of pleasant things would amount to being radically false and indifferent to my self and to the world that has raised me and nourished me because that world is right now burning, raging, roaring smouldering and groaning as a whole. Rich culture has been devastated by the stink of the running and frozen streams of blood, burning human bodies, burning smell of entire residential areas and shopping complexes and on top of al-l the odour of the bestial violence borne by women's bodies.

REFERENCES

1. Simone-de Beauvoir: *The Second Sex*,1949.Trans. and Ed. H.M. Parshley: Hummondsworth Penguin, 1972.

2. Amnesty International: Women in China: Imprisoned and Abused for Dissent: All-International Secretaiat, Easton Street: London, 1995, p. 2.

3. Amnesty International: *Human Rights are Women's Rights* New York, 1995.

4. *Ibid*.

Index